The Sec

Invisible Archi

Uncover the secret history of two ancient brotherhoods in 'The Secret Government', a journey revealing the scripted shadows behind world events.

Ismael Perez

Dedication

This work is lovingly dedicated to my Mother, who now resides in the higher dimensions. As my Earthly guardian and spiritual warrior, she was not only a beacon of resilience but also a fountain of inspiration. She urged me to embark on a lifelong quest for knowledge. Before her transition, she imparted a message of divine significance, urging me never to cease my pursuit of understanding. This sacred counsel became the catalyst for my exploration, leading to the revelations I am honored to share in my forthcoming work, "Our Cosmic Origin." Maria de Guadalupe, my unwavering source of strength and my hero, navigated the trials of her Earthly journey with unmatched grace. Despite her untimely departure, a consequence of a battle with depression, her spirit of perseverance and unconditional love for her children remain my guiding light. Mother, your memory is a treasure I hold dear, and I eagerly await our reunion on the grand day of ascension.

<u>Acknowledgements</u>

I extend my heartfelt gratitude to the valiant souls who have illuminated the path by unveiling the veiled machinations of our world. A special tribute to Alberto Rivera, the courageous ex-Jesuit priest whose sacrifice in revealing the truths about the Jesuit Order will forever be remembered. His martyrdom is a testament to the power of truth. I also wish to acknowledge Ivan Fraser for his enlightening contributions and Myron Fagan, whose bravery in exposing the Illuminati's infiltration of America has not gone unnoticed. To David Icke and Alex Jones, whose relentless efforts continue to pierce the veil of the systemic beast, your resilience is commendable. Above all, this work is in honor of all the unsung heroes and heroines whose ultimate sacrifice for freedom has paved the way for enlightenment and liberation.

TABLE OF CONTENTS

INTRODUCTION

In this remarkable era of information and internet technology, restored to us by the emissaries of light, a long-suppressed truth of history is finally emerging. Despite this, the pace at which people receive information remains relatively slow. Only a handful seek to truly understand what is happening in our world, while the majority remains unaware of many vital issues. It's disheartening that a significant number of people show little interest in global happenings and, even more concerning, many accept media-disseminated information without question. Surprisingly, the media itself is an instrument controlled by the secret government, designed to obscure the truth from the public eye.

In our fast-paced world, masterminded by design, finding time to research and understand the full scope of events is nearly impossible. The demands of daily life compel us to focus on survival and personal needs, leaving little room for deeper inquiry. This compilation is dedicated to those concerned about our world's fate and the pivotal events shaping it.

These events, as marked by biblical scripture, reveal a crucial piece of information that has been conveniently omitted from mainstream narrative. This information, alongside powerful passages from biblical scripture, aids in understanding world events and historical contexts. It reveals that our world has been primarily under the influence of Fallen Angels, or adversarial forces opposed to God's goodness. However, it's crucial to recognize that their power is not absolute.

It is my honor to bring to light what many independent researchers are uncovering — a disturbing revelation about a shadowy cabal that manipulates and influences governments. Moreover, it's essential to expose their agenda. The Bible reveals that the powers ruling this world are of darkness, having influenced our world for millennia. Jesus Christ disclosed that the God of this world is Satan, pending the second coming. Familiarizing ourselves with the Great Awakening and its relation to the diminishing power of these dark forces is timely. The Great Awakening, long prophesied, is unfolding as more individuals become aware of these oppressive forces. The disclosure of such forces is a significant step in the awakening process.

The way this information is revealed is important to note. Emphasizing that "nothing is new under the sun," all knowledge is collective, stemming from a singular source—the omniscient mind of our Creator. In a world of duality, knowledge can be used for both good and evil.

God grants humanity fragments of knowledge, guarding the reservoir of universal wisdom. Those who believe they are originators in any field, be it science, math, or philosophy, are merely accessing glimpses of the omniscient mind of God. We are rediscovering what exists within the universal consciousness of our Creator. Thus, this material is presented as a compilation of discoveries by bold light workers and truth-seekers, consolidating their findings into a biblical perspective to enlighten the masses.

This revelation is dedicated to the brave souls who faced danger to share this information. A special thanks to those formerly involved in secretive societies who, upon turning towards the light, chose to share their knowledge, validating the truth further. For some, this information may be startling, especially regarding the roles and actions of secret societies within our governments. Some readers may already be familiar with these concepts, while others may be encountering them for the first time.

In our universe, driven by intelligence, nothing happens by chance. Every event and occurrence are the result of deliberate, intelligent planning. The term "conspiracy" has been misconstrued; its true meaning involves collaboration towards a common goal, not the nefarious connotations it has been imbued with. In essence, we inhabit a universe of intention, where accidents do not exist, reflecting the intelligent design behind all creation.

Chapter 1: THE TWO FORCES AT PLAY

There are two forces at play, or is it one force with two sides? Truth never remains buried; eventually, everything comes to light. We are living in grave yet exciting times. Our world is faced with many challenges from all different directions: inflation, global warming, wars, famine, diseases, terrorism, the declining third world countries, as well as the gradual decline of second world countries. I will not forget to mention the disintegration of many nations' economic infrastructures resulting from worldwide economic injustice, as well as worldwide massacres and the obvious elimination of the middle-class agenda in the U.S.A. and other leading nations. What most people don't know is that something is causing all these unwanted realities. All the atrocities facing mankind are a manifestation of a covert global agenda known as globalization. Globalization is a threat to the well-being of mankind and our planet.

If we examine globalization from its roots, finding out its overall purpose, intent, and the negative impact it has on our world, we must come to the knowledge of the secret societies that created it. It is well known that not only are secret societies real, but they are the causes of every effect that has shaped our world since antiquity. For example, the globalization programs affecting our world are not new ideas at all; they're part of an ancient plot that could be traceable back to the ancient world. This agenda's overall intention is to effect absolute control of our world in a totalitarian manner. In fact, everything that is happening is part of an unresolved conflict that is now coming to an end. Part of the reason why society is unable to detect the source of these unwanted problems is that the real movers and shakers are perpetrating such acts behind closed doors. Another reason is the veil of great secrecy which surrounds the special elite clubs in which they operate. As a society, we are unable to see how major evil intentions are conceived, germinated, and later manifested since we only experience its effect. This is since all evil is generated in a clandestine fashion, launched within the secret meetings and private halls of the negative secret societies that operate and function from behind the scenes and the highest echelons of our world governments.

More importantly, the existence and operations of secret societies are a reality that must come to light to decipher why our world is facing a major social, political, and economic cataclysm. As natural law proves, every cause has consequences, positive or negative.

Everything that happens, happens for a reason and has been planned or conceptualized by a person or a group before it becomes reality. Our world is a continual happenstance of causes and effects as the result of intelligent planners who are driven by a common desire towards a specific goal. Those who know the truth behind secret societies and their role and influence may understand the subject. For those who don't, eventually, all secrets come to light. After all, isn't it written in the Bible that this world is ruled by evil in high places? Don't be alarmed about the subject. Just keep in mind the age-old prophecy indicating that before the coming of the Son, the works of the devil, the great Satan, would be revealed.

The apparently unconnected incidents plaguing our world are not a happenstance of unrelated accidents but a product of a destructive force that can be traced back to the ancient world. Today, this physical force is the reason why globalization is real and directs and influences governments, corporations, and major institutions and utilizes psychological tools like social engineering on a grand scale. It is an agenda that has always existed in different times and under various forms. It caused Nimrod to do what he did in Babylon with the creation of the Tower of Babel. It is the same agenda that ignited Imperial Rome to do the same 2,000 years ago. Furthermore, the agenda of world domination under an absolute totalitarian form of government—the Empire—is real and it's demonstrated by the Central Banking Financial systems, which were created by evil in high places. Through money and power, they not only manipulate governments but are secretly bringing our world into the One World Government of the Beast system that John the Revelator refers to in the Book of Revelation. After all, isn't it true that the love of money is the root of all evil?

The agenda of world domination is not new, for it has been part of the game played since the Luciferian Rebellion took place in Heaven and is clearly revealed in the Book of Revelation as the system of the Beast. In our modern world, we can detect this type of injustice by witnessing the living conditions.

Imposed by the embodiment of the Antichrist who temporarily rules our world. This system thrives on ignorance and is ignited by fear. Ignorance enables them to skillfully manipulate the masses, as fear and ignorance become their greatest weapons. Secrecy is the manner in which they conquer. These clandestine operations are real and are exploited and executed by the secret society members. They are the working instruments of Satan on Earth. The system of the Beast is the true force behind all terrorism; in fact, they sponsor, organize, finance, and create worldwide terrorist groups. In addition, the same powers also synthetically created many deadly diseases known to men, such as the A.I.D.S. virus, polio, the bird flu, and even the coronavirus. Finally, they are the powers that, through the creation of the United Nations, are gradually encompassing the entire world through a series of unions. Their consolidation of power proceeds into a universal vehicle known as the Global Union, aka the One World Government, the true agenda behind globalization. The creation of struggling living conditions only serves as an excuse, as it is part of their agenda to create a greater need for a New World Order.

Therefore, everything that is happening is nothing more than the maxim of using chaos to create the desired global order. The system of the Beast is "The Hidden Hand", and the ruling powers manipulating events from behind the scenes are the last of the remnant of the embodiment of the Antichrist, known today as the old guard secret government of the Jesuit Illuminati syndicate. They are the representatives of Satan, and they have ruled over empires, religions, and governments for millennia. In the Bible, it is understood that there are two forces at play, or two brotherhoods, and our world is temporarily under the control of the destructive force, the evil of the Dark Brotherhood. However, there is still the force of darkness, the Brotherhood of Light, who have been silently engaged in an everlasting battle against the rulers of this world.

We can conclude that all events shaping our world are a direct result of the cause and effect of the silent warfare between these two forces or two brotherhoods. It is a battle that is not only finishing in our world but a battle that has its origins before the creation of our world, perhaps in the middle of Heavens or pre-mortal existence, when a third of the angels decided to join the ranks of the Fallen One, who in the Bible is known as Lucifer. One of the reasons the Earth happens to be a special place is because it is the chosen location as the last battleground between good and evil. That's why it has been prophesied for millennia that this conflict ends with the "forces of good" prevailing over the forces of darkness, as Archangel Michael and the entire host descend upon the Earth to eliminate the last of the system of the Beast. There is no doubt that in these very days, this battle will come to its end with the "forces of good" triumphing once and for all. This can be discerned by those awakening to the truth and tuning into the changes.

Unfortunately, however, not enough people are aware of the real issue, and that is the purpose of this material. This is not another conspiracy theory, nor is it fictional or meant to frighten. It is the truth, plain and simple, and it's written to educate and inform all who are concerned about what John the Revelator conveys in the Book of Revelation—the true reason why our world is in this condition. It is important to understand the meaning and message in the Book of Revelation and what John the Revelator clearly specifies. There are many passages included in the Bible that clearly reveal all the apparently unrelated events happening in our world as they mark the signs of the times.

For example, the Book of Revelation gives many clues to the perpetrators of such evil calamities and warns mankind of the coming of the system of the Beast and encompassing the entire world under a One World Government, globalization. However, according to actual prophecy, the result is the final defeat of the Beast system, with the restoration of our world. In evaluating diverse spiritual texts and manuscripts from other religions, including the Sanskrit literature of India, we see a correlation indicating the last battle between good and evil taking place in our present time.

In the Book of Revelation, it is called Armageddon. More importantly, this battle will usher in a period of everlasting peace and joy, known as the Millennium in Christian traditions and the Golden Age in Eastern traditions. This truth implies that the system of the Beast does not get a chance to manifest its full agenda of global domination, for it has never been allowed to do so, even in past times. After all, since Lucifer is the father and source of all lies, and since his forces have been the primary rulers of this world, it is obvious that we have been lied to regarding many important matters, especially our true celestial origin.

In like manner, all oppressiveness, bondage, and slavery known to man, which is characterized in the form of an Empire totalitarian system model of government, is known as Luciferian in nature.

This totalitarian, ultramontane system of government is the Luciferian manifesto, and it's the reason why all wars have been fought. In contrast, it is God who is the author and source of all freedom, joy, abundance, and peace everlasting. It has always been the instrument of Lucifer or his followers, the negative secret societies, who have created all oppressive regimes, and why the quest for global domination is real and in motion. This is why we need to understand the Luciferian agenda, which is the same as the Luciferian manifesto. This agenda has influenced, molded, and ruled governments and empires for thousands of years. The Luciferian agenda originated with Lucifer and continues through every level of existence, penetrating and finally affecting our world. Although Lucifer is no longer an active agent of his agenda, for he has been bound by the forces of light, it continues in our world through the last remnant of his instruments.

They are the Brotherhood of Darkness, the embodiment of the Antichrist, and today's negative secret societies. Throughout history, we've witnessed this battle between good and evil in the types of ruling systems, governments we've experienced, and come to know. For example, there is the far right, the totalitarian system of absolute control by a self-proclaimed, unelected elite, whether it is a single autocratic king, dictator, or some sort of tyrannical empirical structure that brings mankind under its absolute and centralized power. Then there is its opposite, a system where we've experienced for a couple of hundred years within a constitutional Republic based on nation-state democracy, where government is by the people and for the people. The Republican model is based on the grounds of a commonwealth and is a workable one, as it reflects the good, modeling opposition to the Luciferian manifesto of absolute tyranny.

It is the struggle between these two forms of government that marks the invisible battle taking place by the two brotherhoods, the "forces of good" and the forces of evil. Today, we can detect this battle taking place in the political arena between the "forces of good", who want to preserve our constitutional Republic and bring the rest of the world under a constitutional democracy, and the forces of evil, who want to eradicate all freedoms and manifest a world empire of absolute spiritual, mental, and physical control that is likened to the Empire of the dark side in the movie "Star Wars". In fact, the same theme that we see in these great movies like "Star Wars" and "Lord of the Rings" is the theme being played out in our world. Therefore, we can conclude that there have been only two forms of government and that two agendas or two forces are at play.

We are at a crossroad, wondering which one of these models will overcome the other as their final battle comes to an end. The question is, which agendas would we like to live under? Anybody in their right mind would agree that the agenda model of the free world would be best. As seen in the "Star Wars" Trilogy, the agenda of Lucifer is characterized by an Empire with an emperor dictator who seeks absolute power. We also know the same logic in "Lord of the Rings" and in "Chronicles of Narnia", which are movies with great spiritual messages. Most importantly, it is the principle in those films which need to be understood as they spiritually relate to the world we live in. The Luciferian agenda of totalitarianism can be traced back to the ancient world, where it originated in Babylon. It was this agenda that corrupted entire civilizations, causing their fall. This includes pre-ancient civilizations that had catastrophic endings, such as Atlantis, which existed in the Atlantic Ocean, and Lemuria, which existed in the Pacific Ocean. They were all subjected to catastrophe, ruined on behalf of the Luciferian agenda.

Unlike other times in our past, however, these times are marked differently. This era marks the time of the Great Harvest and the end of Evil's reign on the Earth. The tables have turned; only the wicked and the entire structure of the Beast system will be rooted out as the last embodiment of the Antichrist crumbles down and its eliminated, aa a outdated, unworkable, competitive and fear-based system driven by lust for absolute power. This is the time when the Earth will be renewed and restored back to a state of perfect balance, as it once was before the infiltration and interception of Luciferians.

In this restoration, only people of good intent will populate the new Earth as they initiate a Golden Age of light and enlightenment. According to the prophecy, the new humanity will be based on Agape, brotherly love, and will act as one. Most people desire peace and prefer to live in harmony with one another. A good number of people want to save our environment from collapse and establish a relationship with nature based on respect and the preservation of our ecosystem. A New Earth and humanity are endeavoring to come forward as a final renaissance. The only element preventing this is the forces that control our world, the secret government of the embodiment of the Antichrist, the cabal. Our understanding of science and technology has once again reached a boiling point.

We have rediscovered the dangers of certain technologies like the atom bomb, nuclear weapons of mass destruction, microbiological germ warfare. Mankind has reached a high level of development, which once again places us at a crossing point, not only in our world but in our evolution. This time, spirituality needs to bypass technology as we may use technology to best serve humanity. Something history will repeat itself, including that humankind is set for another probable destruction by its own hand, as has happened before many times in the past. Others say the world is going to end in a cataclysmic event and will be destroyed by hail, brimstones, and fire. These are all negative approaches that have been imprinted in our minds by the same forces that are serving the Luciferian agenda. Even though mankind has reached a great height in technology, we are also at a decline in our civilization. We must, therefore, use what we know to better our world, especially since we have become a global society standing at a crossroad of our collective destinies. We must take the right direction because nature will run its course, and the outcome will be determined based on whether we've used the knowledge gathered in a positive way.

Humanity is facing a spiritual transformation, not destruction. A special dispensation is upon us, which is why it is important to become informed about the changes that have been prophesied and will transform mankind back into its purity and original blueprint. This transformation will take place on all levels of intelligence and parallels what the ancients mean as the Great Awakening and the restoration of planet Earth.

Part of the awakening process is understanding the long-played-out battle between good and evil and why this conflict is now coming to an end in our world. As mentioned in the past, many civilizations have fallen due to the existing unseen wicked powers in high places, which have ruled through the form of a secret shadow government. For generations, they maintained their power over empires and civilizations because of their ability to remain hidden. However, now that the age of information and a special dispensation is upon us, their secrecy will serve them no more. As more and more people become informed, especially those in government positions, we can redirect the course of events by making sure that the outcome of this silent but deadly war ends in a free world and not in an Empire One World dictatorship. Bear with me as we learn the truth behind every world event and connections to the secret societies that have always existed.

Today, we have the opportunity to take up our humanity for the age of information that's been restored to the Earth once again, as it was in Egypt and in other immemorial Golden Ages. Mankind can use what they know about technology and science and apply it to bettering living conditions. Today, we must stand at the beginning of a new threshold, a threshold that is simply drawing upon us and will change the current structure of our planet forever. We need to be ready. With that said, let me explain one of the most puzzling elements and mysteries that is affecting our world at large. And that is the revelation of the forces of darkness, their methods of operation, and their goal, which lies at the center of their ancient agenda.

The Luciferian agenda is to effect absolute control and domination of our planet Earth by manifesting the Luciferian manifesto. This agenda has its origins from the beginning of the split in Heaven when Lucifer took 1/3 of the angels. Now, the split is coming to a finish as the last forces of evil become absolved into light, resulting from the cleansing Archangel Michael began in the middle of the Heavens 38 million years ago at the onset of the Luciferian rebellion. As we see in "Star Wars", "Chronicles of Narnia", and "Lord of the Rings", light always prevails, for our Earth, as well as our universe, is under divine will.

This book is a testament of truth, revealing the nature of the Beast himself, the great Satan, Baal, as it uncovers the real current events that our media and government officials have hidden under the controlling body of the unseen hand, the secret government that oversees, censors, controls everything we know, except for our minds.

From oppression to corruption, tyranny to disease, to global sensory and surveillance, a literal force causes everything. The force of evil is intangible but real and is represented by the ancient fallen hierarchies operating under the control of high-level sorcerers that lie at the core of the Beast, which is the governing body of the synagogue of satanic, Satan, "The Hidden Hand", the secret government. They've always been known as the Luciferian secret Brotherhood, representatives of Satan on Earth, the Brotherhood of the Snake, all known by different names throughout different times. They have been the leading figures in executing every pain known to humanity and, in an effort to not only oppress but ultimately destroy the human race. The intervention of the forces of light is always here, doing battle with the forces of Darkness, counteracting every attempt made by the Dark Brotherhood.

Secret societies have existed since immemorial times, and their structure, only active participants involved in the Luciferian conspiracy, could plan, and execute their evil plots without the knowledge of the public, giving them the ability to execute their plans more efficiently. This operation of acting in secret for an evil purpose has been perpetuated throughout history through the negative secret societies that serve the Luciferian agenda. On the contrary, secrecy has not always been the reason for all evil intentions.

Until the Dark Middle Ages in Europe, benevolent secret societies flourished in the underground, not only to prevent persecution from the dark forces who dominated the known world but also to preserve the ageless wisdom of the higher sacred knowledge and liberate humanity in our world. The Luciferians have been the prime movers and shakers of every oppressive institution, religion, and empire, they sought to oppress the ultimate truth and higher knowledge of the spiritual realms, which threatens their power and control over mankind. This is why truth bringers, perhaps prophets of God and good, have been murdered throughout history to maintain the masses subject to the existing regime of the embodiment of the Antichrist, ruled by keeping mankind in ignorance. Today, we notice all good men who tried to make a difference eventually are assassinated by the same powers that were.

These negative powers have yielded a vast network of secret societies, the last remnant of the embodiment of the Antichrist, who is desperately trying to bring our world under its absolute power by manifesting a totalitarian empire worldwide. We can intellectually conclude that our world, for the most part, was heading into that direction, especially since the establishment of the United Nations in 1945 and the 21st-century consolidation of the European Union, which is uniting Europe under one federal empire where every nation is to act as a state and is going to be subject to a more centralized ruler. Could this be no other than the resurrection of the Holy Roman Empire that Hitler attempted to revive in his day? The existence of a One World Government, the New World Order, has been emerging by the day until now, the Great Awakening.

Chapter 2: THE REVEALING

To anyone who has been aware for some time, Europe has already united under the banner of the European Union. For over 15 years, there were no borders in Europe; people could freely travel and use the same currency, like the United States. This began with the euro currency, a single monetary system known as the European Economic Community (EEC), one monetary unit for all of Europe. It was predicted that by 2011, Europe would be in full force as another world power, as powerful as, or more than, the United States. The secret European Union has been engineered by the Luciferian Brotherhood and will come into the open, as predicted by John the Revelator, described symbolically as a ten-horned beast, which indicates the unification of Europe. He states the Antichrist will have a crown with 10 horns, symbolic of all the main nations that will unite and comprise a great super government structure, power to be known as the United States of Federal Europe, the revived Holy Roman Empire.

Christ referred to the powers in high places that rule our world as the synagogue of Satan, the hidden head. This makes sense when one considers how the Luciferians have functioned under various names and guises throughout all of history. Christ knew of the intrigues of the Sanhedrin during his time and aspects of "The Hidden Hand" that no one else knew about because of their great secrecy and hidden empire, which acted as a shadow government to the prevailing Roman Empire.

"The Hidden Hand", through the Sanhedrin, became the secret controllers of the Pharisees and seduced the religious men of Judea, who governed the religious policies of the people in those days. What more evidence do we need than the words of Christ himself, who knew they were his archenemies and that they had influenced the skepticism and hatred toward him, which was built upon by the Sadducees and Pharisees, and inevitably led to his crucifixion? Jesus also warned us of the many false prophets who would come in his name to confuse the masses, bearing the name of Christ but acting as a tool for the synagogue of Satan, or "The Hidden Hand". This explains the abomination of the Earth, the great Harlot of Revelation, that deceives many in the name of Christ.

Ultimately, oppression and human enslavement have been the main manifestations of the Hidden Empire of the Beast, which, to God, is an abomination. This Beast system of slavery has been counteracted many times by the forces of light to preserve and continue the concept of freedom, which will cease to exist the moment the Empire becomes absolute. God has repeatedly proven this by not allowing the forces of Darkness to fully manifest their agenda of absolute world domination, thereby maintaining the world in a state of balance until the time of the Great Transition. Nonetheless, there have been times where it almost tilted toward the dark side, like in the Dark Ages following the fall of Rome. It is still unbalanced today, through Central Banking institutions that dominate our world's governments.

Perhaps the hardest challenge is still to come. Yes, this period in our world's timeframe marks the greatest and best time in which to live, due to the restoration process, which is in progress. There is a new era that is coming, known by various names: the Millennium, the Golden Age of Enlightenment, also known as The Age of Aquarius, where the Earth and humanity will reach ultimate liberation from the bondages of oppressive forces, and all suffering and oppression will end.

According to various researchers and investigators of truth, particularly Ken Adachi, Ivan Fraser, David Icke, and others, the current name of the hidden evil secret government and the source of the central banking system is known as the Illuminati. There is more to the Illuminati than that, for this is just the financial arm of the Beast system. Nevertheless, the secret organization was set up in Germany under its original name, the Bavarian Illuminati, and despite its controversy, it has been acting as a vehicle for the Luciferian Brotherhood in modern times.

The purpose of the Illuminati is manifold, but it was designed to serve as a financial institution for the Beast. The Illuminati became the new oligarchy within the oligarchy of the already existing monarchs, who wanted to keep their power intact after the Reformation. It was the Illuminati who set up the British East India Company, and it's the vehicle behind the modern-day Central Banking Empire, which is the reason the world is suffering and facing a monetary catastrophe. Today, they are so powerful that no one dares to challenge them because they employ killing mercenaries and soldiers who have been trained to execute murders and assassinations worldwide. They control most of the world's oil resources, governments, and finances. By conquering the Middle East and manipulating wars, they are gradually globalizing the entire world into a one-world government. In fact, it has been documented that all the major and minor wars, political and economic depressions, since their inception in 1776, ironically when our constitutional Republic was born by the good guys, have been carefully planned and instigated by them through their secret society networks. Many have agreed that there has been no political

turmoil that has not been influenced by these negative secret
societies.

They own most of the major corporations in our world. They
dominate the corporate world through their multinationals,
which are a conglomerate of super corporations that, in turn,
are controlled by the international bankers of private banking
interest groups, who are the controlling body and backbone of
the Illuminati syndicate. Another suppressed fact is that they
set up what is known to most intelligent researchers as the
pharmaceutical cartel and the American Medical Association,
which is run by David Rockefeller. Its purpose is to suppress
the natural remedies that Earth provides for all diseases and to
make billions of dollars in the process. In fact, next to the oil
industry, the pharmaceutical industry cartel generates
enormous money for the global elite controllers. Research has
concluded that at the highest echelons of the Illuminati, the
inner council, known as the Council of 13, are families that are
genetically related to one another. This helps explain how a
handful of families have been in control of our world for many
centuries.

This concept is what is referred to as the 13 Bloodlines of the
Illuminati, including the royal families of the European House
of Lords. However, the main families are the Oppenheimer's,
Rothschilds, and at the top, we have the Orsini family, as well
as some of the most powerful American families like the
Rockefellers, the Brahmins, Harriman's, etc. The 13 Bloodlines
are the primary families that are beyond rich, who comprise
the Council of the Inner Court. In collaboration with these
minor yet powerful families, we also have the DuPont's, the
Astors, the Warburg's, the Windsor's, etc. They make up the
secret order of the Illuminati's centralized network, which
together make up the world management team, aka the elite.

It has been discovered by Kent Adachi, Carol Quigley, and others that our world's major governments, policy think tanks, media, educational organizations, and world foundations are among the visible parts of their structure to the public. There are many layers of this shadowy group that remain hidden from the public. They're highly organized and have formulated different compartmentalized levels in a pyramidal structure; from the top, we have the Black Pope, including all figures involved within him, his cabinet, also known as the community of sorcerers, to the 13 bloodlines that operate under their direction.

The structure of this Luciferian modern-day secret Brotherhood is as follows: at its core, which is a small group of sorcerers known as Black Magicians, to its innermost highest council or the outer core of the Illuminati, is the Council of Six, which have been known to be practicing Satanists, blood drinkers, conducting sinister acts like human sacrificing and eating human flesh. Then there is the Council of Nine, who answers directly to the Council of Six, and the Council of 13, which are the 13 Bloodlines who answer to the inner councils, or the three highest grades of the Illuminati syndicate. Underneath these three councils, we also have the Committee of 300, which is composed of the world's most powerful billionaires that are associated with the Illuminati syndicate, commonly known as the current system of the Beast.

In 1992, Dr. John Coleman published "Conspirators' Hierarchy: The Story of the Committee of 300." Dr. Coleman summarized the intent and purpose of this committee as follows: a one-world government with a single worldwide monetary system, a global digital currency. According to Coleman, this one-world government system would be run by a non-elected hereditary oligarchy who will self-select from among their members, in the form of a feudal system as it was in the Middle Ages. He further goes on by stating that in this one-world government system, people will be restricted to controlled, computerized cities and will not be allowed to have more than a certain number of children. Part of their agenda is to create the necessary conditions, such as diseases, wars, and famines, to arrive at such a global governing body that will be controlled by a ruling class. There will be no middle class, only rulers and servants. This is exactly the nature and structure of the Luciferian manifesto. Anyone with a sound mind would decipher that NATO is the umbrella housing of the One World International military force, as described in the Book of Revelation. All financial processes will be conducted through an inserted ID chip that will be linked to technology controlling everyone's transactions. It is well-known that even the implementation of credit cards was a steppingstone towards this one-world digital economy. The abolishment of cash money is also part of the program of the system of the Beast and was laid out in the Protocols of the Learned Elders of Zion, which I will share in Chapter Seven. It is also known that the biometric system has already been implemented in certain states and parts of the world by this evil syndicate.

Dr. Coleman continues by stating that this system will be based on a welfare system, and those who are obedient and subservient to the One World Government will be rewarded with the means to live, while those that resist will be placed in various concentration camps that will be controlled by artificial intelligences in the future. This is the same blueprint designed by the secret government in Nazi Germany before Hitler came to power. The disturbing reality of the concentration camps, AKA smart cities, that are being developed by these billionaires, is no longer a hidden reality. Soon, the people of this Earth, still unaware of this tyranny brewing beneath their feet, will snap out of their hypnosis and regain their power. There is no difference between what the Nazis were doing and what the globalists are doing today; the only difference is that the globalists are doing it in a clandestine, covert method.

The reason people of the Earth have not been aware of this brewing agenda is because this is a silent dictatorship, which seems to be the most effective. David Icke himself stated that there are two types of dictatorships: one is an overt coup, as with Nazi Germany and the old-world Empires tried to do, and then there is the covert method, which is a more efficient one that is being executed through the Illuminati families. Icke further states that the method of overt dictatorship proves ineffective because it allows an opposition to arise from freedom fighters who don't want to live under any oppressive regime.

The covert dictatorship, depicted by David Icke, has always proven to be more successful because people would never oppose a system when they think that they are already free. This is the case in America, which has fallen under the control of the Luciferian Brotherhood secret society networks through the Executive Council on Foreign Relations. Another example of the covert method is the way that the United Nations has been formed under a global vehicle that was established in 1915 and then later consolidated in the 1940s, eventually leading to the unification of Europe, which I strongly believe is the resurrection of the Holy Roman Empire. This UN organization was formed to act as a housing umbrella of the one-world government system through the covert method.

Now, you might better understand that the secret government is secretly in control and has been manipulating all the major industrial nations like Europe, Australia, Canada, and, through the Bolshevik Revolution, even controlled Russia for a while. Latin America is also covertly under their control, and our country, of course, through the Council on Foreign Relations. Nonetheless, most leaders throughout the world have been actively full cooperative participants in this conspiracy, knowingly or unknowingly, for many of them are involved through their global network.

It is no mystery that following the first and second world wars, there has been a major consolidation of world power through the rise of the European Union, leading to the international police force, as well as through the idea of hand-picking individuals groomed since childhood to be in positions of power like presidents, prime ministers, and leaders of nations. Many researchers believe that since the inception of the Federal Reserve, all the presidents have been selected, not elected, so it never mattered if the Republicans or the Democrats won; they would have been playing for the same team. It is also well-known that the elites have always financially financed both sides, Democrats and Republicans, to further their secret agenda, making the public believe they had a choice, and in this regard, they are able to put any of their puppets in office or in a position of power. Anyone that opposes them gets eliminated; for example, President Kennedy, Ali Bhutto from Pakistan, Aldo Moro from Italy, and Colosio from Mexico, who were men that would have made a difference and were all assassinated by the secret world government of the Illuminati.

All research has pointed to the fact that the New World Order conspirators manifest their agenda through the skillful manipulation of human emotions, especially fear, since fear acts as their fuel for power. The more people they manage to keep in fear, the more people give away their power to those who wish to control us. The secret government operates extremely intelligently, and since they act in secrecy, they get away with high-level crimes. At times, they operate under the cover of the Secret Service, above all three-letter agencies.

In addition, the secret government has always manipulated the problems necessary to execute a war, a political agitation, or if they needed to create a coup d'état to overthrow a particular regime not aligned with their interest. One of the methods they have always implemented, which has worked well for them, is the "problem-reaction-solution", also known as the Hegelian Dialectic. This technique is as follows: the secret government masterminds' strategies, creates problems by financing, assembling, and training any opposition group to stimulate conflict in a particular area they wish to overthrow. If they are successful in overthrowing that government, they immediately impose their desired puppet.

By creating conflict, the secret government always offers their own solution to the reaction of the ignorant masses, who react to situations without the proper knowledge. Since the secret government has always operated through secret societies, it has been impossible for people to know what's going on. For example, all evidence conducted by multiple researchers concludes that in recent decades, so-called opposition groups are usually identified in the media as freedom fighters or liberators. Not only does the Illuminati finance and sponsor the opposition group, but also, they target groups so the masterminds of the secret government can control both sides of every conflict to facilitate their desired solution.

According to Ivan Fraser and other researchers, the leaders of the established political party that are controlled by the

Illuminati not only finance opposition, but when they are ready to take them out, they demonize them. That's what happened to Hitler, Stalin, Saddam Hussein, Milosevic, Gaddafi, and Osama bin Laden. Ironically speaking, all these people were groomed by the secret government. In truth, all these men have been pawns in a game of chess, being orchestrated by "The Hidden Hand" of the secret world government of the Illuminati. This ancient art of war, known as divide and conquer, has been employed by powerful despots and dictators throughout history, as they were all influenced to exercise the Hegelian Dialectic. One of the primary reasons the secret government strategists are equally involved in covertly arming and advising both the leaders of the established power and their opposition is that the Illuminati Secret World Government always profits from armed conflict by loaning money and supplying both sides.

In the last century, we have seen this conflict being pushed forward by the Mockingbird C.I.A. media outlets. These conspirators have been known to fabricate photos, videos, and reports of horrific and bloody atrocities suffered by innocent civilians themselves. At which point, the civilians react to the violence and ask for or accept the help that these conspirators originally had planned for them. To give you an example, Black Lives Matter was a recently fomented, orchestrated coup by the secret government to create the woke movement, which led to the idea of racial conflict. This orchestrated race war was also presented in their 24 Protocols of the Learned Elders of Zion, which again, I will be presenting in Chapter 7.

What is even more disturbing is that this cabal employs the same rhetoric in bringing about gun control in the U.S., as in the case of the Columbine atrocities, sniper incidents, and the most recent Vegas shooter. A lot of the evidence regarding these shooters has been revealed within the classified information of the C.I.A. programs under the title of Mind Control MK Ultra. This cabal has also been known to run rings of sex slaves. One of the sex slaves that broke out of her mind control was Kathy O'Brien, who was rescued by Mark Phillips. Kathy O'Brien has documented the truth about how she was used as a sex slave to many of the presidents within the last 20 years.

Perhaps the most disturbing facts that have been exposed regarding the cabal families involve the idea of human blood drinking, child sacrificing in torture rituals for a chemical substance known as adrenochrome, which has been documented to regenerate their lifespan and keep these cabal families looking younger. This chemical compound, adrenochrome, is known to be extracted and released through a child's emotional body when they are in a state of fear and torture.

Using the same technique of "problem-reaction-solution" , the establishment of the United Nations was executed as the last consolidating effort of the secret government over the world. This should not be surprising, for John the Revelator in the Book of Revelation clearly states that the coming of the government of the Antichrist is modeled in the same way the United Nations was designed. Studying the biblical prophecies beyond its allegory and symbols, one can clearly understand how this Revelation would unfold, as it parallels the formation and operation of the UN. In the Book of Revelation, John the Revelator signals the coming of the one-world government system, aka the New World Order. He makes it clear that the Antichrist first comes as a peace-bringer, which is exactly what the UN has been set up to do by the secret government as a major part of their globalization programs.

According to the Book of Revelation, this Antichrist rises and disguises itself as a restorer of world peace, which is precisely what John the Revelator said, and it's exactly what the UN is doing and has been designed to consolidate all the national states and sovereignties of all countries into a single fascist world system known as the new world order.

Most scholars, theologians, and so-called learned people have failed to recognize that the U.N. is the exact description that John the Revelator was talking about, that is, to act as a housing umbrella of the coming one-world system. What else needs to be understood is that the Antichrist is not just one man alone who is expected to come in the last of days. The truth of the matter is that the Antichrist has always ruled this world, as stated in the Bible. The powers of this world, however, have been unable to accomplish its full-blown agenda of enacting the Luciferian manifesto, which is the underlying core of the system of the beast. It is the influence and desire of the dark force that have us believing that the Antichrist is coming when it has always been here as the system of Babylon.

This agenda has obviously been counteracted many times by the forces of light that are also prevalent in our world, acting as custodians and guardians of sacred divine knowledge, truth, and the protectors of the concept of the Republic. In the past, however, there have been times when the Beast system has come close to executing its full agenda. As we end their reign, their control of the financial and political centers of the world has been prophesied to eventually crumble.

For instance, in premortal existence, this war was fought for the control of our entire universe. The Fallen Angel, Lucifer, has, since his separation from God in the Heavens, believed it was his right to bring under his absolute control the entire universe. This separation from God began the great Universal battle that is now coming to an end here on our planet. It is also important to know that 98% or more of our universe, except for our world, has been won by the light, and it's now reaching our reality. This has been revealed by various spiritual sources that are now restoring the truth to the people of this Earth. The victory of the light began first in the celestial spheres and descended into the galactic spheres, cleansing all the fallen intelligences and species that fell under the control of the Fallen angelics. The only planet still lurking in darkness is our own little Earth, which is a great part of the Divine Universal plan and is soon to be restored.

It is good to reveal that most of Lucifer's fallen angels have been defeated and neutralized by Archangel Michael, and his forces are also getting ready to fully cleanse and neutralize the last remaining forces of darkness still on the Earth. Without a doubt, one can clearly see that the warnings and signs of this momentous event are here. This information has been confirmed by various spiritual sources who are attempting to bring forth the good news that the kingdom of the most high is at hand. Unfortunately, many people remain asleep to the changes that are upon us, ignoring the signs of the times as they become hypnotized by the mass media and control institutions of the Secret Government.

The truth is coming forward as people are now beginning to see for themselves since the 9/11 event. Also, the age of information is making it possible, and has for the last 25 years, for this information to finally come out to the public, to wake up and understand the operations of the secret government. A lot of the substantial evidence regarding this cabal has come from multiple independent resources from every field of knowledge, documented within the political arena by economist and political insider Lyndon LaRouche in his Executive Intelligence Review. Lyndon LaRouche, with the Executive Intelligence Review, has been exposing the corruption of the modern-day neo-cons that are masquerading under the control of the corporations.

The truth is that throughout all of history, every war, every conflict has been executed by the secret government. For example, World War I and II, and all the wars between the last three centuries all the way up to the Iraq War, including modern-day Hamas and Israel, have been maneuvered and orchestrated by these globalists, who have been the masterminds of all the conflict everywhere. The war waged today is no different than the war that was waged in Heaven; it is just in its last phase. It is important to understand that the "forces of good" have always been here, counteracting the forces of evil from behind the scenes, as well preserving the constitutional Republic and then later manifesting as the White Knights, hence the plan. The forces of evil, on the other hand, are fighting for the same reasons that Lucifer opposed God in the premortal realm, which was to eradicate free will, the greatest gift of the universe. That is why the remnant family, that are the bloodlines of the Luciferians today, the Leviathan lineage, are attempting to do the same, and why the quests for world domination continue to be pushed by these families that are trying so desperately to manifest their age-old agenda that could be traceable back to the war in Heaven.

The core that created the Illuminati, the financial interest groups, are the Jesuit priests of the Vatican. As mentioned, there are only two types of government or community structures: one is based on agape love, freedom, and prosperity, which is the structure of a free world. On the other hand, the structure of the Luciferian system is based on bondage and suffering brought about by the totalitarian system of universal absolutism, otherwise known as totalitarianism. This is why it is important to know the true meanings and reasons behind every political action, revolution, and war. They are all driven by one of two true forces: the "forces of good" are the people behind the free world Republic, and again, the forces of darkness are those that have been pushing for tyranny.

While most believe that the 13 bloodlines, the international bankers of the cabal families, were the most important extension of the Beast system, it is not its core. However, the embodiment of the Antichrist always concealed itself like onion layers, with various secret societies surrounded by the core of the Beast itself, a community of sorcerers. This community of sorcerers, as mentioned, are the Society of Jesus, also known as the Jesuits. The Jesuits are the missing link between the modern-day Illuminati New World Order and the old, struggling Roman Holy Empire. The Jesuits came to power in 1501 as a counteract to the 15th-century Reformation. When the pope issued the Council of Trent, which was the old Holy Roman Empire's way of reorganizing themselves by orchestrating all the religious wars in Europe from the 1500s to the 1790s, when they switched their methodology to the Babylonian fiat money system.

During the period of the 1500s to about the 1780s, when Adam Weishaupt came into the scene, who was educated by Jesuit-run universities, the Jesuits attempted to bring back power to the Pope through all the wars they caused until finally, through the House of Rothschild, who used to be known as Bauer or "Red Shield," shifted the power of the Vatican over into a new structure that evolved into the corporate conglomerate that runs the world today.

All history books conveniently left out the information regarding the oppressive nature of the Jesuit order. One of the prerogatives of the Jesuit is that they wielded a great deal of control over the top universities and colleges in the Western world, especially in Europe, which is why they have substantial influence and power over most educational curriculums. In truth, the Jesuits represent the true meaning and core of the embodiment of the Beast, the system of the Antichrist, "The Hidden Hand" of Satan. At least, they were the last order of darkness to evolve out of the Old Guard during the days of the Roman Empire.

For simplicity, let's refer to this order as a modern-day Brotherhood of the embodiment of Babylon. This Dark Brotherhood has kept us in ignorance by placing a monopoly over the right knowledge all throughout history and has repeatedly revised books to conceal the truth to serve their agenda. They control what we know and have been for the last thousands of years, which is why they remain hidden. We can see the trace of this Hidden Hand throughout history, the synagogue of Satan during the times of the Roman Empire that controlled the Pharisees, Sadducees, and, of course, Rome, to "The Hidden Hand" behind every overt empire that has ever existed on the face of our Earth.

Even though the world has only known about the Illuminati but not so much about the Jesuits, the core that has been running all criminal and secret society networks since the 1500s, being the last arm of an ancient agenda that could be traceable back to Nimrod. Therefore, in modern times, the

Jesuits have been at the core of this Luciferian manifesto, controlling the financial arm known as the Illuminati or the international bankers, but also controlling the organized crime families through the mafias, the Knights of Malta, and, of course, the Knights of Columbus. The knowledge of this order came to light when certain priests defected from the Jesuit order, like Alberto Rivera.

Thanks to Alberto Rivera, the truth of who the Jesuits have been has come to light, and he did confirm that everything that has been going on in this world has been controlled by the Supreme Jesuit General himself, who is known to be the second most powerful man in the world, next to the great Pope Pepe Orsini. For the record, this international order, the military Society of Jesus, the Jesuits, have been the force behind all the wars, the death of uncontrollable presidents, including the 9/11 attacks. With this new understanding, we can now state that the Jesuits have been the force behind the globalization programs of the European Union, the expansion of NATO, and the world government.

Anyone in their right mind would know that the total existence of the U.N. was never about bringing peace to the world but was about consolidating national sovereignties of the world's nations into one universal global government, the resurrected Holy Roman Empire. A perfect example of this "problem-reaction-solution" was when the Jesuits and their Illuminati financial arms orchestrated the first and second world wars with the ultimate desire of bringing these countries into union after terrorizing them with war. This lie of great proportion led to the rise of the European Union, which is at the head of the world government through the World Health Organization, the World Economic Forum, and NATO.

The existence of the U.N. was never about bringing peace to the world, even though it posed that way. In consideration of this global movement, one must consider the words described in the book of Revelation by John the Revelator. It is, therefore, important to understand the operations of the Beast system in today's world as it parallels the events that took place in the premortal realm of the Heavens. As is now known, the intention of establishing a world government based on a totalitarian regime structure is a reality that reflects the reason why the war in Heaven was fought. Lucifer wanted to take away free will from all living things throughout the universe, which is the same thing that today's secret government has been trying to bring about a global union through the continued consolidation of world power. Those of us who discern the truth behind the fake liberation of globalization programs understand that the European Union is a secret government of the Jesuit Illuminati syndicate manifesting a revived Holy Roman Empire. With the erection of the Holy Roman Empire, aka the European Union, hence Global Union, the Beast system would have tried to encompass an entire world under absolute tyranny and control. This, my friends, is known as the new world order.

In examination of further pain and afflicted suffering, it is important to understand some aspects of the globalization programs implemented by the beast. The total indebtedness of millions, inflicted by the secret government, is also part of a eugenics secret project, which was initiated during and after the wars as another satanic worldwide political plot against our humanity to kill off as many people as possible before they execute their Luciferian old-age agenda of a one-world government. It is well-known that part of their intention is to disseminate 3/4 of the world population, as revealed by Dr. John Coleman. This plot is real, and the primary deadly weapon that the secret government has been using, like HIV among other diseases and many more that were to come, all developed by these private scientists, one was Dr. Robert Gallo, and the other was his colleague, Anthony Fauci.

The creation and manufacturing of all these diseases are ultra-top-secret projects of the eugenics programs, which were set up after World War II when the Illuminati world government changed their power structure from Germany over to the United States of America through Project Paperclip. These atrocious, satanic, hidden programs explain why people have been dying by the millions because of what's been happening from behind the scenes, not to mention the poisoning of our food supply and the contamination of our air through chemtrails.

In the Book of Ephesians, it is well known that we are not at war with flesh and blood but with powers and principalities that are not of this world. Many discoveries agree that the evil that generates from the synagogue of "The Hidden Hand", the secret government, comes from the lower fourth dimension where actual demonic forces, AKA Draconian, exist and operate from. As mentioned previously, the core of the Jesuit Illuminati Syndicate secret world government is being driven by malevolent modern-day sorcerers who, in turn, are guided and directed by entities that are not from this dimension, as revealed in the Book of Ephesians.

Further evidence of these fourth-dimensional, extraterrestrial demonic entities comes from mind control victims that have snapped out of their mind control. For example, in the book called "Transformation of America," Kathy O'Brien clearly exposes not only the truth behind the secret government and their intentions but also reveals in detail that at the highest levels of the Illuminati, they are indeed practicing Satanists who, in turn, answer to off-world entities. Another deprogrammed individual, Brice Taylor, the author of "Thanks for the Memories," Things Remembered while being under mind control, confirmed that at the highest echelons of the secret government are off-world entities. All these individuals, from Kathy O'Brien to Brice Taylor, have been exposing what's been going on since the end of World War II. They've also admitted that the Oklahoma City bombing was also an orchestrated event, as well as all the snipers and killings that have been going on in America.

Another clue in the Bible that reveals the nature of the system of Babylon is that the love of money is the root of all evil, not some evil but all evil. This implication is also true and examines how the financial arm known as the Illuminati managed to gain control of our world governments, especially the United States government, by seizing control of our economy since the establishment of the Jesuit-run, privately-owned Federal Reserve system. It is, therefore, through the control and manipulation of money that the Illuminati prosper and can buy out and control anyone willing to sell their soul for a price. The top families involved in this organization within the secret government are rich beyond rich and can use their money to get anything they want.

This sinister group even established an isolated island that was set aside by this cabal to take possible candidates groomed for positions of power worldwide to have them blackmailed with evidence of them having sex with young women under the age of 18. The top families involved in the organization have established a worldwide pedophilia network that is being run by them and kept secret by the politicians and celebrities that have participated in such blasphemy. Within the secret government rich beyond rich and can use their money to get anything they want. This cabal has been hoarding money for centuries, unsatisfied until all power resources and world economies are controlled and administered by them. They continue to make billions per year at the expense of our world through their industries and cartels, which account for a great proportion of their accumulation of wealth, which is why corruption exists. Money, just like anything else, could either be used for good or evil, but the love of money, which implies service to self at the expense of others, is what leads to corruption.

The truth of the matter is that these secret organizations and secret societies exist and have always been posing a great threat to our world. The only reason they haven't taken over the world is because of the great nation that gave mankind the gift of freedom, the United States Constitution, which was given to us by God through His emissary, the Brotherhood of Light, thus making it impossible for the Jesuit Illuminati syndicate to corrupt it overtly. Other regions impeding the secret government's full takeover are India, Tibet, Brazil, and many other countries that are building a worldwide resistance against this globalization program.

Furthermore, globalization is the reason why General Motors collapsed, as well as other major companies that once provided millions with jobs in the states. Globalization is also playing a key role in the elimination of the middle class. The elimination of the middle class brings us back to a state of feudalism, where there is only a small number of rich and a large volume of poor. This Luciferian system has been dominating Europe for the last 1700 years, and it's exactly the type of system that the secret government today wants to resurrect. With the globalization programs taking effect, the Jesuit Illuminati

Syndicate World Government Elite can subjugate all the remaining nations that are not in alignment with the new world order. That is the sole purpose of this evil globalization program.

The Executive Intelligence Review, written by Lyndon LaRouche, an insider economist and political activist who is out to expose the international fascism of the syndicate, as he would call them, reveals that our country, the United States of America, with its Constitution, is being threatened by the synarchist international bankers, another term used to identify the Illuminati. He exposes fascism in our country as exercised by the Bush administrations, as well as the Clinton administration, with Dick Cheney, who is a puppet for the synarchist cabal international bankers. LaRouche has proven this with impeccable evidence coming from multiple sources in the political, economic, and social spectrum. In the Executive Intelligence Review, it is reported that a group of private interest groups, as Linden calls the synarchist, is currently and has been manipulating the office of the United States government, exemplified with Truman, Carter, Johnson, Nixon, and both Bushes.

LaRouche has solid, documented evidence that this powerful cabal group of powerful private banking houses is deliberately trying to overthrow and undo our constitutional Republic in a coup d'état to create a totalitarian fascist police state in our own country, and hence the entire world. He unveils people like George Schultz, Carl Smith, Henry Kissinger, and George Soros. Since 2000, Lyndon LaRouche has clearly put out evidence regarding this disrupting element that has been undermining the U.S. Constitution, destroying our constitutional Republic for more than 20 years.

All researchers agree that all the world's problems are arising from this secret government of financial interest groups and private banking houses known as the international financiers. They incurred an enormous financial debt to pardon our nation and upon every individual, not only within the states but in all the other countries around the world. This debt exists because of their privately owned Central Banking system, the Federal Reserve, which has been loaning our nation's money since its inception. The central banking system has affected not only our economy but the global economy. Their main agenda is to collapse the economy to insert a worldwide single currency.

The disaster of economic ruin is part of their blueprint of global domination, causing further harm by the secret government through the Bank of International Settlements. The IMF has been deliberately destroying the economies of the world. In addition, the gradual collapse of our physical economic infrastructure is resulting from this economic injustice by sending jobs to third-world countries who make people in other parts of the world work for cheap labor, which is modern-day slavery. In short, the Federal Reserve and the IMF are privately owned by international bankers and the 13 most ultra-wealthy families in the world, the 13 Bloodlines of the Illuminati.

All these socially engineered catastrophes and more have been deliberately orchestrated by the worldwide agents of the secret government. By using the Hegelian Dialectic, the globalists destroyed countries' economies, then offered financing to rebuild them, "problem-reaction-solution". This puts them in deeper debt to the New World Order synarchist gang. So, every nation is in major debt to a group of powerful genius bankers who consider themselves the elite of the world. When a nation is unable to pay the debt, the bankers begin controlling the nation's policies, which is part of their Protocols of the Learned Elders of Zion.

People will always react to a problem, as proven in physics, cause and effect. In this case, when people have no knowledge of those causing the problems, they are rendered helpless and will accept any solutions. Usually, this solution is the original one desired by the masterminds of the secret government. In short, all these contrived maneuvers, wars, monetary collapse, elimination of the middle class, coup, etc., have been socially engineered, designed to bring the entire world to its knees. If they succeed, this will ultimately eliminate the entire middle class, bringing us into a global fascist state of feudalism.

Using solid reason, the system of the Beast, the embodiment of Babylon, is a source of all evils affecting our world. From the fomenting of wars and terrorism to the engineering of worldwide poverty, the creation of lethal diseases to the fact that millions are dying daily, all are because they won't rest until all power is concentrated in the hands of a self-proclaimed elite who are continuing an ancient old plot that has descended throughout their secret society networks. This age-old plot has been passed down through generations from family to family, and it is believed that these families have suffered from a high concentration of reptilian genetics.

Unfortunately, most people in our world have been clueless to the real powers and movers and shakers that have operated from behind the scenes. One major reason is the fact that these powers and shakers have gained absolute control of the mass media as well as all educational systems through the Jesuit order and the medical system. Some believe that they even control the religious system of organized religions, keeping mankind from having a direct experience with the divine and divided. So once again, our humanity is facing a crossroad, as we have many times in the past during different eras. We, the people of the world, need to wake up and demand change for a better tomorrow because it is not only our lives, we are fighting for but the lives of our children and our children's children.

According to prophecy, we are in the times of the Great Awakening, and the material presented in this book is presented to help trigger the Great Awakening process, for it is essential information that needs to be known by every individual on this planet. We need to come to terms with the last bastion of this ancient cabal so that we can regain our power back. Therefore, our quality of living, as we become aware, can together demand change and make a better world. It is the awareness of the real problems and identifying the sources of all these problems, and as a collective, planning to no longer tolerate these evils.

Before one can remedy any problem, one must first discover its root cause and eliminate the problem from its roots. To better understand the evils going on in our world, we must examine its roots, which could be traceable back to Babylon. For even the mafia is an organized crime family that is an extension of these hidden groups, commonly associated with the secret government. The crime family organizations operate under the Knights of Malta and are needed to run the black market, which, with its other cartels like the oil, banking, and pharmaceuticals, etc., generate enormous amounts of money for the elites. The embodiment of this evil is like an octopus with many arms and tentacles; it can only be defeated if we eliminate it from its core, not just cutting off an arm or a tentacle, for it will just grow another one.

Learning about the nature of malevolent secret societies, we can decipher the real masterminds and authors of terrorism are the powers within the secret orders, not the killing mercenaries that they have trained, sponsored, financed, and molded by the same wicked powers in high places that are orchestrating wars, controlling the international black market, coordinating coups, assassinations, and launching the evil exploitations of globalization. Therefore, the secret government was and is the source and power that created, directed, and financed all terrorist groups, from Bin Laden to Al-Qaeda and even ISIS. They are only pawns in the chess game of World Domination, while the real chess masters are functioning from behind the scenes in the highest echelons of world government. This revelation may be difficult to digest but considering that the One World Government Elite is willing to go to any measure to assure their takeover of our planet, it is all true, as the end justifies the means for them. For example, rationalizing it and considering their famous technique, the creation-reaction-solution method, this one-world secret government can create their own terrorist attack, which is the problem created, the people respond, and they offer the solution that they want.

According to Lyndon LaRouche, as well as many other researchers, there is ample evidence that supports the claim that 9/11 was an inside job from the same secret conspirators that are operating from Washington DC. The order came from the Black Pope himself, and through the secret society network, the C.I.A. was able to orchestrate the event. This is no different than when Nazi Germany blew up the Reichstag Bank, which served to impose the Nazi regime in Germany in the early 1930s. This is the same tactic that the globalists have been using since they orchestrated the 9/11 attacks.

Of course, any type of atrocity will be followed by a mass response reaction by the people, and the solution imposed by these hidden groups that have been controlling our world from behind the scenes. Like I said before, there is nothing different between what Nazi Germany was trying to execute and what these globalists are trying to do. It has been revealed that our country's freedoms have been diminished since the 9/11 attacks, and the National Security Agency has become more dictatorial by passing the treasonous Patriot Act, allowing our government to spy on its own citizens. The people in power, who are public agents of the secret government, are attempting to suspend our Constitution and impose martial law through FEMA, and they have been for many years. This explains why FEMA did nothing after the Katrina disaster or any of the other disasters since then. The real purpose is to serve the dictates of the secret controllers who are in control of our government. Its purpose serves as the secret agenda for an organization that would immediately take over the country in case of any natural, social, or economic catastrophe, giving full power to the executive branch.

In summary, there is ample evidence surfacing, indicating that there is a conscious conspiracy that exists and is attempting to exercise world domination. These are the kinds of social, political, and economic disasters that would be engineered by the secret government to suspend the Constitution and allow the corporations to assert absolute power and control. Despite what we are sold through the controlled media that is manipulated by the secret government, the truth is that there is a powerful body of extremely evil people in high places who have been directing the forces and the affairs of our world events and have been the cause of all our problems. They are the secret government of the ancient Babylonian Brotherhood, the Brotherhood of the Snake, and their goal is absolute domination of our world, and their agenda has been boiling not only for centuries but for thousands of years by the same powers, the same bloodlines that have been shifting their power from region to region since the beginning of recorded time. This world is being ruled by powers of wickedness in high places that have been dominating all the institutions for the last 6,000 years, and their time is up.

In summary, there is ample evidence surfacing, indicating that there is a conscious conspiracy that exists and is attempting to exercise world domination. This reality is being executed by the powerful and wealthy who think that they own the world and their alien overlords. These families are members of various secret societies that have been operating in secret for thousands of years. They are the ultra-secret groups of extremely evil people who are secretly running the world from behind the scenes and have absolute control over think tanks, media, educational systems, government, and economic districts. That said, here are some statements and words from some presidents who have become aware of this cabal and various prominent political figures who have admitted to having knowledge of a secret shadow government operating behind the visible government of the world, manipulating both the European, North, and South American governments since the Second World War.

Chapter 3: THE EVIDENCE OF A CONSPIRACY

President Franklin Roosevelt, prior to being elected, wrote a letter to Colonel Edward Mandell House, President Wilson's close advisor, stating, "The real truth of the matter is, as you and I know, that a financial element of international bankers in the large centers has owned every government since the days of Andrew Jackson." That there exists a cabal of power brokers who control governments from behind the scenes has been detailed several times this century by credible sources. After making such statements, a few weeks later, President Roosevelt was murdered.

Professor Carroll Quigley, Bill Clinton's mentor at Georgetown University, in his magnum opus "Tragedy and Hope" published in 1966, states, "There does exist, and has existed for a generation, an international network which operates, to some extent, in the way the radical right believes the Communists act." In fact, this network, which we may identify as the Round Table Groups or secret societies created by Cecil Rhodes in 1889 to further the plan for global dominance, has no aversion to cooperating with the Communists or other groups and frequently does so. Professor Quigley further states, "I know of the operation of this network because I have studied it for twenty years and was permitted for two years in the 1960s to examine its papers and secret records. I have no aversion to most of its aims. I have objected, both in the past and recently, to a few of its policies. But, in general, my chief difference of opinion is that it wishes to remain unknown, and I believe its role in history is significant enough to be known."

The term "New World Order" was first used by none other than Adolf Hitler himself. "National Socialism will use its own revolution for the establishment of a new world order." The Associated Press reported that on July 26, 1968, New York Governor Nelson Rockefeller said in a speech to the International Platform Association at the Sheraton Park Hotel in New York that as president, he would work toward the international creation of a new world order.

Edward VIII became King of England on January 20, 1936, but was forced to abdicate the throne 11 months later when he married a commoner. He became the Duke of Windsor and in July 1940 became the governor of the Bahamas. He went on record saying, "Whatever happens, whatever the outcome, a new world order is going to come into the world. It will be buttressed by public power."

Richard Gardner, former deputy assistant Secretary of State for International Organizations under Kennedy and Johnson, and a member of the Trilateral Commission, a modern-day front for a secret society involving the world's most powerful, wrote in the April 1974 issue of the Council on Foreign Relations (CFR) journal Foreign Affairs, "In short, the 'house of world order' will have to be built from the bottom up rather than from the top down. It will look like a great 'booming, buzzing confusion,' but an end run around national sovereignty, eroding it piece by piece, will accomplish much more than the old-fashioned frontal assault."

During the 1976 presidential campaign, Jimmy Carter said, "We must replace balance of power politics with world order politics." In a February 14, 1977, speech, Carter said, "I want to assure you that the relations of the United States with other countries and peoples of the world will be guided during my administration by our desire to shape a world order that I believe will be more responsive to human aspirations. The United States will meet the obligation to help create a stable, just, and peaceful world order." He's using the same bait, obviously, as the U.N.

Harvard Professor Stanley Hoffmann wrote in his book Primacy or World Order, "What will have to take place is a gradual adaptation of the social, economic, and political systems of the United States to the imperatives of world order."

Conservative author George Weigel, director of the Ethics and Public Policy Center in Washington, D.C., said, "If the United States does not unashamedly lay down the rules of world order and enforce them, then there is little reason to think that peace, security, freedom, or prosperity will be preserved."

The man who put the New World Order in the limelight and did more than anyone to bring about its acceptance was President George Bush senior. In a February 1990 fundraiser in San Francisco, Bush Senior said, "Time and time again, in this century, the political map of the world was transformed. And in each instance, a new world order came about through the advent of a new tyranny or the outbreak of a bloody global war, or its equivalent."

On Saturday, August 25, 1990, the United Nations Security Council voted unanimously to allow a joint military force to use whatever means necessary to enforce a U.N. blockade against the country of Iraq. That afternoon, Lieutenant General Brent Scowcroft, a CFR member and former aide to Henry Kissinger, the National Security Advisor to Bush, was interviewed by Charles Bierbaur of the Cable News Network (CNN) and used the term "the New World Order" during a September 1990 speech at the U.N., announcing that "we are moving toward a new world order." In the fall of 1990, on his way back to Belgium, Secretary of State James Baker said, "If we really believe that there is an opportunity here for a new world order, many of us believe that we can't start out by appeasing aggression."

In a September 11, 1990, televised address to a joint session of Congress, Senior Bush said, "A new partnership of nations has begun. We stand today at a unique and extraordinary moment. The crisis in the Persian Gulf, as grave as it is, offers a rare opportunity to move "toward an historic period of cooperation". Out of these troubled times, our fifth objective—a new world order—can emerge. When we are successful, and we will be, we have a real chance at this new world order, an order in which a credible United Nations can use its peacekeeping role to fulfill the promise and vision of the U.N.'s folders." The Jesuit Illuminati syndicate.

The September 17, 1990, issue of Time Magazine said that the Bush Administration would like to make the United Nations a cornerstone of its plans to construct a new world order and a long era of peace. Jeanne Kirkpatrick, former U.S. ambassador to the U.N., said, "One of the purposes for the Desert Storm operation was to show the world how a reinvigorated United Nations could serve as a global policeman in the New World Order." Prior to the Gulf, on January 29, 1991, Bush told the nation in his State of the Union address, "What is at stake is more than one small country; it is a big idea—a new world order, where diverse nations are drawn together in common cause to achieve the universal aspirations of mankind: peace and security, freedom, and the rule of law. Such is a world worthy of our struggle and worthy of our children's future." Of course, this is what the president tells the public, what they want to hear. In an interview with CNN at the height of the Gulf War, Scowcroft said he had doubts about the signature Middle East objectives regarding global policy. When asked if that meant he didn't believe in the New World Order, he replied, "Oh, I believe in it, but our definition, not theirs."

In a speech to the families of servicemen at Fort Gordon, Georgia, on February 1, 1991, Bush said, "When we win, and we will, we will have taught a dangerous dictator, and any tyrant tempted to follow in his footsteps, that the United States has a new credibility. And what we say goes, and that there is no place for lawless aggression in the Persian Gulf in this new world order that we seek to create." Following a February 6, 1991, speech to the Economic Club of New York City, Bush answered a reporter's question about what the new world order was, by saying, "Now my vision of a new world order foresees a United Nations with a revitalized peacekeeping function." He said in a speech to Congress on March 6, 1991, "Now we can see a new world order coming into view." On August 11, 1991, after the failed coup in the Soviet Union, a CNN reporter said that the president's new world order is "back on track, now stronger than ever." On January 25, 1995, Clinton's Secretary of State, Warren Christopher, said in a CNN interview, "We must get the New World Order on track and bring the U.N. into its correct role in regard to the United States."

On September 10, 1878, Disraeli said, "The governments have not to deal with emperors, kings, and ministers, but also with secret societies which have everywhere their unscrupulous agents and can at the last moment upset all government plans."

In 1987, Henry Edward Manning, Cardinal Archbishop of Westmoreland, spoke of the trouble in the Balkan states: "It is not emperors or kings, nor princes, that direct the course of affairs in the east. There is something else over them and behind them, and that thing is more powerful than them."

In 1902, Pope Leo XIII wrote of this power: "It bends governments to its will sometimes by promises, sometimes by threats. It has found its way into every class of society and forms an invincible and irresponsible power, an independent government, as it were, within the body corporate of the lawful state."

Walter Rathenau, head of German General Electric, said in 1909," there are 300 men, all of whom know one another, direct the economic Destiny of Europe and choose their successor from among themselves." John F Highland, mayor of New York City from 1918 to 1925 said in a March 26th, 1922, speech," the real Menace of our Republic is the Invincible government which, like a giant octopus sprawls it's slimy length over city-state nations. At the head is a small group of powerful banking houses generally referred to as the international bankers. This group of powerful International bankers virtually runs the United States government for their own selfish purpose." President Woodrow Wilson said." There is a power somewhere so organized, so subtle, so watchful, so interlocked, so complete, and so pervasive that no one better not speak in condemnation of it."

According to the California state investigating committee on education 1953." So modern communism is apparently the same hypocritical and deadly world conspiracy to destroy civilization that was founded by The Secret order of the

Illuminati and Bavaria on May 1st, 1776, and that raised its working hand in our colonies here at the critical period before the adoption of our federal constitution." Dr Tom Berry, who was pastor of the Baptist Bible Church in Maryland, said." at most there are only 5,000 people in the world who have a significant understanding of the plan." Senator William Jenna said in a February 23, 1954 speech," Today the plan to total dictatorship in the United States can be laid by strictly legal means, unseen and unheard by congress, the president, or the people. Outwardly we have a constitutional government and political system, inwardly we have another body representing another form of government, "bureaucratic elite" which believes the Constitution is outmoded and is sure that it is the winning side. All the strange developments in foreign policy agreements may be traced to this group who are going to make us over to suit their pleasure. This political action group has its own local political support organizations, its own pressure groups, its own vested interests, and its foothold within our government." Senator Russell Long of Louisiana, who for 18 years was the chairman of the Senate Finance committee said, "our government is completely and totally out of control. We do not know how much long-term debt we have put on the American people. We don't even know our financial condition from year to year." He also said," we have created a bureaucracy in Washington so gigantic that it is running that government for the bureaucracy the way they want, and not for the people of the United States."

The terms New World Order and one world government have been a topic in the 20th century, so the conspirators have camouflaged the concept under the banner of the global union. Just as we have the European Union in Europe emerging, we also have through NAFTA the North American free trade agreement, which is to evolve into the American

Union and APEC the Asian Pacific economic cooperation is to evolve into the Pacific Union, which once in format will Encompass all the Asian superpowers such as Japan China and Korea, the three most powerful Asian nations in the east. and finally, the African Union is to bring all the countries of the African continent into a centralized body politic. All four unions are scheduled to evolve into the global Union that is to manifest as the One World Government, New World Order government of the Beast. The name has shifted but the agenda remains, and this has perpetuated throughout history.

Chapter 4: THE ANCIENT WORLD

In order to understand the plot for world domination and the problems challenging our world, we must understand what took place in the ancient world. After the flood, Noah and his selective people were destined to repopulate the Earth. Noah had three sons, Shem, Japheth, and Ham. All brothers were learned in the ways of their father, Noah. As far as we know, these three figures became the most significant persons that helped in the repopulation of the Earth after the flood. After the cataclysmic event known as the Great Deluge in the Bible, the world had been wiped out for its wickedness. But there was more to the story than just wickedness, for before the Great Deluge, the civilization that existed prior to our known world had reached a high level of development and technology that by far surpassed our civilization today. It was the world before our own, and of course, all records indicating a world before Egypt were eradicated through various cataclysms and the many generations of people who seem to have rewritten history over and over, forgetting the pre-diluvian age.

The key point is, what kind of civilization existed before the Egyptians or Sumerians? To our discovery, and in the light of today's wonderful age of information, there is proof that there was an even more advanced ancient civilization that existed prior to our own ancient world. Apparently, this pre-ancient civilization was using advanced technology for evil purposes. In order for the human race to continue evolving according to divine will, that wicked civilization needed to be destroyed. This was the ancient civilization of Atlantis. Central to their wickedness was their attempt to dominate our world. This fact reveals how the quest for world domination really originated with the powers that took over the Atlantean empire. Technically speaking, it was the Atlanteans that wanted to dominate the world about 12,000 years ago that led to their civilization sinking and the destruction of the firmament, that was a band of thick moisture in the atmosphere, which kept our world in some constant tropical season. The destruction of that firmament caused the Great Flood of the Bible. We can trace the Luciferian manifesto to the days of Atlantis, which became a corrupt empire Controlled by a community of sorcerers. This suppressed event took place approximately 12,000 years ago.

After the fall of Atlantis, it was time for God to give the human race another chance to develop according to the Divine plan, which was to first evolve spiritually so that our humanity could be ahead of technological development and not the other way around, which was the case of Atlantis. It was decided to preserve a remnant portion of the ancient survivors through Noah and his family, who were righteous Atlanteans. In spite of the corruption and wickedness that caused the fall of Atlantis, they remained loyal to the highest good. After the flood, Noah was also given the opportunity to continue the body of knowledge of the ancients, which became known as the ancient sacred knowledge or ageless wisdom of the ancient ones.

This wisdom later became the secret tradition of esoteric knowledge of certain hereditary priesthoods and benevolent orders that tried to preserve it and guarded it because it was considered such a high level of knowledge. It was preserved and taught to those who showed signs of readiness. When the time was right, they would reveal it to the world at large. Had no one preserved the priceless wisdom of all ages, our civilization would have evolved as the Atlanteans did, being only one-sided technologically, and we would have destroyed ourselves long ago. This ancient knowledge was the wisdom that existed in our world before the flood. This wisdom was passed on to the three sons of Noah by their father, marking the beginning of the oral tradition. All three sons were given different regions of the Eastern hemisphere, mainly the Mesopotamia area where officially Western world history began.

Shem's people began settling and building communities of people who were willing to work together to help build a great civilization in ancient Sumer. One of them became known as the greatest and oldest civilization next to Egypt. According to history books, it is one of the earliest civilizations recorded by man after the flood. Japheth's people also contributed to building these first civilizations, but they spread further into Asia. The descendants of Shem became known as the Semites, thus beginning the origins of the Semitic people.

At least that's how they got their name, from Shem, Noah's most righteous son who had educated his family in the ways of God, as exemplified through his grandson Abraham. It was his descendants who made a pact with God to establish the Kingdom of Heaven on Earth. Shem was the progenitor who was considered the most righteous man to ever live after the flood. Some researchers have stated that the mysterious figure known as Melchizedek of Salem would have been Shem.

The process of contending with God till the End is the true meaning of Israel. It was never supposed to be a specific religion, nation, or an exclusive people. It was a name given by God to those who were supposed to contend with light despite the opposition till the end of the cycle. This program, Israel, was designated for the people that were trying to evolve spiritually first and not succumb to the indoctrinations of Babylon. Through Shem's lineage, his grandson Abraham inherited the promise that Shem made with God as he proved to be a righteous inheritor of teachings of the light.

How did Evil emerge after God had wiped out the Earth in the flood? How did the Dark Brotherhood of Satan form again after they had been destroyed in Atlantis? It was believed that the people of Shem were building good societies around Mesopotamia, Middle East, and Asia Minor area. We not only had Sumer, but other developing areas were beginning to pop up, including the great civilization that became known as one of the greatest societies that ever existed in its prime glory, Egypt.

Both the people of Shem and Japheth contributed, traded, and even resided in Egypt when it was ruled by righteousness. It was these two civilizations, Sumer and Egypt, that began constructing our new world. Both reached marvelous heights in spirituality and maintained this aspect ahead of their technological progress. The new world was beginning to take shape, and the first civilizations known to man were magnificent until Ham, a son of Noah, decided it was his destiny to rule the world. He began devising a plan that would give him and his lineage dominance over the new world. This meant establishing absolute power over his brethren and their descendants. The reason behind his indifference to his brothers is unknown, but it has come to light that Ham made a pact with the dark side in order to continue the Luciferian agenda that destroyed Atlantis.

Noah shared the ancient wisdom with all his sons, but it was up to them to either use it for good or evil. Apparently, Shem and Japheth used their knowledge for good, as exemplified in the building of great civilizations like Egypt and Sumer, and continued the ageless knowledge by establishing the ancient mystery schools, even reaching the island of Crete where the ancient Greek civilization was beginning to take form. This knowledge became transmitted by the ancient oral tradition that began with the mysterious Melchizedek, Shem. On the other hand, Ham thought it was in his best interest to misuse the sacred knowledge of the Ancients to create a pact with the adversary, all because he longed for his descendants to rule the new world over Shem and Japheth's descendants. This family feud began the battle of Good and Evil in the new world and is the reason why the world today is in a state of final conflict between their descendants.

What happened to Ham's nature is a mystery. Hypothetically speaking, he could have fallen into the possession of some dark fallen entities/demons/reptilians who promised Ham that if he contended with them, Ham's people would rule absolutely over all the Earth. This implied that his descendants have the right to do whatever they wish to his brother's descendants, including enslavement. Of course, we know he was lied to because the father of all deceptions is Lucifer. However, he took the bait and allowed the forces of evil that controlled Atlantis to once again take root here. For it is written in the prophecies that the powers of this world would have been those of Darkness until the second coming of the angels, which will finally restore peace, freedom, and balance to the Earth, ending the reign of evil in our world.

What is known in ancient esoteric records is that Ham became the first instrument of Marduk, Satan, after the deluge. A follower of Lucifer, he used his occult knowledge for evil purposes by becoming one of the very first sorcerers, establishing the Luciferian Brotherhood once again. It was later that they became known as the Sanhedrin. This hidden hand, established by Ham, began operating through underground, shady secret societies. As a sorcerer, he became influential and wielded great power over many of his people through the dark arts of black magic. I believe that it was Ham who planted the seeds of voodoo in Africa, since Voodoo was the cradle of black magic dating back to the ancient world.

After the flood, the ultimate betrayal to the light and mankind was inserted by Ham. There is evidence in the ancient records that Ham was into necromancy and dark ritual sorcery, so he conjured up a demon and committed a terrible abomination. This resulted in a curse being placed on his people by God. According to the Bible, this was the curse of Canaan.

Through his high-level sorcery, Ham performed a ritual using both a human woman and a fallen entity (demon/reptilian/Marduk/Belial) and himself. In an act of pure evil, he allowed this entity, one of Lucifer's fallen consorts operating from the lower fourth dimension, to use his body to impregnate this woman with his seed. Ham's body was used in an attempt to once again bring forth the seed or the gene of Leviathan, the serpent seed, back into the Earth, since the forces of light had wiped out the Earth from earlier contaminations of this seed by the flood.

According to some revelations, it has been stated that Cain, Abel's brother, was not the offspring of Adam and Eve, but the offspring of Eve and the serpent. This is truly why mankind fell from a state of grace. The seed of Cain contaminated the Earth for thousands of years by introducing mankind the sin of murder, which is associated with the principles of Lucifer, as exemplified when Cain killed his brother Abel. Considering this, Ham committed one of the most abominable acts in the face of God, bringing to the Earth once again the seed of the serpent race that could be traceable to Lucifer. In the pre-mortal realm, they were identified as the Fallen Angels incarnating in grotesque physical forms not of the blueprint of God, that did wage a war against the Sons and Daughters of light, the Adamic race.

It was through Ham's seed that his genealogy continued through his children. However, not all Canaanites carry the gene, only his lineage, which is why his descendants would always intermarry among themselves to keep intact the gene that carries in it the urge to rule absolutely. The first son born out of this demonic act was the first carrier of what became known as the gene of power and control of the seed of the serpent. This act once again gave birth to the Luciferian agenda after the flood.

The identity of this serpent gene could be identified as being genetically tied to a race of extraterrestrials known as the Reptilians, whose sole purpose was to bring worlds under absolute domination as instructed by their father and progenitor, Lucifer, the first Draco Reptilian. The serpent people have been known by many names in different cultures in the ancient world. In the more mystical esoteric writings of the Kabbalah, there is a manuscript that gives full details of the cosmic battle between the sons of light, the human seed of God, and the sons of darkness, the serpent seed of Lucifer. According to prophecy, this battle would continue on Earth until the time when the children of light finally defeat the children of darkness.

Due to the cleansing that Archangel Michael conducted and executed from the lower higher Heavens reaching the lower middle Heavens, it is important to understand that some of

Lucifer's Fallen Angels, whether in gross physical form or in spirit form, have changed sides and rejoined the light. This implies that not all the serpent people are evil as they once were at an earlier stage of our universe. Many of them are now settled in light, thanks to Archangel Michael and his forces.

This is the true meaning of purging or transmuting fallen energy back into its proper wavelength of the infinite living light of the infinite way. That is why the last battle takes place here on the Earth in the lower Heavens. As mentioned, this cleansing process has been going on for millions of years and is about to finalize any day now as a fullness of time unfolds and the restoration process envelops the Earth plane. All accurate prophecies and ancient manuscripts, including those of the Aboriginals, indicate that the last battle between these two forces is to take place on planet Earth, which is biblically known as Armageddon.

To Ham, this serpentine gene would give his particular offspring an extra lust for absolute power over the Earth. In either case, this serpentine was carried through his firstborn, his son's sons, and so on. Ham's grandson, Kish, was the carrier of the gene and erected the first empire to fulfill its genetic blueprint for world domination. This Empire was erected in the region we know today as Iraq, but then it was known as the infamous Babylon. According to all the ancient records, Babylon was the cradle and beginning of all evil in the Western world. Eventually, this chain of power continued with Nimrod of Babylon, the grandson of Kish. We read in all accounts that Nimrod tried to build the Tower of Babel to reach the Heavens. Nimrod was the firstborn of his father, who was the firstborn of Kish. Therefore, Nimrod was Ham's great-great-grandson, who became the dominant carrier of the

Leviathan gene and demonstrated it when he tried to take over the entire Earth during the times of Babylon.

One must understand that because the dark powers dominated the institutions of this world, they tampered with all records and the stories in the Bible. Many believe that is why most of those stories have become allegories rather than literal explanations. This is probably why the Bible has been written in four levels of understanding, concealed in symbology, so that the forces of Darkness would fail to understand the entire prophecies in their fullness. However, those who were ready to understand it on its most profound level would be able to pierce through the veil of allegories and capture its authentic message.

The story of the building of the Tower of Babel in the Bible was written as an allegory, though it refers to a very important passage in the Bible which clearly reveals one of the most important events in history in connection to the quest for world domination throughout all of history, as we shall see. Now we are beginning to see a connection between the cabal families of today and the tower of Babel. According to the allegories of the symbolic interpretation, the creation of the Tower of Babel was attributed to a literal building or tower that was constructed high up so as to reach the Heavens. And deciphering the true meaning behind this passage, one must come to know that the Dark Brotherhood has always concealed their plots and intentions from humanity, otherwise, they would fail in their endeavors.

The truth concerning the creation of the Tower of Babel is that Nimrod was not building a vertical Tower in an attempt to reach the Heavens. Remember, they had knowledge of cosmology because Nimrod was part of the early Brotherhood of the snake created by his grandfather Ham. It's preposterous to think that someone with knowledge of the Stars would try to build something knowing that it is impossible to reach the Zenith of the Heavens as he knew of space. It's like someone today trying to use a rocket ship to reach the Heavens. The Luciferians, the remnant embodiment of the last of the sons of darkness, had knowledge of cosmology back then as they do today.

The creation of the Tower of Babel was an attempt by the Babylonians, particularly the ruling body of Babylon, to bring the entire planet under the empire, erecting absolute control of the Earth. This hierarchy was the reorganized Luciferian brotherhood, which through Nimrod attempted for the first time in recorded history to bring about the absolute domination of the entire known world under his Babylonian empire. This is the true reason behind the creation of the Tower of Babel as he was trying to build a spacecraft through advanced alien tech that was given to him by his off-world masters so that he would use technology to establish a one-world government. The attempt in Babylon by the Dark Brotherhood was the first out of many failed coups although the quest for world domination didn't stop with the Babylonians. Though Babylon fell, the Dark Brotherhood survived and flourished in the underground, keeping alive the flame for absolute control and power.

New revelations have reported that the Dark Brotherhood through Nimrod was working with negative extraterrestrials who were directing him and guiding his every step. Could Babylon be the work of powers and principalities that are not of this reality? This explanation indicates that the Babylonians were given not only guidance by these off-world entities but advanced rocketry technology by the fallen entities, who were the real masters behind the Luciferian brotherhood. Perhaps this is why God confused mankind's language so as to impede the rate of technology that was blooming during Babylonian times, which under the Babylonian Brotherhood was once again going to bypass mankind's spiritual growth and repeat again what happened in Atlantis.

The rulers of this world did well in concealing their identity and agenda of world domination as demonstrated by the Luciferian brotherhood. This is why the biblical passage was twisted to mean something totally different than what it really meant. In fact, this became the first cover-up out of many by the Dark Brotherhood. Since then, every attempt at global domination has been conveniently left out from all written records. On the other hand, just as the forces of light prevented the Atlanteans from dominating our world before the deluge, they did it again with the Babylonians in 3400 BC. Therefore, the efforts of Nimrod to achieve full control of our planet were counteracted by the "forces of good", which is the real reason why Nimrod's Tower of Babel failed.

Now that we have pinpointed the beginning of the quest for world domination back to Babylon, which was not only controlled by the Luciferian Dark Brotherhood during their earliest days but became the first expedition in world domination by the forces that have been controlling this world ever since. The Babel failed coup was to the Dark Brotherhood the beginning of a battle that has continued in secret throughout all of history, as we shall see. After Babylon, they began infiltrating all of the surrounding prosperous communities that were developing according to God's plan. They were the great civilizations of Egypt, who were then ruled by the sons of righteousness, descendants of Shem, the first pharaohs, and the original biblical Israelites who were the descendants of the children of light. Egypt during its golden era was a rather prosperous living harmonious society, and all went well until the infiltration of the Dark Brotherhood from Babylon began to take effect.

It is important to understand the nature of Babylon. Essential information regarding the system of the Babylonian Empire with all its corruption and wickedness that we now know originated there. For instance, it was the Babylonians who first created the system of lending money with interest providing the grounds in which an elite maintained power over most of the masses by virtue of keeping them in poverty and perpetual debt. This sounds familiar today as history repeats itself. They were the first merchants and bankers to hold a well-controlled monopoly over the masses financially by instituting the concept and practice of fractional banking. It is this satanic practice that later continued in Rome and dominated the medieval ages through the old Venetian ultramontane system imposed by the oligarchs of Europe. This is the same type of illegal banking practice being incorporated today by our own Federal Reserve System under the Anglo-Dutch imperialist cartel movement, which is dominated by today's international bankers.

Today it is known that when banks are centralized and privately owned by an elite, it creates an incompatibility that only serves the interest of the already rich and wealthy, the elite, while at the same time creating further poverty for those who are already in a state of impoverished living conditions. In truth, the central banking system perpetuates and expands the existence of poverty, and now we know it's Babylonian in nature. This type of injustice is based solely on the principles of the Babylonian Luciferian agenda that we see today. The concept and practice of tyranny were also demonstrated by the

Babylonians as they created the first oligarchs in the ancient world, when only a few prospered and maintained decent living conditions, while the rest of humanity suffered. Therefore, tyranny and the concept of the central banking system go hand in hand. The Babylonians became the progenitors of all unbalanced, unworkable systems and the force behind all corruptions that have, unfortunately, transpired over and over again throughout all of history in our world. That is what John the Revelator refers to as the system of the beast and the abomination of desolation.

In addition, the Babylonian Brotherhood also became the projectors of a false sense of religion. Idolatry and the worship of many gods originated in Babylon. They did it because the Babylonian hierarchy wanted to rule as gods in the ancient world, thus creating the first centralized organized religions, contaminating the truths of the higher spiritual knowledge that they stole from the people of Shem and Japheth and inverted it. The Babylonians established the worship of idols and images, rendering God as something outside of us, in order to control the people. That sounds like religion today.

In Babylon, the beginning of all dogma was born in an attempt to separate humanity from the sacred. The Babylonians developed control over people through fear for the first time as their corrupt priesthoods only served the oligarchy of the Babylonian hierarchy. It was this erroneous concept of men being of a beastly nature, rather than a spiritual one, that caused people to fall away from forgetting the truth of their divinity and so humanity, who had regressed after the fall of Atlantis. As a result, humanity had fallen into a fear-based Consciousness and became subject and enslaved by the Babylonian empire. Unfortunately, this fallacy still rules in the minds of most humans today. Since like attracts like, most of us allow the secret government to rule over our lives by virtue of harboring a co-dependency behavior towards them.

These are the same recurrent principles that have been practiced and accepted for centuries by the Holy Roman Catholic Church, who, according to many biblical scholars, is considered the second Babylon and the whore of the Earth Revelation 13 and 17. Even today, the practice of idol worship and worshiping graven images dominates the practice of the Roman Catholic faith.

This mentality subjects humans by giving their power away to the clergy or church system designed to perpetuate control and power over people's lives. In addition, this Luciferian theology also became the progenitor of future organized religions which place mankind as an irrational animal, rather than a great spiritual being made in the image of God. For centuries, mankind has been kept in the dark regarding their divine nature. In truth, the control of humanity through a centralized dogmatic religion serves to throw us into more fear by keeping us distracted and shut off from our own connection to the divine. Since then, fear and ignorance have become the Dark Brotherhood's secret weapons and tools over a sleeping humanity. Unfortunately, this system of religious control is still being practiced today by many religious institutions, who, perhaps unknowingly, are serving the Babylonian system and are only doing it for the money.

Furthermore, I also discovered that the Dark Brotherhood behind Babylon also created the first group of assassins to create order out of chaos that they would engineer. This is the same "problem-reaction-solution" known as the Hegelian method that the elite families practice today. It's part of a method where the ends justify the means, a technique that the

Dark Brotherhood still implements today. There is no doubt that this desired empire was created by the Luciferians through Nimrod, endeavoring to accomplish what they failed in Atlantis as Nimrod became the first emperor following the flood.

We can now trace this evil back to Babylon that had sought to corrupt the new world after the flood. It is believed, as revealed in the secret records, that the Luciferian agents were planted everywhere, even in Egypt where they were able to infiltrate after the demise of Sumer. The process of infiltration began after the fall of Babylon in order to contaminate the new world. Because of this infiltration process, it wasn't long before the Babylonian Luciferian Brotherhood also caused the downfall of Egypt. For the most part, Egypt rose to its peak as one of the greatest civilizations enjoyed by the ancient people of Israel; those who followed the blueprint of light. It flourished for centuries until the Luciferians were able to penetrate it by planting their agents in Egypt, especially in their ruling body. These agents became the forerunners that gave us Ramses and the corrupt Egyptian empire.

However, right before the infiltration of Luciferians in Egypt, the ancient wisdom that was passed on to Shem and Japheth culminated as the ancient mystery schools, which restore the ancient higher knowledge back to the Earth via the prophets and seers of the "forces of good". This spiritual wisdom in Egypt was demonstrated by the beauty and splendor of their first dynasties. All people were important and cared for as the righteous leaders, the original high priests and Priestesses of light implemented the concepts of the Commonwealth of the people as practiced by the early original council of Atlantis. During the Golden Age of Egypt, justice prevailed for there was no corruption, famine, poverty, or struggle. All was good in this great civilization until the lineage of Nimrod penetrated and planted their seed in the ranks of the Egyptian ruling body. This caused the original Egyptian dynasty to become corrupt as the Luciferian Brotherhood took it from within. This corruption gave us Ramses the Tyrant of Egypt and the second major Luciferian Dark Brotherhood's tool after Nimrod.

Under the reign and control of Ramses, Egypt went into a state of decline. Their perfect system of a utopian Commonwealth was gradually declining, as it was replaced by an oligarchy which had its roots in Babylon. On the other hand, the original inhabitants of Egypt who didn't conform or associate with the precepts of Ramses fell into bondage and were forced into slavery by the numbers. This is recorded in the Bible as the bondage of the people of Israel. This is the type of plot that was part of the blueprint which fulfilled the desires of Ham's lineage to captivate and subdue the descendants of Shem, Japheth, and all the people that had multiplied on the Earth after the flood.

By this point, the Luciferians had already created a secret network of power that mainly flourished in the underground through clandestine operations as today's modern-day secret societies do. That's why when they infiltrated and destroyed the great civilization of Egypt, no one had any inclination of the existence of the resurgence of the secret Dark Brotherhood of the snake despite their failure in Babylon after the flood. The secret Brotherhood of the Luciferians continued their quest for absolute control of our world in various forms and auspices as we shall see. In a chronological line of circumstances, the fall of Egypt was their second attempt at arriving at world domination, but this coup failed, thanks to Moses.

Unfortunately, Egypt fell due to the infiltration of the Babylonian Brotherhood and immediately implemented the institution of slavery on a large scale. For the Luciferian brotherhood, this was their second attempt at gaining full control of our world after Babylon. It was at this point that Moses came into play as an emissary of God. His purpose was to restore the balance of power and free the slaves, the people of Israel, from the bondages of slavery which originated in Babylon.

One of the most important incidents in this scenario, as well as in history, was the battle of magic between Moses and Ramses. The display of supernatural forces that participated in this battle between the Luciferians through Ramses and the forces of light through Moses gives light to two important facts. Both Ramses and Moses possessed not only great knowledge of the supernatural realm but both became instruments of the supernatural forces that were working through them. Ramses became a human instrument for the dark forces, while Moses became a channel for the forces of light. According to the secret knowledge, Moses was one of the greatest white magicians next to Merlin, capable of harnessing cosmic power from the forces of the light, proving to pharaoh that his God was more powerful in might and power than Ramses' off-world masters that were the Demonic reptilians (negative Anunnaki) who were the real Powers behind the Brotherhood of the snake.

In this battle, Moses comes out victorious, liberates Israel (the slaves) out of the bondage of the fallen Anunnaki that were controlling Egypt through the evil Pharaoh, providing once again that the forces behind Moses of the light and that explains why Moses was even able to part the Red Sea which was another feat of mystical power. Overall, Moses became the instrument and restorer to counteract the establishment of a Luciferian takeover of Egypt. Not only did he restore universal truths, but he also became the instrument that attempted to wipe out the fallen system of idolatry and the worship of the pantheon of the gods that had originated in Babylon under the direction of the ET Marduk. Moses had become the forerunner of Christ in the sense that he restored the Torah, The Ten Commandments, and continued the original Covenant that Melchizedek left with Abraham. After Moses' death, however, it wasn't long enough before the Luciferians corrupted the Israelites (who were the early good humans of Atlantis that survived through the line of Noah) into false image forms of worship.

After the fall of Egypt, there was another great civilization that developed in the Northeast of Egypt, known as ancient Greece by the descendants of the righteous son of Noah, Shem. As a result of implementing and practicing the spiritual teachings of Heliopolis from the golden age of Egypt into Greece, Greece reached a peak of beauty and glory in their civilization in many ways. The rise of the golden age of Greece resurrected the old academies of higher learning once again the age of the philosophers, mathematicians, and great wise men was born. This glorious moment in Greece also lasted of course until the agents of the Babylonian network began to infiltrate it from within as is always the case.

The evidence of the fall of the golden age of Greece lies in later periods as well. Before the infiltration of the Babylonians took effect in Greece, Greece had a great commonwealth, a Republic that was created by the "forces of good" through the Brotherhood of light. In fact, it was ancient Greece where the first Republic in our world was established. This was actually one of the first times besides Egypt that a commonwealth existed, resulting from great figures like Solon of Athens who was the righteous lawgiver who had been tutored by Plato, the genius behind "The Republic" and its original context before the Dark Brotherhood twisted it to serve the totalitarian agenda. This type of free-world government was a direct violation and threat to the Luciferian Brotherhood and their plans for global domination. So, they did what they do best and began infiltrating from within like they did in Egypt. This is the same type of infiltration method they are utilizing today in their attempt to take over the Constitution of the United States government from within as we shall see.

In Greece, evidence of Luciferian control was demonstrated in the people known as the supposed learned man of Athens the Sophist, resembling the Pharisees and Sadducees from the days of Christ. The Sophists were produced when the Dark Brotherhood began controlling the educational curricula of those days. It is well known that these men had limited knowledge that resembled the dogmatic centralized structure of the then polytheistic system that dominated the great culture. This formed the second basis of controlled religion, denying the very existence of man's soul that Socrates argued for, resulting in his innocent death.

When one studies "The Apology", one of Plato's classics referring to the last days of Socrates revolutionizing the polytheistic model with the monotheistic one in Greece it is evident that the Sophist were involved in secret societies. The Sophists' main objective was to destroy the higher knowledge circulating in Greece, which was brought about by the temple of Delphi. Delphi was a Godly inspired School of higher learning and perhaps a continuation of the first mystery schools of Heliopolis that originated in Egypt. The Sophists attempted to establish a rigid structure of basic knowledge that was stagnant and served to keep mankind in perpetual darkness, especially regarding their true nature as Spiritual Beings of light. There was nothing intellectual about the Sophists; they were only interested in sucking up to the state that had been infiltrated and controlled by the Luciferian brotherhood.

We can witness the control of the Luciferian Brotherhood when the high powers of Greece felt threatened by Socrates, Who challenged them with truth and righteousness. In light of this, there is no doubt that the powers of Greece were manipulated by the Luciferian Brotherhood and had, therefore, manipulated the death of Socrates. The Luciferian Brotherhood had secret control over those in positions of power, especially those in the state and jury of the court. By this point, Greece had been corrupted and began its decline from its original pristine and classical beauty, as proven in the death of their most knowledgeable philosopher and truth bringer Socrates.

In either case, there was a connection between the Egyptians' storehouse of knowledge to that of the Greeks. In fact, it was Pythagoras who had been learned in the ways of the Egyptians. He was perhaps educated in Heliopolitan Giza who brought to Greece a great deal of knowledge. Together with other philosophers, he created great schools of thought and higher learning, culminating in the Greek mystery schools. That is why knowledge of the Greeks reflected a continuation of the great knowledge of the Egyptians before they became corrupt and poisoned by "The Hidden Hand", the synagogue of the Brotherhood of the snake. Socrates, the greatest philosopher of truth that ever lived in Athens at the height of

Greek culture, was the figure that influenced Plato's Academy of higher learning.

In classical Greece, this was the type of atmosphere that brought people together to discuss topics ranging from the perfect form of government known as a sovereign nation-state Republic, which the founding fathers installed for us a couple thousand years later. Classical Greece also provided a ground for science, art, medicine, and mathematics to resurface as it was in Egypt, which boosted civilization into a more refined society when it reached its zenith. We had philosophers and mathematicians like Euclid, a student who was influenced by Pythagoras, known for his discoveries in geometry. Euclid discovered sacred geometry, the root essence of a spiritual type of geometry involving metaphysical symmetry.

The greatest asset to mankind that the Greeks solidified was the concept that man was more than just a human being. Since he was made in the image of God he had an immortal aspect that was considered to be the real divine self. Plato's academy of higher learning was instrumental in circulating among the lovers of truth and wisdom (Sophia) many of the great truths of God, which were later altered and suppressed by The Babylonian brotherhood who caused the fall of Greece. To the dark Babylonian brotherhood any form of knowledge, especially the type that would lead to spiritual awakening was considered their greatest enemy in terms of controlling humanity. How can a group of evil men affect control over an enlightened humanity? Ignorance has become the Dark Brotherhood's greatest weapon against humanity time and time again in fulfilling their age-old plot of world domination. All suppression of the higher knowledge started in Babylon and continued in Egypt after the fall of Greece.

On the other hand, great bodies of truth and knowledge circulating in Greece and their golden period were a terrible blow to the Luciferian brotherhood, who had been working hard since Nimrod's time to suppress such truths, especially those that stated that humans were made in the image of God and had a divine essence. This implies that we have a divine immortal soul and were more than just mere mortals. It appears that all these universal truths and bodies of knowledge brought out of Classical Greece were in indirect opposition to the deception of the Babylonian secret Brotherhood, who by creating a system of religion that forces man to find God outside of himself, made it impossible for human beings to discover the great immortal spirit within.

In every generation and era, ignorance of the truth has allowed the Babylonian Brotherhood the ability to keep humanity in bondage. This is why the Dark Brotherhood always attempted to suppress Universal truths, making ignorance their first and greatest weapon against humanity, next to the creation of a centralized dogmatic religion based on control, political and economic gain.

Not only did the Luciferians infiltrate Greece, which was demonstrated in the death of Socrates, but they fomented the wars that ended in the destruction of classical Greece. This brings us to another truth. In light of everything we have uncovered up to this point about the forces of Darkness as the Luciferian Brotherhood, their ways of infiltration, and how the end justifies the means for them becomes more obvious that they were the force behind all the wars that brought ruin to all the classical periods and golden ages. History repeats itself as today they have continued to foment our modern wars in order to bring about a One World Government New World Order system of absolute totalitarianism.

Nevertheless, the Dark Brotherhood also was the instrument behind the wars that broke out between Greece and Sparta. There is no doubt that "The Hidden Hand" of this brotherhood was the force behind it. The only war that the Brotherhood of light fomented is our own Revolutionary War of Independence when our constitution was born in 1776, but this war is what gave us the long-repressed Republic that hasn't existed since classical Greece.

The truth of the matter is that the war that ruined Greece brought about by the Dark Brotherhood was more of an attack on knowledge that was generated by the Brotherhood of light through the philosophers and great thinkers. Eventually, the Republic of Greece fell and it became a dictatorship.

In Greece, the Dark Brotherhood used the Spartans to destroy the great classical era. Just like the Dark Brotherhood orchestrated the Civil War, which will be discussed later in an attempt to destroy the Republic of the United States of America. They likewise fomented it thousands of years ago in Greece with the Spartans and succeeded as history repeats itself. In some cases, good wins over evil, as in the victory of the North in our civil war. Moreover, this method is none other than the divide and conquer technique the Dark Brotherhood has been employing since its beginning in Babylon.

Unfortunately, the fall of classical Greece resulted in the end of arts, science, mathematics, and medicine, all beautiful assets of the Western world. In short, Greece became an ancient renaissance whose fire of knowledge was put out by the machinations of the Luciferian brotherhood.

After the fall of Greece was maneuvered by the Luciferians, another leader by the name of Alexander the Great began the quest to conquer. We know that he was the person who conquered most of the Mesopotamian world after the decline of Greece. According to history, he was tutored by Aristotle, a student of Plato. The Luciferian Brotherhood will use certain figures to serve their own needs, as in the case of Alexander the Great. After all, the real conquerors behind him were "The Hidden Hand", the secret government during those days who perhaps sponsored and financed his conquest. We can see these types of covert operations in today's world with conquering figures like Napoleon and Hitler, who are both sponsored and financed by the same secret government.

Since the creation of Babylon, the Dark Brotherhood had yielded a great deal of riches by means of economic injustice through the fractal banking that they imposed every time they had a chance. They also have been using religion as a money-making machine and by taking people's wealth by force through wars. Alexander the Great was executing the Luciferian agenda as he was trying to consolidate world power. We also know that right after Alexander the Great conquered most of the Mesopotamian world, he died, and his empire was divided among his three generals. The cause of his death is a mystery, and because the winners of wars always rewrite history to suit their agenda, there is no evidence suggesting that he died of a normal cause. It seems like he would have been used by "The Hidden Hand" who deposed him later to expedite their next plan.

What is known is that after the death of Alexander the Great, Mesopotamia was divided among his three generals. According to history, one of his generals, Mark Antony, had fallen in love with Cleopatra. He could have initially been involved in a power-hungry Luciferian secret society and was therefore supposed to pretend to fall in love with the queen of the very last Egyptian dynasty. On the other hand, Mark Antony really did fall in love with Cleopatra. This could explain the wars between him and the other two generals, implying that those generals were also involved in a negative secret society serving "The Hidden Hand". This conflict brought about a consolidation of power for "The Hidden Hand", the real powers behind all oppressive and conquering regimes who were preparing to erect one of the most powerful empires known to man.

The Babylonian Brotherhood is well-trained, and they mold figures to do a particular task, whether it is to infiltrate a peaceful system or to blend as an imposter to wreak havoc in a particular region in order to bring it to ruin. They will do whatever it takes to fulfill their agenda of world domination as laid down by the patriarchs of the Luciferians through their Babylonian lineage.

It is possible that Alexander the Great was used by the Dark Brotherhood to capture most of the known Mesopotamian world that was being occupied by different peoples and different empires like the Persians, Assyrians, Phoenicians, etc. What is a fact is that when people turn against other people, it is because there is a conspiracy involved. Nonetheless, the end justifying the means has always been the primary maxim for the Luciferian Brotherhood regardless of the circumstances.

Chapter 5: THE RISE OF THE SECOND BABYLON

At this time, most of Mesopotamia had been conquered by Alexander the Great and his generals, enabling the Luciferians to once again erect an empire that would fulfill their secret agenda of world domination. Despite some alterations in history books, this empire became known as one of the most brutal, tyrannical, and corrupt living social systems on Earth, second only to its predecessor, Babylon.

This new empire continued the same models and practices that ruled Babylon. Known as the second Babylon, or the Roman Empire, it demonstrated every Luciferian element since its inception. In truth, the Roman Empire was based on a tyrannical system of oligarchs, similar to Babylon, with a provincial form of government where all of Mesopotamia was divided among rulers or governors, all under the absolute control of the emperor. The new Babylon was in effect once again, albeit under a different guise and name. As this empire grew incredibly powerful, it became the perfect vehicle for the Dark Brotherhood, designed and ready to bring the entire world once again under its absolute control.

The fire for global domination was the underlying agenda of this empire, controlled by the secret government. However, a very important event transpired, changing the direction of our world. This event became the catalyst for change, especially since the new Roman Empire, under the direction of the Luciferian hidden government, was bringing our world under its absolute control. Herod, the Judean governor, was also subject to the Romans. Just as Socrates became a threat to the

Luciferians 500 years prior in Greece, so did Jesus the Christ, who arrived just in time, becoming a significant threat to this new Luciferian regime, the Roman Empire.

References to "The Hidden Hand" in the Bible are found in the King James Version, where Christ mentioned "The Hidden Hand", the Sanhedrin, talking about the secret government of the Luciferian Brotherhood that controls this world. Christ was well aware of his enemies but saw them as nothing more than lost souls in need of love, hence his addition of the commandment to love our enemies. Nevertheless, some biblical passages in the King James Version where Christ mentions "The Hidden Hand" were removed from current bibles.

The openly powerful religious zealots, such as the Pharisees and Sadducees, were also manipulated agents of the Luciferian secret Brotherhood of the Snake. Just as the Dark Brotherhood controlled the Sophists in Socrates' times, the Pharisees were controlled by the high powers that Christ referred to as the Sanhedrin, "The Hidden Hand", or the synagogue of Satan, the high despots that ruled Rome.

Therefore, we may conclude that the real murderers of Christ originated with the secret government because they knew Jesus the Christ was prophesied to liberate the entire world from the strongholds of the synagogue of Satan, who had been the primary rulers of our world, keeping mankind in a state of bondage. Jesus, however, came as a peaceful truth-bringer, preaching peace, love, forgiveness, tolerance, and agape love to all men. He came to fulfill the prophecies of old by introducing the most important commandment: to love your neighbor and pray for your enemies. Love, peace, and compassion for all people are what this peaceful messenger demonstrated.

To the secret government controlling the Roman Empire, Jesus became the greatest threat. It was with this assumption that, through the Pharisees, "The Hidden Hand" manipulated hatred towards Jesus and managed to condemn him to death without a hearing. Any true Christian knows that Jesus was put to death and condemned for blasphemy for no reason when he was the embodiment of perfect divinity, goodness, and purity. He came to show us the way to the Father and how to live, and he demonstrated it very well. During his ministry, he touched, healed, and saved many souls from their misery. It was precisely this divine act that caused problems in the eyes of the Sanhedrin, "The Hidden Hand". When he proclaimed to be the Son of God, that was the final straw for the Sanhedrin and the Roman rulers. Jesus always knew that the so-called religious leaders, the Pharisees and Sadducees, were manipulating agents of the Sanhedrin, who in turn was a manipulated agency of the secret government of Satan, the Luciferian Brotherhood.

It is apparent that Jesus became the Sanhedrin's greatest enemy, who commissioned his death by crucifixion, the Roman method of capital punishment. This is another example of the connection between the powers of Rome and the Sanhedrin, the secret government during the Roman Empire. In their eyes, Jesus committed blasphemy. In reality, it was they, the Sanhedrin, who were blasphemous. When the messenger of light, who came to show mankind a better way of life, was punished to death by the existing powers of the same models and practices that ruled Babylon. Known as the second Babylon or the Roman Empire, it demonstrated every Luciferian element from its inception. In truth, the Roman

Empire was based on a system of oligarchs, similar to Babylon, with a provincial government dividing Mesopotamia among rulers or governors under the emperor's absolute control. This new Babylon was, in effect, the same entity under a different name and guise. As the empire grew incredibly powerful, it became the perfect vehicle for the Dark Brotherhood, designed and ready to bring the entire world under its absolute control.

The underlying agenda of global domination was controlled by the secret government. However, a significant event changed our world's direction. This event became a catalyst for change, especially as the new Roman Empire, under the direction of the Luciferian hidden government, was bringing our world under its absolute control. Herod, the Judean governor, was also subject to the Romans. Just as Socrates became a threat to the Luciferians 500 years prior in Greece, so did Jesus the Christ, who arrived just in time and posed a great threat to this new Luciferian regime, the Roman Empire.

References to "The Hidden Hand" in the Bible are found in the King James Version, where Christ mentioned "The Hidden Hand", the Sanhedrin, referring to the secret government of the Luciferian Brotherhood that controls this world. Christ was aware of his enemies but saw them as lost souls needing love, as he introduced the commandment of loving our enemies. However, many biblical passages in the King James Version where Christ mentions "The Hidden Hand" were removed from current bibles.

The openly powerful religious zealots, such as the Pharisees and the Sadducees, were also manipulated agents of the Luciferian secret Brotherhood of the Snake. Just as the Dark Brotherhood controlled the Sophists in Socrates' times, the

Pharisees were controlled by the high powers that Christ referred to as the Sanhedrin, "The Hidden Hand", or the synagogue of Satan, the high despots that ruled Rome.

For the record, the new Babylon, known as the Roman Empire, became the most dominating force in the old known world and was able to begin bringing the rest of the world under its empire, manifesting the Luciferian agenda.

However, the arrival of Jesus at such a perfect time changed the world's direction from falling completely under the Luciferian agenda through the Roman Empire. Additionally, other factors contributed to the collapse of the Roman Empire. The first was the significant following Jesus left behind. Originally known as the followers of the Way, the Covenanters, or the Nasoreans of the Essene community, the first Christian followers and disciples of Jesus faced persecution by the Roman Empire. They were fed to lions as entertainment for the ruling emperor, massacred in large numbers. However, regardless of the massacres, volumes of people from all levels of society, especially the poor, were converting to the principles Jesus left behind.

The message of a universal brotherhood based on agape love spread like wildfire, posing a significant problem for the Roman Empire, which battled to keep its empire intact. This was affecting the Roman government and their religions, which were based on sun worship and polytheistic theologies, a replica of the same religious idolatry practiced in Babylon. Apparently, the followers of the Way caused great turmoil for Rome.

Secondly, the major contributing element that saved the world from the Luciferian conquering agenda of the Roman Empire was the ransacking of Rome by what history books consider barbaric tribes from the North, such as the Vikings, the Nordics, etc. In truth, those tribes contributing to the fall of Rome were some of the lost ten tribes of ancient Israel. Ten out of the twelve tribes of Israel were never lost; some traveled eastward to Tibet, others to areas known as Russia and the British Isles. One tribe from Phoenicia, 600 years BC, even crossed the Atlantic Ocean to the Americas, 2,100 years before Columbus. The rest traveled north after the fall of Greece to escape the corruption of the coming Roman Empire a few hundred years later before the establishment of Rome.

God made it possible for the lost tribes, only lost to the old known world, to later resurface and serve a blow to counteract the Dark Brotherhood's attempt at world domination. Note that even though control of this Earth was temporarily given to the forces of Lucifer, God is still the final author of what ultimately transpires because we are under a divine plan, and therefore even the powers of evil are limited. In truth, God knew beforehand about the coming power of Rome as a Luciferian tool and therefore allowed the lost tribes to disappear for a few hundred years, not only to preserve them but to allow them to once again be the unknown armies that brought Rome down to its inevitable collapse.

With the collapse of Rome, the secret Brotherhood of the Luciferians knew their plans for world domination had been thwarted again. They realized they needed to formulate another methodology to continue their secret draconian agenda of bringing the entire world and its people under a totalitarian system of absolute control. Immediately, the intelligence of the secret Brotherhood began to use the circumstances to their advantage in continuing the Luciferian manifesto. With keen and effective planning, conspiring, and immediate mobilization, the new solution came about when "The Hidden Hand" transformed the fallen Roman Empire into a new universal central power structure of control.

Since many Christian followers of the Way were emerging in large numbers, creating enormous momentum during the days of Rome, it was decided by the hierarchy of the secret Brotherhood to turn the situation to their advantage. We could say that "The Hidden Hand" had the Caesars of Rome quickly switch their togas for religious robes and costumes. Through the synagogue of Satan, individuals were trained, including Constantine, who established the second Babylon, organized universal religion with a very centralized dogma of control, similar to the first Babylonian religious system in 3400 BC.

This marked one of the world's greatest deceptions and cover-ups. The establishment of the Roman Catholic universal church was set up as an imitation Christian Church by the Dark Brotherhood to covertly continue the agenda of world domination under the disguise of religion. This institution became the exact replica of the earlier Babylonian religion, with an overall political and economic agenda and vehicle that suppressed the great truths regarding our connection to the spiritual realm. That is why dogmatic religion has always used clergy as a type of intermediary between man and God when, in essence, every man and woman has the capacity to connect directly with the divine. This long-veiled truth lies at the center of true Christianity or any spiritual organization.

The year 325 AD marked a resolution by the community of secret government-controlled bishops, all educated by the institution of the Beast, Babylon. The embodiment of the Antichrist maneuvered the Nicene Council right after they established the Edict of Milan, which was born out of the ashes of the fallen Roman empire. This new institution became a combination of the old Babylonian practices with the same methods and structure but under a different name. Jesus had become the new Apollo as Baal in Babylon, which is why they moved his birthday to the 25th of December, when any learned scholar agrees he was born sometime in the spring. Mary, the Blessed Virgin Mother of Jesus, took over the position of Venus Semiramis of Babylon, the Mother and wife of Baal, implementing the same practices of the Roman Saturnalia religion.

From the beginning, the Babylonians corrupted the true meaning of the ancient mysteries to suit their agenda of achieving absolute control over the planet. As far back as Babylon, they manipulated the true meaning of religious spirituality from its original form into a system of control based on the polytheistic model used by the Luciferians for centuries, until the organization of the Roman church. At this point, the Dark Brotherhood replaced the polytheistic model with the monotheistic concept and perverted it to fit their agenda as a new state religion, continuing the hidden plan of the fallen Roman empire. The true concept of monotheism was corrupted and twisted by the secret government to consolidate the power of spiritual control over to one man alone, the Pope, thus establishing the apostolic succession of priests.

The Roman Church became no more than a continuation of the old exoteric practices of the fallen teachings categorized as Saturnalia, which dominated Rome.

Saturnalia, the religious system of idolatry that originated in Babylon, was reinstated under the camouflage of Christianity, becoming a powerful force for the Luciferian Brotherhood as the Holy Roman Church took power. Furthermore, this institution, posing as a Church of Christ, was an imposter church consolidating all the religions in Rome with no spiritual principles whatsoever. This is exactly what Christ meant when he warned about the coming of many false prophets who would come in his name and deceive many, referring to the apostolic succession of the popes. In light of this, it became logical that the first wolf in sheep's clothing had become the new pontiff because this new vehicle had engineered one of the world's biggest deceptions and cover-ups, not to mention the bloodshed of millions of people.

In the Book of Revelation, this institution is regarded as the whore of the Earth, the Mother of all abominations. Author and researcher Alexander Hislop provides documented evidence indicating that the Holy Roman Catholic Church is, in fact, the second Babylon, the Mother of all abominations. Technically, the Roman Empire was the second Babylon, and the Holy Roman Catholic Church became the third Babylon. Perhaps the European Union today is the 4th and final Babylon. In light of this, we can conclude as truth that the position in the hierarchy of the apostolic succession was a fraud; the pontiffs were and are used as false prophets by the Luciferian Brotherhood. History has clearly shown that their actions have been proven to be evil in nature. Peter was never the first pope of Rome; in fact, the Romans killed him in Jerusalem, and that's where he was buried. According to the Yah revelations, it was Peter Simon, the sorcerer, who became instrumental in the organization of this new religion.

This makes perfect sense when one considers that the synagogue of Satan is controlled by a community of sorcerers following in the ways of Ham.

That is why, despite what we have been taught, it is important to understand that the Holy Roman Catholic Church was created by the synagogue of Satan, the Brotherhood of the snake, that serves the dictates of the community of sorcerers who have become the pope's advisors since its inception. This was again a covert regime that the Luciferians designed to gradually bring the world under their absolute control following the fall of Rome. With this in mind, let it be known that it was Constantine who became the first pope, not Peter the Apostle of Christ. In light of the new revelations, it was James the Just, the brother of Jesus, and John the Revelator who were instructed by the master to spread the message of love. With the establishment of this imitation church, the Dark Brotherhood would once again begin the process of bringing the entire world under absolute domination, starting with the region of Europe and then the rest of the world, manifesting their age-old plot of absolute tyranny.

The fact remains that since the inception of this institution, the world has experienced some of the most painful and suffering realities known to man. Torture and killing in the name of God became the new holocaust of "The Hidden Hand", who are the agents that created the term "heretic" as a reason to murder unconvertible souls. In addition, the Dark Brotherhood, through this institution, was once again able to suppress all bodies of knowledge, including science, mathematics, the arts, etc., which were brought about in the Hellenistic era by Alexander the Great. The Dark Ages continued for a period of 1,300 years until the Reformation came about in the 15th century. In this darkest period, anybody who showed signs of genius or talent was killed immediately, as they were a threat to the new Babylon, the papacy, which saw itself as the only bridge and mediator between men and God. This perpetuated a false theology based on control through fear, a system that could only be experienced within the structures provided by the forces of darkness.

The age of information is now bringing to light substantial evidence regarding the satanic attributes and corruption behind most of the reigning popes, especially the first five popes who have been documented as the most corrupt popes in the history of its existence. It has also been revealed that Constantine killed his own Mother to silence her because she saw through the deception of this new state religion that was driven by pure evil and political and economic gain, not by spirituality. Many researchers have also discovered that Constantine was a sun worshiper of the Sol Invictus cult that dominated religion in Rome as the corrupt Luciferian occult version of the Saturnalia religion. Some even believe that the Roman Church was a continuation of the Sol Invictus Saturnalia, using the name of Christ. Another theory suggests that the Roman Church became a merger of the many religions that existed in Rome in those days to appease all the rivaling religions while bringing them all under one universal control.

While the popes were suppressing all forms of spirituality and metaphysics and killing anyone suspected of any spiritual activity, behind closed doors, they were secretly guided by sorcery, black magic, and the occult. However, they were obviously misusing this knowledge for evil purposes. The popes, like the Roman emperors, became more like puppets for the secret government and loved to serve in positions of power. Despite some of the power-hungry popes who sought personal power, some popes genuinely believed they were serving God. Therefore, they supported killing in the name of God, regardless of breaking most, if not all, of the Ten Commandments. Since we are dealing with powers and principalities that are not of this world, they could have been under a spell or possession through black magic by the sorcerers that oversaw this evil religious institution.

In addition to the greatest deception ever imposed on mankind, the creators of the new Catholic Church used the word "Catholic," which means universal, as a way to imprint in the minds of men that there should be no other church but this single one. Universal doctrine has absolute dogma, allowing these false powers to eventually obtain absolute control of the world by virtue of religion. The results of this abominable institution manifested in the killing of true saints, mystics, and millions of what they called heretics that were killed in the name of God. This type of system later evolved into historical inquisitions.

Since their inception, all other practices that were not convertible to the new universal faith were annihilated. For instance, it is now well-known that spiritually oriented groups known as the Gnostics, who believed in having a direct connection to the Divine as exemplified by Jesus, were all condemned as heretics and became one of the first martyrs of the long enduring Inquisition that killed millions for hundreds and hundreds of years. It is evident now that this new Dark Brotherhood's vehicle not only killed millions in the name of God but really in the name of Satan. As ignorance became the greatest weapon against humanity, the new Babylon, the Roman Church, became instrumental in the destruction of ancient records, thereby succeeding in the suppression of all knowledge, including science, mathematics, medicine, astronomy, etc.

These forms of knowledge were once again being eradicated from circulation by the hands of this new Dark Brotherhood front. It was documented that they even destroyed one of the world's oldest libraries that contained information predating the flood. This library was the last of the Egyptian storehouses of knowledge, known as the Library of Alexandria. The Dark Brotherhood and its new vehicle knew that if they managed to destroy all knowledge out of ignorance, all of the people of the world would be forced into absolute control of the church. That was the reason why they plunged the world into the darkest ages known in history.

This evil church, controlled people through fear, just as they did in Babylon. Fear of hell was preached as a weapon to convert every living soul into submission. Since 325 AD, the new Universal Church knew that by becoming a centralized structure and establishing a rigid dogma posing as a religion of good, they would be able to control and appoint all of the new rising kingdoms that eventually evolved into the European monarchies.

Generally, the European region is and has been the first major land continent the Luciferian brotherhood attempted to bring under their absolute control since their power originated in the Mesopotamian world. They used the excuse that the pope was Christ's representative on Earth, so by divine command, all kings and queens had to become Roman Catholic and therefore become subject to the pope. In return, the pontiff vicar would grant them a kingdom or a region of land of their own to rule. Just as in Babylon and Rome, this instituted a provincial form of government where all of the governors, in this case, the new monarchs, would rule under the reign of the pope, being the new Caesar. For centuries, the monarchies were under the absolute control of the papacy. In today's rising knowledge, it has been known that the dark ages ensued for many centuries as a result of this tightly centralized control over the monarchies by the church, as well as the eradication of knowledge. Only the clergy were eligible to learn. This rigid system of education is a main feature of the Luciferian agenda.

For hundreds of years, this new move by the Dark Brotherhood led to the long-dreaded period known to men as the Dark Ages, allowing the Luciferian to resurrect their Babylonian form of government and prevail in a feudalistic monopoly where the lords appointed by the popes became the ruling aristocracy of the new world. This corrupt system provided once again for only the wealthy few to live lavishly, while the vast numbers of people suffered the worst poverty conditions ever in the history of our world during the Dark Ages. The kings proved to be tyrannical as they controlled the affairs of medieval Europe, but only as long as they remained under the spiritual control of the pope, the harlot of the new monarchs.

The established monarchs provided the pope with armies for the Crusades and inquisitions, which further strengthened the power of the popes. They were sold on the reward that all soldiers who died for the new faith would have immediate entrance to Heaven. It is very clear that this new vehicle dominated the new world in early Europe through the fear of hell. For it is clearly stated in Genesis that God created the Heavens and the Earth, not the hells, and in this case, only the church would have the power to save humankind from this hell. It was well known that if one wanted to reach Heaven, one needed to conform to all the mandates of the Holy Roman Church while confessing all sins to the priests. This is the same doctrinal substance that dominated the idolatrous religions of Babylon, which was once again applied in the new Babylon, the Roman Church. This idea of everlasting pain, torture, and suffering in a state of fire, which burns for the sins of the world, was their way of subduing the masses. This false theology had its origins in Babylon. Any true spiritual person understands that hell was taken out of context by the church's doctrines.

In addition, since we are immortal spiritual beings of light, there is no way that any fire could burn the living substance of light. Similarly, today in the new light of quantum physics, it's been found that energy never gets destroyed; it only changes form. In this sense, our spirit, our real self, is a form of immortal energy that is indestructible at its essence. Only the vehicle, its outer shell, is capable of being destroyed. Unfortunately, this Luciferian Doctrine has dominated the Christian world up to the present time, not only in the Catholic traditions but in Protestant ones who had inherited Catholic doctrines. Back then, however, we didn't know of quantum physics.

On this note, it is extremely significant that the Dark Brotherhood misinterpreted the higher knowledge during the times of Nimrod and fabricated their own literal damnation, giving religion a sense of fear instead of the sense of peace and tranquility, which was practiced by the original primitive Church before the penetration and corruption of the Babylonians.

In medieval Europe, the control of fear through the condemnation of the soul burning for eternity ruled heavily among the monarchies. For example, there came a time that certain monarchs tried to break away from the absolute power of the church. The reigning pope of that time forged a document and called it the Donation of Constantine. This fabricated letter ensured their absolute control over the kingdoms of Europe, who might have been trying to separate from its stronghold. For centuries, there was no literature or advancement, only the centralization of further power by the new Luciferian vehicle, the Roman Church.

The historical Inquisition and purges conducted by this institution were to ensure total control not only of Europe but of the entire world, as vowed by Nimrod and his great-grandfather Ham. There isn't much history to cover during the Dark Ages, as there was no literacy or scribes to document anything. There was no progress, only pain, suffering, and torture as the direction of the world was heading again towards the fulfillment of the Luciferian agenda, using religion and ignorance as their weapon.

At this point, another act of God was in process to counteract the third Babylonian attempt at arriving at world domination. Anyone in their right mind could see that the entire world would have fallen under the absolute control of the Pope as the ruling Antichrist if it hadn't been for another godly intervention that inspired what became known as the Reformation and the Renaissance in the late 14th century.

Chapter 6: **THE REFORMATION**

Just as the forces of light preserved the original ten tribes of Israel, they also became the force behind the Reformation that weakened the spiritual control of the Luciferian Holy Roman institution. Historically, this mobilization became known as the Protestant Reformation. Yet, it was more than a reformation in religion. The fifteenth-century Reformation was driven by the forces of light to move out of the Dark Ages into the age of light and literacy.

This Reformation came about through positive orders and secret societies opposing the Luciferian Brotherhood. This event not only hindered the power of the Papacy, but it also paved the way for the Renaissance, the Scientific Revolution, and the Enlightenment, which brought our world out of the long period known as the Dark Ages into a world with a resurgence of knowledge. People were beginning to read the Bible for the first time, enabling them to understand the hidden teachings behind the metaphors without the mediation of the church's clergy and hierarchy. Monarchs like King James the First and King Henry the Fourth of France wanted to convert the monarchy into a parliamentary system that would eventually turn into a Republic, as practiced in ancient Greece. Furthermore, the Reformation not only paved the way for religious liberty through figures like William of Orange, Cromwell, and Saint Coligny but also allowed the concept of the sovereign Nation-State Republic and the Commonwealth to finally emerge into our world from its long suppression.

If it wasn't for the fifteenth-century Reformation, the concepts and practices of freedom and knowledge would have never come to fruition; the Brotherhood of Darkness would have been victorious, and America and the free world would have never existed. The fifteenth-century Reformation not only changed the course of history but served as another act of God to thwart the Dark Brotherhood's plot from achieving world domination through the imitation Satanist Church of Rome. However, the Luciferian Brotherhood was not going to give up. As in Babylon and in Rome, they created another plan that would enable them to preserve their power in the spiritual domain as well as in the temporal one.

At this point, the Dark Brotherhood took a different direction and evolved into a military order that continued the existence of the synagogue of Satan, who was losing control as a result of the Reformation. They became more modern and technical this time. After years of planning and organizing, they created another military order to counteract the Reformation. This new and improved synagogue of Satan became the modern-day core of the beast. This organization aimed to ensure their plans for global domination. In the process, the Dark Brotherhood raised another figure instrumental in creating the new organized vehicle with an omnipotent leader that would pave the way to continue the inquisitions but also created the atmosphere that would continue the quest for global domination in the hands of what many discovered to be the beginning of the Black Nobility in Europe.

Since the Reformation brought an end to the absolute religious spiritual control of the Dark Brotherhood over mankind, the Dark Brotherhood, through their new militant order, formulated another plan to give the descendants of Nimrod control over mankind and institute their lineage in power as vowed by Ham four thousand years ago. They raised a figure that was conceived as the second reich Antichrist, as Constantine was the first reich. This second reich was Ignatius

De Loyola, a practicing sorcerer who was already part of the Dark Brotherhood involved in a notorious secret society in Spain called the Alumbrados, which later became translated as the Illuminati in English. He apparently became the chosen one by the secret government then to continue the quest for world domination as the omnipotent leader of the new Dark Brotherhood vehicle, the Jesuits.

The Dark Brotherhood, through Ignatius De Loyola, organized a secret society that created a counterattack to the Reformation by destroying the Protestant revolution in Europe. Later, it was used to evolve a new vehicle that gave the Luciferians a new ability and methodology to take over the world since they were losing their spiritual and temporal control of humanity. This time, instead of using religion as in the guise of the Holy Roman Church, they developed another tactic. This secret society became the missing link between "The Hidden Hand" of Rome and the Illuminati of today. This new Dark Brotherhood front, devised by Loyola, became known as the Jesuits, and they have been known to be the modern-day core of the NWO we see unfolding today.

For the next couple of hundred years, the Vatican's Council of Trent brought about the international military order of the Society of Jesus, the Jesuits, who condemned any form of freedom in Europe. Even though the Reformation gave us political and religious breaks, the next hundred years had become a living hell following the Reformation because of the new and reformed hidden hand known as the Jesuits. During the Reformation, there were several times in Europe that the forces of light were attempting to resurrect the old Constitutional Republic of Classical Greece as practiced by Solon of Athens, but to no avail because of Loyola's new order was a constant Pandora's Box in Europe, doing the opposite and counteracting all of the reformers.

This new vehicle prevented any form of democracy or freedom from existing; they fought the Reformation head-on. This resulted in the first European wars beginning with Spain with the expulsion of the Jews. The monarchs took sides. We know that King James the First, King Henry IV, and King Louis VI all tried to change for a better world as a result of the Reformation as they tried to take us out of the long dark ages which were ruled by the concepts of the Ultramontane Catholic oligarchy. Despite the changes, some monarchs sided with the Jesuits and the pope and began inflicting devastating war upon Europe, fighting for supremacy and the resurrection of the Holy Roman Empire.

Since the late 1400s, the Pope obviously made it impossible for other religious groups to live in Europe. After various conflicts, Loyola's Jesuit order added to the flame by plunging Europe into what became known as the first Thirty Years' War from 1618 to 1648. According to Ridpath's history of our world, published in 1899, the true perpetrators of the early European wars were the result of the Jesuits trying to combat the Reformation. The Jesuits were the force behind every conflict as they fomented these wars in an attempt to stop the implementation of The Sovereign Nation State Republic as well as to stop the new reformist.

These wars were devastating, for they killed ten million people or more, reveals researcher and author John Eric Phelps. Luckily, those wars ended with the victory by the Snow King from Sweden, the Great Gustavus Adolphus, who defeated the Jesuit-controlled General Wallenstein and his partner Tilly. This temporary victory of the light resulted in the establishing of the Treaty of Westphalia, which brought an end to the religious and political wars waged by the Jesuits and their oligarchs. On the same token, it was the order of the Jesuits that assassinated all figures who brought religious and political freedom to Europe. These heroes were William of Orange, King Henry the IV, Oliver Cromwell, and St. Coligny, not to mention St. Patrick, who liberated the Irish.

The Jesuits were also behind the Gunpowder Plot of 1605 and an attempt to destroy the writings of William Howitt, who wrote a popular history of priestcraft. His writings expose the truth behind the Jesuit order who were endeavoring to overthrow the good people who wanted to bring freedom. The Jesuits were also behind the Irish Massacre that lasted for almost 10 years from 1641 to 1649. They also killed off about 500,000 French men as a result of their religious freedom brought about by the Edict of Nantes through Henry the 4th, who was another exponent of freedom and the Commonwealth of the people. As a result, he fell victim and became assassinated by the Jesuit order. Apparently, many good people had become victims of the company of Jesuits, including future presidents of the United States like Lincoln, Garfield, McKinley, and Kennedy.

The power structure of this group is held together as follows: The malevolent leader running the secret organization was known as the Black Pope. The name was derived from the hidden powers that control the Papacy from behind the scenes before the formation of its structure. Since popes have been puppets of the secret government of the synagogue of Satan since the beginning of the Roman Church. In like manner, Ignatius de Loyola thought it would be a good idea to consider himself the first Black Pope in the new organized Dark

Brotherhood, like his forebears who have been doing it for centuries following the collapse of the Roman Empire.

It appeared that every member of this new secret Sanhedrin needed to undergo complicated spiritual exercises as ordered by Loyola and the demonic forces behind him. All early members who became Jesuits underwent such exercises to be a productive functioning soldier of the new Dark Brotherhood military order. Although conventional history records state it was another religious order within the Catholic Church, in truth, it was a ruthless military underground network. They were a power to reckon with, for they not only controlled the Vatican since their inception but became the driving force of the embodiment of the Luciferian agenda till the present day.

According to the research work of John Eric Phelps, they would dispose of any good Popes who would run the Catholic Church to their liking and Monarchs who were not in alignment with their dictates of preserving a centralized oligarchy power structure under the control of the Vatican. During the beginning, as a new secret society, it was notorious and considered dangerous by some of the monarchs who knew of their evil intrigues. As a result, they were expelled several times. Yet, they were powerful enough overall to keep coming back. Every time they did, they became even more powerful as if they were being led by something else, like demonic forces. Remember the Bible phrase that we are not at war with flesh and blood but with powers and principalities that are not of this world.

The Society of Jesuits at the highest level are a group of practicing sorcerers led by demonic forces outside of this realm, as described in the biblical passage. At first, this organization was small but quickly grew into the thousands.

Loyola organized the order in a pyramidal structure where the Black Pope would only allow certain high professed Jesuits to meet with him, while the others were functioning in compartmentalized levels, taking orders from on high. Note, this is the same structure that the Jesuits laid down for the Illuminati, which, as mentioned earlier, was an extension of the Jesuit order.

The professed Jesuits are the highest in the order of what became known as the worldwide evil cabal. As a result, each professed Jesuit was given a certain region in our world to govern and rule on behalf of the Supreme Jesuit General, the Black Pope. The professed Jesuits are like smaller generals for the inner counsel of the order, which are a group of sorcerers that make up the inner highest circles of the Black Pope's council members. After the high level of professed Jesuits, there are various levels or orders underneath them, as each level answers and follows directives from the levels up. In this way, the Black Pope can command an army of perhaps thousands of men.

Since ancient times, throughout their existence, these Luciferian groups of sorcerers developed a power so strong and so secretive that they were able to infiltrate their agents not only into monarchs, governments, and religions but also other secret societies like the Freemasons, who started off as a good society produced by the Knights Templar, which were the Brotherhood of Light during medieval times. This was before they became infiltrated and taken over by the Jesuits through their Illuminati vehicle.

A Brief History of the Masons

The order of masonry dates back to the ancient world. We can actually trace their origin to Egypt, where it originated with Ptah, the great and original architect of the pyramids and the sphinx. They were the first Stone Guild builders of the ancient temples under the leadership of Ptah, who was actually the spiritual father of the biblical Enoch, who became known as the builder of the ancient pyramids. Their knowledge derived from the ancient mystery schools, which were prevalent in the old world before the corruption of the Babylonians set in. They first began using the divine art of sacred geometry as given to them by Enoch, the great initiator of the living light and master of sacred geometry.

Enoch was also known as Hermes Trismegistus to the Greeks and helped in building the ancient temples and cities in both lands. The craftsmen initiated by Enoch-Hermes were known as the Dionysian builders, who built all of the great temples of ancient Greece. Since then, the original Masonic order was created as a branch of the great white brotherhood, who became instrumental not only in the sacred art of temple building but at times acted as custodians of truth, ancient knowledge, and representatives of the light here on Earth, rivaling the Luciferian Brotherhood of the snake.

Overall, the orders of light were instrumental in preserving the ancient knowledge of not only the art of building and architecture but the higher knowledge of sacred geometry and other great esoteric works of the secret tradition, which was given to them by Enoch, the first great revealer and initiator of ancient sacred knowledge. It appeared that they took a different direction in the times of Solomon when the hierophant Hiram Abiff died a mysterious death. Some say his death was a metaphor for his failure to achieve ultimate ascension, a process of completion when one is ready to integrate his form with his Spirit Light body. As a result, he left the order without the last keys to achieving the Lakh Boymer, which is the completion of ascension.

Another theory holds that he was to come together with three other high-level initiates, Solomon being one of them. Together, they were to unite and bring forth the final solution, the last key in completing the Lakh Boymer, which is the highest level of initiation before a human is ready to ascend into their divinity. This was to be accomplished by combining three keys that each one of the three carried. However, according to this theory, Solomon became greedy and conspired with the other king to kill Hiram Abiff so that Solomon could become the omnipotent ruler of the order and therefore become the wisest man on Earth.

Apparently, the order wasn't the same after the days of Solomon and perhaps vanished for a while until it resurrected when a group of Gnostic descendants, who derived from the Essene sacred order in which Jesus was a part of, survived and continued in secret the practices throughout the dark ages, preserving the ancient knowledge and wisdom, including Neoplatonism and Pythagorean mathematics. It was through secrecy that the righteous orders of light survived during the dark ages.

In middle-age Europe, before they were Masons, they were known as the Stone Guild craftsmen. The only reason they weren't killed off in the Inquisition was that they were needed to build most of the cathedrals, temples, and palaces in Europe. The pope realized that their knowledge of architecture was needed. Of course, the Stone Guild Masons pretended to be good Catholics as well, in order to fool the Pope, while in secret, they were planning to strip the church from their stronghold over Europe. The Stone Guild masons were also protected by another positive order of light known as the poor Knights of Christ, which later became known as the Knights Templars.

In either case, the Stone Guild builders essentially evolved into the new modern lodges that originally became known as the Blue Lodge masonic order that reorganized in Scotland. This new Blue Lodge of Freemasonry was dedicated to the concepts of freedom, liberty, the seeking of knowledge, and the sharing of ideas and philosophy. The Blue Lodge, with the assistance of another order of light known as the Rosicrucians, who had been the depositary of ancient knowledge, became the flaming force and instrument in giving birth to the free world.

The sovereign modern nation-state Republic in America, just like in other times in the past, the Jesuits managed to infiltrate the European lodges of the Freemasons through a powerful oligarch by the name of Frederick the Great, a high-level Jesuit who infiltrated the Masonic order as planned by the Jesuits. The Jesuits became his master during their suppression by a righteous Pope known as Ganganelli. Ganganelli wasn't your usual Pope, for he was secretly working for the Knights Templars, who knew of the Luciferian traits of the Jesuits. During this suppression, the Jesuits planned for Frederick the Great and Catherine of Prussia to create the last of the Scottish rites and their attempt to cause a division in the Masonic order as a result of the infiltration.

With the new dark infiltrated Freemasonry under the control of the Black Pope, the Jesuits became more influential in Europe, and most of the grand lodges of masonry had become corrupted, with the exception of those who continued the faction of the Blue Lodge in secret. Unfortunately, under the direction of the Black Pope, the powerful oligarchs like Frederick the Great, King George III, and others had all been aligned with the Jesuits to make sure that Europe did not get a taste of freedom.

On the other hand, since the forces of light failed to bring about a commonwealth in Europe, they began sending voyagers across the Atlantic as early as the late 1300s. These were remnant Knights of the Templars who sought refuge in Scotland under the St. Clair's and other Rex Duex family descendants of the Holy Grail of King David, who had become the leading proponent in the attempt to establish a Republic in Europe. This was to no avail; however, though this success came about in the American continent when our founding fathers established our constitutional Republic. The reason why the St.Clairs and their associated families were unable to establish a commonwealth in Europe was that the oligarchs, controlled by the Jesuits, had too much influence and power. They blocked every opportunity possible, preventing the Republic from existing in the European region.

On a good note, the free world became established by the works of all of the positive orders of light that remained hidden. The primary order behind the free world had been the order of the rosy cross, a.k.a. the Rosicrucians, the Knights Templars, and the Blue Lodge faction of the Freemasons here in America that had not been corrupted by the Jesuits. Members of the original uncorrupted lodges were John Hancock, George Washington, Madison, and Jefferson. All this was possible because a few hundred years earlier, a remnant group of the Knights Templars had escaped annihilation from the Roman Church in the Inquisition of 1307 and therefore preserved the blueprint of the sovereign nation-state Republic, which had been carefully guarded for centuries by them under the guise of various orders of knighthood.

Our founding fathers, who gave us the free world, were men who were well-educated in the Rosicrucian order and learned in the higher knowledge of universal brotherhood and truth. However, the attempts before 1776 were many, as exemplified in the Massachusetts Bay Colony fight for independence as early as 1650. For centuries, our world had neither a true Republic, a taste of freedom, nor a democracy until 1776, which was not only a great achievement for the Brotherhood of Light but a major impediment to the Dark Brotherhood and their attempt at dominating our world.

While the good orders were busy engaged in the new world, attempting to implement freedom and a new way of life, the Jesuits and their infiltration of the European Masonic lodges through Frederick the Great were also busy planning and reorganizing another vehicle that would gradually bring the world into the Luciferian agenda of absolute power. The Dark Brotherhood knew that the battle of religion had been lost in Europe due to the Reformation, the Renaissance, the Scientific Revolution, and the establishment of the Republic in the Americas. The Jesuits were planning a new method; they needed to counteract the new arrival of the Republic and bring it down from within. At this point, the Dark Brotherhood made another move that was going to severely affect the outcome of our world, which is why our world today is plagued with economic injustice. This new vehicle became an extension of the Jesuit order, with a new methodology for them to secure power not only in Europe but all over the world. We had now become transcontinental.

The power of domination through religion, as portrayed through the Roman Church, was not the case anymore for the Luciferian Brotherhood, so they shifted methodology, like they did at the collapse of the Roman Empire. Their control through religion shifted to control through economics by implementing the models of the central banking system, controlled by the new hidden hand, the Jesuits, and their chosen family, the Rothschilds. The new method would not only bring our world under their control again over time, but it would ensure that Jesuits' control over the existing Lodges of Freemasonry that have spread in the new continent. Originally, the Blue Lodge Masonic fraternity is what helped give us the free world. The dark force sought power over this worldwide fraternity, so they infiltrated it and eventually penetrated it from within, gradually coercing all lodges to conform to the dictates of the new Illuminati vehicle on behalf of the Black Pope.

From the beginning, the Jesuits were training individuals as they gained influence and control over the universities in Europe and indoctrinated new individuals to rise to power since their childhood. One of them that they recognized as a descendant of Nimrod was Adam Weishaupt. Another one was Moses Bauer, the father of Mayer Amschel Bauer. Both received special education on behalf of the order of the Jesuits. Mayer Amschel Bauer changed his name to an emblem that was hanging on his father's door that spelled "Red Child." The beginning of this system of control became congruent with the rise of the House of Rothschild, which became the embodiment of the Luciferians' new tool and vehicle for the new power base structure of economic control.

The Bauers had changed their name to Rothschild and began their exploitation to create a strong central Financial Empire that would dominate Europe financially and politically. After all, he who controls the money of a nation also controls the politics of that nation. This family reorganized and formed what became known as the European financial oligarchy elites. The financial oligarchy elite fell under the guidance and secret leadership of the Rothschilds, who apparently evolved to become the most powerful family in Europe. The Rothschild became the First Knights of Malta, operating directly under the guidance of the Black Pope.

The rise of the House of Rothschild overshadowed all of the negative secret societies that became known as the black nobility in Europe. With the reorganization of the Jesuits' black nobility, the new hidden hand had a network of people working for them, and they managed to establish the first major central banking system in Europe, based on the old Venetian oligarch model that dominated Europe during the Dark Ages under the Vatican.

The renegade tyrants and the black nobility wanted to hold on to their power and uphold the mandates of the old aristocracy. They believed it was their birthright to rule the world by covertly and overtly warring the concepts of freedom and the Republic. In truth, they became the unwitting pawns of the international military order of the Jesuits. The rise of the House of Rothschild gave rise to the black nobility in Europe. They were all banding together because of the love of money and the centralization of preserving power in their hands. Thus began the agenda of reviving the old Roman Empire once again. The love of money began the ripping root of all evil as the new modern-day Dark Brotherhood plunged the world into a different type of Inquisition known as the modern-day political wars.

Through the rise of the House of Rothschild, the black nobility elites of Europe, and their masters, the Jesuits, formulated their financial enterprise, which became known as the Bavarian Illuminati. It was formulated by the Jesuits and financed by the House of Rothschild. The person they used to organize this order was trained by the Jesuits and was a professor of canon law at Ingolstadt University by the name of Adam Weishaupt. Ever since the establishment of the first banking system in 1679 in England, the House of Rothschilds, the Jesuits had been creating this new secret society to act as a consolidator of money in the hands of the new powerful oligarchies, the black nobility. The creation of the Bavarian Illuminati allowed the power-hungry families of the old European aristocracy, along with the new house of Rothschild, to work secretly to bring all of the nation's monetary systems under their control, not only in Europe but also in the United States.

Ironically, the Bavarian Illuminati was founded on the same day the free world was established in the west in 1776. Nonetheless, the Illuminati financial apparatus enabled the Black Pope to gain control over the international Lodges of the Freemasons. This move and the infiltration of the Masonic lodges gave the Dark Brotherhood a worldwide network of people who, for the love of money, were willing to sell their soul to the Luciferian agenda, thus giving birth to the modern-day agenda of the New World Order. Most of the Masonic fraternities became an outer lodge for the more secretive members of the Illuminati, who are now operating at the highest levels of corrupted Freemasonry. The old Blue Lodge or what remained of the original loyalist to the Republic became absorbed into the order of the Rosicrucians, who were the Guardians of our Republic and disseminators of ancient and metaphysical knowledge wisdom since the birth of our nation. On the contrary, the Bavarian Illuminati attempted to hoard all metaphysical and esoteric knowledge for themselves.

Perhaps 1776 marked the beginning of the last battle between the two brotherhoods to see which government system would eventually envelop the world in the twenty-first century. This was not only the year of the birth of the free world but also the year that the Empire of the embodiment of the Dark Brotherhood grew into a global secret government through the rise of the Bavarian Illuminati. The Supreme Jesuit General, the Black Pope, had worked out an international apparatus of secret networks all controlled through their new Illuminati Financial vehicle. Overall, this move with the organization of the black nobility of Europe and the infiltration and takeover of the Masonic lodges gave birth to the secret government of the Black Pope as the final manifestation of "The Hidden Hand" on a global scale. Since then, this global secret network has become the executioners' representatives as the working bees of Satan/Marduk in our modern world.

Moreover, as revealed earlier, the Illuminati system of control through the centralization of money in the hands of a few has been practiced for generations, beginning in Babylon, where it originated. We also see it in Imperial Rome and the ultramontane system of Venetian financial rule in Europe, forming the basis of feudalism. This type of unworkable system is associated with the system of the beast, who is only utilizing this apparatus as its final resource to bring the world under absolute control.

It's apparent that absolute power corrupts all power, and nothing else matters when the end justifies the means for this Dark Brotherhood. It is the power to manufacture money out of thin air by using paper money and transforming its value.

This is where the corruption comes in. They lend this paper money at high interest rates and expect it back in actual valuables, such as silver and gold, as returns. This practice of fractal central banking was formulated in Babylon to control the entire people of the first empire and maintain its hierarchy and power by keeping the people in perpetual poverty.

Unfortunately, this is the type of system most of our world's banks have been operating under the effects of the international bankers in modern times. Today, it is well understood that he who controls the money currency can indirectly gain control over its government. This conspired intention is why the House of Rothschild became the star players for the Jesuits. This type of financial witchcraft demonstrated by the Rothschilds enabled them to be set apart as the highest single family to run the new international money today's most known as the international banking cartel.

This family is one of the world's most powerful and influential families, controlling approximately one-third of the world's wealth. Due to this central banking enterprise, they and their comrades have maneuvered our world into economic slavery. It has been estimated that the House of Rothschild has hoarded a few trillion, and today, in the Luciferian last stage, they remained as major key players in the quest of world domination.

It has been revealed that their power began within the courts of Hesse-Kessel, as Amschel Mayer Rothschild became appointed personal financier to Prince William of Hesse-Kessel, who was reported to be the wealthiest monarch in the seventeenth and eighteenth centuries. Mayer Rothschild became extremely close to the prince and offered his assistance and service as planned by the masterminds of the Jesuits.

According to the hidden archives, the prince went off to war and entrusted all his wealth and assets in the hands of the Rothschilds.

However, what Prince William of Hesse-Kessel wasn't aware of was that the war he had to attend had been orchestrated by the very man that created the Rothschild dynasty, the Jesuits. Apparently, even the Treaty of Westphalia did not stop the Jesuits from continuing their war machine (modern-day inquisitions) until all power rested in their hands once again.

With the wealth of Hesse-Kessel in the care of the Rothschilds, the balance of wealth in Europe shifted into the hands of the Jesuits once again. The Jesuits were now ready to make the move that would allow them to seize absolute control of the economies of both England and France, and therefore, their governments. The Rothschilds, as their key players, were conducting a two-fold operation for the Jesuits. They knew that they could make large amounts of money by agitating conflict between different nations and financing both sides of every conflict in secret. In today's light, it is the fact that every war since the 1700s had financial backing aid from the House of Rothschild.

Some sources even claim that our own revolutionary war of Independence was also financed by the Rothschilds in an attempt to weaken the power of the British. England was the greatest power in Europe in the eighteenth century. The plan became as follows: The Jesuits' House of Rothschild union would take the opportunity of making large sums of money by pitting countries against each other and financing both sides of the conflict. These covert actions would not only put countries in debt to the new international clan but also gradually destroy the national sovereignties of nations they wish to control in secret.

The organizations represented the newly organized European financial alliance that became known as the British East India Company of 1763, the "Paris Treaty". The House of Rothschild formulated this in Europe to consolidate all of the world's wealth in their hands. The ultimate result would be a worldwide centralized banking system, which is today the IMF, based on the Babylonian concept of the financial oligarchy rule by a few, as demonstrated in the concept of the medieval Ultramontane system of the Venetian powerful lords.

The idea of creating the wars to impose the Central Banking systems worldwide became the apparatus and final master plan for the newly organized House of Rothschilds and their masters, the Jesuits. With this mobilization, the torch for world domination was well underway once again.

Apparently, the creation of the Bavarian Illuminati served many purposes for the synagogue of the secret government of Satan. However, it was primarily designed as an extension and vehicle that became the financial arm of the beast corps system and a final cloak to the last core of the Luciferian agenda.

Despite what many researchers had gathered, Adam Weishaupt was used as a pawn in this conspiracy, as many men have in the past. He had been educated by the Jesuits and had defected from Christianity to embrace the Luciferian agenda when he joined the Jesuit order. He went off to become the professor of Canon law at Ingolstadt University in Germany. The Jesuits used him because he was not only driven by a zeal based on the destruction of all governments and religions of the world, but because the Jesuits needed a front man to take the heat for the formulation of the new secret society. One of the most important elements that went along with the creation of the Bavarian Illuminati was an actual blueprint and outline that they were going to use to arrive at absolute world domination. The Jesuits and the Rothschilds perfected an outline of Protocols titled "The Protocols of the Learned Elders of Zion."

In essence, "The Protocols of the Learned Elders of Zion" were written by the Black Pope, the supreme ruler of the new hidden global secret government. They, however, made it appear as if the Protocols were written by Jews by placing Adam Weishaupt as the nominal founder of the Bavarian Illuminati and the sole author of the Protocols because the Protocols became outlined as the perfect blueprint for world domination. Adam was to take the blame, a clever move by the Jesuits to place Adam in the front line so that in case the nefarious Protocols leaked out, it would appear as if the entire conspiracy was masterminded by the Jews.

This was the beginning of what we call today Zionism, which served to create a massive hatred for the Jewish race at the same time. Why would the Dark Brotherhood want to cast the blame of world domination on the Jews? This could be explained by examining who the original Jews were in the Old Testament among the twelve tribes of Israel. In the old world, the term Jew was given to those who came from the royal house of Judah. Judah was one of the twelve sons of Jacob, whose descendants became the line of the original messianic lineage of King David.

This line gave us Moses, Elijah, and all of the great prophets of the Old Testament, who were part of the Melchizedek tradition of the Brotherhood of Light. This lineage was the bloodline in which Jesus was born into, the royal house of Judah, otherwise known as the Davidic bloodline of the Messianic lineage that the Knights Templars protected during the Dark Ages as the holy grail blood.

This royal line of Judah (the lion) has been the rival lineage to the Babylonian Nimrod/Ramsey's line of the Dark Brotherhood. Since ancient times, the Dark Brotherhood has been conspiring to do away with the royal house of the messianic lineage, as this lineage proved to be the greatest threat to their agenda of world domination. Most importantly, the Dark Brotherhood always understood the tremendous power in this bloodline and that a promised Messiah who would liberate the world would be born of this bloodline. Therefore, it was always a requirement by the Dark Brotherhood to succeed in the elimination of that original lineage.

To preserve this bloodline after the rule of King David and Solomon, this bloodline needed to go into hiding following the Babylonian exile and after the Maccabean revolt. The original royal house of Judah fled to safety, seeking refuge, and began their own spiritual private community that later became known as the community of Qumran. This community was a community based on righteousness that flourished parallel but in secret from the rest of the surface world. As a result of the Hasmonean dynasty that gave us King Herod, who was an imposter king of Israel. As to why Jerusalem fell under Roman jurisdiction.

Therefore, this threat regarding the existence of the messianic lineage is the real reason why "The Hidden Hand" throughout history has always been victimizing the Jewish descendants. Under this impression, the Jews had been killed in numbers to put an end to the Davidic bloodline of the holy blood. For example, when King Herod heard word that the real king of the Jews had been born, he and his Roman superiors quickly set out to kill all the male children in Judea and Galilee. We can see this pattern continuing down the ages and, in most recent times, the Holocaust by the Nazis.

According to ex-Jesuit priest Alberto Rivera, following the fall of Rome, the Holy Roman Catholic Church continued this agenda through their Crusades and inquisitions, as to why they primarily targeted the Jews throughout the European Dark Ages. For some strange reason, the Dark Brotherhood always believed that if any trace of the Davidic lineage had survived, it would exist within the Jewish race. Boy, were they wrong. It's unfortunate that many innocent Jewish people, though, had to be killed for centuries due to this assumption.

In either case, "The Protocols of the Learned Elders of Zion" did leak. According to multiple sources, the plot was unveiled in 1784 when a Rothschild agent was struck by lightning on his way to France, carrying a copy of the Protocols. As a result, the Bavarian government raided all Weishaupt's lodges, while the real masterminds had gone deeper into hiding. The irony in all of this is that the very same people that the Protocols were written for are the same people claiming to be Jewish today.

 These modern-day proclaimed Jews, political Zionists, are the Rothschilds and their associated families of the elites, which claimed to be Jewish, was apparently a big part of the conspiracy and a deception.

These powerful families of the Illuminati claim to be the descendants of King David to justify their power over the Earth. This is a lie and part of their plot to bring the entire

Earth under their control. Remember, initially, the Rothschilds had changed their name from Bauer to Rothschild to pose as Jewish because, in the Protocols of the Learned Elders of Zion, they place themselves as the chosen people of God and descendants of King David, which they're not. This implies that the rest of the world are the non-chosen people of God and are therefore considered goyim or human cattle, as stated in the Protocols, and must become subject to the true chosen.

In truth, the Rothschilds are not real Jews but fake Jews, descendants of the Nimrod Babylonian bloodline, not King David's, and neither are their circles of political Zionists. On the other hand, the real descendants of the royal house of Judah have always been protected by the Brotherhood of Light and the angels that have secured their existence throughout all of history; however, they have been blending in society as commoners today.

There is more to the Nimrod/Ramseys bloodline. In the Bible's Book of Genesis, we find the story of Esau and Jacob, the two twin brothers born from Isaac and Rebecca. Esau was known as the oldest son, born a few minutes before his younger brother Jacob. It was well known that, according to Abrahamic tradition, the firstborn was the one to receive both the blessings and the Covenant of ancient Israel to carry out their father Abraham's duties. The Covenant is a spiritual contract that Abraham established with Melchizedek.

When Esau and Jacob grew older, Esau thought it would be nice to sell his birthright. Both his blessings and the promise of the Covenant were sold to his brother Jacob for a bowl of pottage, as recorded in the bible. So Jacob, instead of Esau, received the promise. However, Esau wasn't too thrilled about it and decided that he also wanted his father's blessings and promise, but it was too late, for Jacob was the one who had received it.

According to the Bible, Rebecca favored her youngest son, Jacob, out of the two, and arranged for only Jacob to receive his father's blessings and promise. This incident not only enraged Esau, making him rebel, and he married outside the tribe of his father, who were the descendants of Shem. As a result, Esau ended up marrying a descendant of Ham's lineage of Babylon, which were the carriers of the leviathan serpent seed of power. These were the ancient Canaanites that the early Israelites were prohibited from mixing with due to their heavy concentration of reptilian genetics. In the Bible, this was camouflaged as a blemish.

Now, this is the lineage that has continued in today's world as the Illuminati cabal families.

Regardless of Esau's refutation, Esau didn't care. Esau was cast out by his father, but he vowed that his descendants would one day destroy the descendants of his brother Jacob, as explained in the Protocols of the Learned Elders of Zion today. This explains why the Dark Brotherhood's intentions have been to place descendants of Esau mixed with the descendants of Nimrod in positions of power for the last 3600 years. That explains the evil aristocracy and why it's always been a small group of people, the oligarchs, descendants of Nimrod and Esau, trying to dominate the world and enslave the rest of humanity.

The plot of Esau's descendants seeking retribution against Jacob's descendants is seen as a continuation of the Ham-Nimrod strategy, passed down through generations by the Dark Brotherhood's secret societies within the Luciferian networks. This narrative is now associated with the thirteen Bloodlines of the Illuminati, who are said to carry a high concentration of serpent genetics. Today, these descendants are portrayed as Jews but are essentially identified as Zionists and Khazarians working under the direction of the Black Pope. This framework suggests that for generations, only a select group of families has maintained power and amassed a significant portion of the world's wealth throughout history.

The predisposition towards absolute power and control is evident in key figures who have played roles in the establishment of tyranny, such as Ignatius de Loyola, the first Jesuit Black Pope, Constantine of Rome, Napoleon, Hitler, and, notably, Mayer Amschel Rothschild. Their rise to prominence and influence is not seen as accidental but rather as a result of their lineage and alleged connection to the Luciferian agenda, rooted deeply in their genetics. Hence, "The Protocols of the Learned Elders of Zion" are perceived as the culminating blueprint for global domination, authored by the descendants of the Nimrod-Esau bloodline.

These Protocols are Marduk-Satan's ultimate strategy, recognizing the finite nature of his influence and time. The attribution of these plans to the Jews serves as a protective measure. It's intended to deflect scrutiny, and blame away from the true architects of this scheme—those posing as Jews today, aligned with Zionist ideologies. In essence, the Protocols were crafted to undermine the authentic descendants of Israel, who are of non-Canaanite, non-Babylonian origin.

Chapter 7: THE PROTOCOLS

The information was taken from Victor E. Marsden, who translated the 24 Protocols into English before the Jesuit Illuminati eliminated him. The Protocols will help in understanding world events today as their implications have been applied in almost every world event that has transpired. The Protocols are listed in order, but not in their entirety, for space reasons. Bear in mind that these Protocols are also the exact opposite blueprint of our constitutional Republic and the Ten Commandments. They are the outline and precepts of a totalitarian tyranny.

Protocol 1: The Basic Doctrine

Right lies in might, politics versus morals, the end justifies the means, is the new conspiracy. It must be noted that men with bad instincts outnumber the good. Therefore, the best results in governing them are attained by violence and terrorization, not by academic discussion. Every man aims for power; everyone would like to become a dictator if only he could.

There are indeed men who would not be willing to sacrifice the welfare of all for the sake of securing their own welfare. political freedom is an idea but not a fact. This idea one must know how to apply whenever it appears necessary to attract the masses of the people to one's party for the purpose of crushing another who is in authority. This task is rendered easier if the opponent has been infected with the idea of freedom, so-called liberalism, and, for the sake of any idea, is willing to yield some of its power. It is precisely here that the triumph of our theory appears. The slackened reign of government is immediately cut up by the law of life, cut up and gathered by a new hand because the blind might of the nation cannot for one single day exist without guidance and merely fits into the place of the old already weakened by freedom. Only the Jew can govern the goyim (human cattle) for the goyim are like cattle that need to be governed. It is important to understand that in this case, the Protocols are referring to the Babylonian Bloodlines of the Rothschilds and the black nobility that are posing as modern-day Jews, which are not, as they consider everyone else human cattle.

Moreover, politics has nothing to do with morality. According to this Protocol, the ruler who is governed by morals is not a skilled politician and is therefore unstable on his throne. He who wishes to rule must have recourse both to cunning and to make-believe. Great national qualities, like frankness and honesty, are vices in politics for they bring down rulers from their thrones more effectively and certainly than the most powerful enemy. Such qualities must be the attributes of the kingdoms of the goyim, as human cattle. The right lies in force according to this Protocol. The word is an abstract thought and proven by nothing. Our power in the present torturing conditions of all forms of power will be more invisible than any other because it will remain invisible until it has gained such strength that no cunning can undermine it. It is therefore only with a despotic ruler that plans can be elaborated extensively and clearly to distribute the whole properly among the several parts of the machinery of the state.

From this conclusion, it is inevitable that a satisfactory form of government for any country is one that concentrates in the hands of one responsible person; without absolutism, there can be no existence for civilization to be carried on not by the masses but by the despots. Only force conquers in political affairs, especially if it is concealed in the talents essential to statesmen. Violence must be the principal, cunning and make-believe rule for governments which do not want to lay down their crowns at the feet of agents of some new power. This is a brief description of Protocol number one.

Protocol Number 2: Economic Wars

It is indispensable for our purpose that wars should not result in territorial gains; wars will thus be brought onto the economic ground, where actions will not fail to perceive, through the assistance we give, the strength of our predominance. This would put forth sides at the mercy of our international agency which possesses millions of eyes ever on the watch and is hampered by no limitations whatsoever. Our international rights will wipe out national rights in the proper sense of rights and will rule the nations precisely as a civil law of state rules that relate other subjects among themselves.

The administrators whom we will choose among the public with strict regard to their capacities for servile obedience will be persons trained in the arts of government and will therefore easily be pawns in our game in the hands of men of learning and genius who will be their advisors, specially bred and reared from early childhood to rule the affairs of the world. The information they need from our political plans from the lessons of history, from observations made of the events of every moment as it passes. The goyim, the human cattle, will be considered slaves in a totalitarian fascist system. We do not, therefore, take any account of them until the hour strikes, letting them live in hope of new forms of enterprising pastimes or the memories of all they have enjoyed. Let them play the principal part which persuaded them to accept as the dictates of science. It is this object of ours that we constantly, by means of our press, arouse blind confidence in these series.

The intellectuals of the goyim, descendants of the twelve tribes, will puff themselves up with their knowledge and without any logical verification of them, will put an effect on all the information available from science which our agent Illuminati specialists have cunningly pieced together for the purpose of educating their minds in the direction we want.

Do not suppose for a moment that these statements are empty words. Think carefully of the success we arranged for Darwinism, Marxism, and Nietzscheism. It is indispensable for us to take account of the thoughts, characters, and tendencies of the nations to avoid making slips in the political and in the direction of administrative affairs. The triumph of our system, of which the component parts of the machinery may be variously disposed, according to the temperament of the people met on our way, will fail if the practical application is not based upon a summing up of the lessons of the past and the light of the present.

Today there is a great force that creates the movement of thought in the people, and that is the press. The part played by the press is to keep pointing out requirements supposed to be indispensable, to give voice to the complaints of the people, to express and create discontent. But the golden states have not known how to make use of this force, and it has fallen into our hands. Through the press, we have gained the power to influence while remaining in the shade. Thanks to the press, we have the gold in our hands, notwithstanding that we have had to gather it out of the oceans of blood and tears. But it has paid us, though we have sacrificed many of our people. Each victim on our side is worth in the sight of God — referring to, of course, their god Satan.

Protocol Number 3: Methods of Conquest

The Constitution scale will break down, for we have established them with a certain lack of accurate balance in order that they may oscillate incessantly until they wear through the pivot on which they turn. The goyim are under the expression that they will make them sufficiently strong. However, the pivots—the kings on their thrones—are hemmed in by their representatives, who play the fool distraught with their own uncontrollable and irresponsible power. This power they owe to the terror which has been breathed into the palaces. As they have no means of getting at their people, the kings on the thrones are no longer able to come to terms with them. Both have lost all meaning, for like the blind man and his stick, both are powerless apart.

To incite seekers of power to misuse power, we have set all forces in opposition to one another, breaking up their freedom tendencies towards independence. To this end, we stir up every form of enterprise; we arm all parties; we set up authority as a target for every ambition. Of states, we have made gladiatorial arenas where a lot of confused issues contend. Disorders and bankruptcy will be universal.

Protocol Number 4: Materialism Replaces Religion

Who and what is in the position to overthrow an invincible force? This is precisely what our force is: Gentile masonry blindly serves as a screen for us and our objects, but the plan of action of our force, even in its very abiding place, remains for the whole people an unknown mystery. In order to give the goyim no time to think and take note, their minds must be diverted toward industry and trade. Thus, all the nations will be swallowed up in the pursuit of gain and in the rat race for it, not taking note of their common foe. But again, in order that freedom may disintegrate and ruin the communities of the goyim, we must put industry on a speculative basis. The result will be that what is withdrawn from the land by industry will slip through the hands and pass into speculation, that is, into our classes.

The intensified struggle for superiority and shocks delivered to economic life will create, and have already created, disenchanted, cold, and heartless communities. Such communities will foster a strong aversion towards higher political and religious ideals. Their only guide is to gain gold, which they will erect into a veritable cult for the sake of the material delights it can give. Then will the hour strike when, not for the sake of attaining the good, not even to win wealth, but solely out of hatred toward the privileged, the lower classes of the goyim will follow our lead against our rivals for power, the intellectuals of the goyim.

Protocol Number 5: Despotism and Modern Progress

Centralized government as a super-government administration. What form of administrative rule can be given to communities in which corruption has prevailed everywhere, communities where riches are attained only by the clever surprise tactics of semi-swindling tricks, where looseness reigns, where morality is maintained by penal measures and harsh laws, not by voluntarily accepted principles like the Ten Commandments?

We shall create an intensified centralization of government to grip in our hands all the forces of the community. We shall mechanically regulate all the actions of the political life of our subjects by new laws. These laws will withdraw one by one all the indulgences and freedoms which have been permitted by the goyim, and our kingdom will be distinguished by a despotism of such magnificent proportions as to be at any moment and in every place in a position to wipe out any goyim who oppose us by deed or word.

Protocol Number 6: Takeover Technique

We shall soon establish huge monopolies, reserve warriors of colossal riches upon which even large fortunes of the goyim will depend to such an extent they will go to the bottom, together with the credit of states, on the day after the political smash.

At the same time, we must intensively patronize trade and industry, but first and foremost, speculation, which provides a counterpoint to industry. The absence of speculative industry will multiply capital in private hands and serve to restore agriculture by freeing the land from indebtedness to the banks. Industry should drain from the land both labor and capital and by means of speculation transfer into our hands all the money of the world, thereby throwing the goyim into the ranks of the proletariat. Then the goyim will bow down before us if for no other reason than to have the right to exist.

To complete the ruin of the industry of the goyim, we shall bring to the assistance of speculation the luxury which we have developed among the goyim. We shall raise the rate of wages, which, however, will not bring any advantage to the workers, for at the same time we shall produce a rise in prices of the first necessities of life, alleging that it arises from the decline of agriculture and cattle breeding. We shall further undermine, artfully and deeply, sources of production by accustoming the workers to anarchy and to drunkenness, and side by side therewith, taking all measures to extricate from the face of the

Earth all the educated forces of the goyim. In order that the true meaning of things may not strike the goyim before the proper time, we shall mask it under an alleged ardent desire to serve the working classes and the great principles of political economy about which our economic theories are carrying on energetic propaganda.

Protocol Number 7: Worldwide Wars

The intensification of armaments and the increase of police forces are all essential for the completion of the aforementioned plans. There will be in all the states of the world, besides ourselves, only the masses of the proletariat, a few millionaires devoted to our interests, policies and soldiers. Through Europe, and by means of relations with Europe, in other continents, we must create foments, discord, and hostility. Therein, we gain a double advantage. We keep in check all countries, for they will know we have the power wherever we like to create disorders or to restore order. All these countries are accustomed to see us as an indispensable force of coercion.

Secondly, by our intrigues, we shall tangle up all the threads which we have stretched into the cabinets of all states by means of the political, economic treaties, or loan obligations. To succeed, we must use great cunning and penetration during negotiations and agreements, but regarding the official language, we shall keep to the opposite tactics and assume the mask of honesty and complacency. In this way, the peoples and governments of the goyim, whom we have taught to look only at the outside of whatever we present to their notice, will still continue to accept us as benefactors and saviors of the human race. We must be able to respond to every act of opposition by war with the neighbors of that country which dares to oppose us. But if these neighbors should also venture to stand collectively against us, then we must offer resistance by a universal war.

The principal factor of success in politics is the secrecy of its undertakings; the word should not agree with the deeds of the diplomat. We must compel the governments of the goyim to act in the direction favored by our widely conceived plan, already approaching the desired consummation, by what we shall represent as public opinion, secretly promoted by us through the means of the so-called great power—the press—which, with few exceptions, is already entirely in our hands.

Protocol Number 8: Provisional Government

We must arm ourselves with all the weapons which our opponent might employ against us. We must search in the very finest shades of expression and the knotty points of the lexicon of law. We must find justification for those cases when we must pronounce judgments that might appear abnormally audacious and unjust, for it is important that these resolutions should be set forth in expressions that shall seem to be the most exalted moral principles cast into legal form. All directorates must surround themselves with all of the forces of civilization among which it will have to work. It will surround itself with political, practical, judiciary, administrators, diplomats, and with persons prepared for a special super-educational training in our special schools.

These people will have cognizance of all the secrets of the social structure; they will know all of the languages that can be made up by political alphabets and words. They will be made acquainted with the whole underside of human nature, with all its sensitive chords on which they will have to play. These chords are the cast of mind of the goyim, their tendencies, shortcomings, vices, and qualities. The talented assistance of the authority of whom I speak will be taken not from among goyim who are accustomed to performing their administrative work without troubling to think what its aim is and who sign papers without reading them; they serve either for mercenary reasons or ambition.

We shall surround our government with a whole world of economists. That is the reason why economic sciences form the principal subject of the teaching given to the Jews. Around us will be a whole constellation of bankers, industrialists, capitalists, and millionaires because in substance, everything will be settled by the question of figures. Until there will no longer be any risk in entrusting responsible posts in our state to our brothers, we shall put them in the hands of persons whose past and reputations are such that between them and the people lies an abyss, persons who, in case of disobedience to our instructions, must face criminal charges or disappear. This is to make them defend our interests to their last gasp.

Protocol Number 9: Re-education

In applying our principles, let attention be paid to the character of the people in whose country you live and act. A general, identical application of them, until such time as the people are re-educated to our pattern, cannot have success. By approaching their application cautiously, not a decade will pass before the most stubborn character changes, and we will add new people to the ranks of those already subdued by us. For us, there are no checks to limit the range of our activity. Our super-government subsists in exact legal conditions which are described in the accepted terminology by the energetic, enforceable word "dictatorship." We are the head of all troops mounted on the steed of the leader. We rule by force of will because, in our hands, are the fragments of a once powerful party, now vanquished by us. The weapons in our hands are limitless ambitions, burning greediness, merciless vengeance, hatreds, and malice.

It is from us that the all-engulfing terror proceeds. We have in our service people of all opinions, all doctrines—restorers of monarchies, demagogues, socialists, communists, and utopian dreamers of every kind. We have harnessed them all to the task; each one of them, on his own account, is etching away at the last remnants of authority, striving to overthrow all established forms of order. By these acts, states are tortured; they exhort tranquility, ready to sacrifice everything for peace, but we will not give them peace until they openly acknowledge our international super-government and submit to it. We fooled, used, and corrupted the youth of the goyim by rearing them in principles and theories which are known to us to be false, although it is by us, they have been inculcated. Above the existing laws, without substantially altering them, and by merely twisting them into contradictions of interpretations, we have erected something grandiose. These results found expression in the fact that the interpretations masked the law. Afterward, they entirely hid them from the eyes of the governments owing to the impossibility of making anything out of the tangled web of legislation.

Protocol Number 10: Preparing for Power

We count on attracting all nations to the task of erecting new fundamental structures, the project for which has been drawn up by us. This is why it is indispensable for us to arm ourselves and to store in ourselves the reckless audacity and irresponsible might of the spirit, which, in the person of our active workers, will break down all hindrances on our way.

When we accomplish our coup d'état, we shall say to the various peoples: "Everything has gone terribly badly; all have been worn out with suffering. We are destroying the causes of your torment—nationalities, frontiers, differences in coinages. You are at liberty, of course, to pronounce judgment upon us, but can it possibly be a just one if it is confirmed by you before you make any trial of what we are offering you." In order to produce this result, we shall arrange elections in favor of such presidents who have in their past some dark, undiscovered stain, then they will be trustworthy agents for the accomplishment of our plans out of fear of revelations and from the natural desire of everyone who has attained power, namely, the retention of the privileges, advantages, and honor connected with the office of president. The chamber of deputies will provide cover for, protect, and elect presidents, but when we shall take from it the right to propose new laws, or make changes in existing ones, for this right will be given by us to the irresponsible presidents—puppets in our hands.

Naturally, the authority of the presidents will then become a target for every possible form of attack, but we shall provide him with a means of self-defense in the right of an appeal to the people, for the decision of the people over the heads of their representatives an appeal to that some blind slave of ours—the majority of the mob. Independently of this, we shall invest the president with the right to declare war. We shall justify this right on the grounds that the president, as chief of the whole army of the country, must have at his disposal for the defense of the government the right to defend it, which will belong to him as the responsible representative of this constitution. By such measures, we shall obtain the power to destroy little by little, step by step, all that we are compelled to introduce into the constitutions of states to prepare for the transition to an imperceptible abolition of every kind of constitution, and then the time will come to turn every form of government into our despotism.

Protocol Number 11: The Totalitarian State

Having established our motives agenda, we will occupy ourselves with details of those combinations by which we still have to complete the revolution during the machinery of state in the direction indicated. By those combinations, I mean the freedom of the press, the right of association, freedom of conscience, the voting principle, and many others that must disappear forever from the memory of man or undergo a radical alteration the day after the promulgation of the new constitution.

It is only then that we shall be able to announce all our orders, for afterward every noticeable alteration will be dangerous for the following reasons: If this alteration is brought in with harsh severity and a sense of severity and limitations, it may lead to a feeling of despair caused by fear of a new alteration in the same direction. If, on the other hand, it is brought in a sense of further indulgence, it will be said that we have recognized our own wrongdoing, and this will destroy the prestige of the infallibility of our authority, or else it will be said that we are alarmed and compelled to show a yielding disposition, for which we shall get no thanks. Both are injurious to the prestige of the new constitution.

What we want is that, from the first moment of its promulgation, while the peoples of the world are still stunned by the accomplished fact of the revolution, still in a condition of terror and uncertainty, they shall recognize that we are so strong, inexhaustible, and superabundantly filled with power, that in no case shall we take any account of them, and so far from paying any attention to their opinions or wishes, we are ready and able to crush with irresistible power all expression or manifestation thereof at every moment and in every place, that we have seized at once everything we wanted and shall in no case divide our power with them. Then in fear and trembling, they will close their eyes to everything and be content to wait for what will be the end of it all.

Protocol Number 12: Control of the Press

What is the part played by the press today? It serves to excite and inflame those passions needed for our purpose or else it serves selfish ends of parties. It is often vapid, unjust, mendacious, and much of the public have not the slightest idea what ends the press really serves. We shall settle and bridle it with a tight curb. We shall do the same also with all productions of the printing press, for what would be the sense of getting rid of the attacks of the press if we remain targets for pamphlets or books? The product of publicity, a source of heavy expense owing to the necessity of censoring it, will be turned by us into a very lucrative source of income to our state. We shall lay on it a special stamp tax and require deposits of caution money before permitting the establishment of any organ of the press or printing offices. This will then guarantee our government against any type of attack on the parts of the press. For any attempt to attack us, if such still be possible, we shall inflict fines without mercy. Such measures as stamp tax, deposit of caution money, and fines secured by these deposits will bring in a huge income to the government.

It is true that party organs might not spare money for the sake of publicity, but they shall shut up at the second attack upon us. No one shall with impunity lay a finger on the aura of our government's infallibility. The pretext for stopping any publication will be the allegation that it is agitating the public mind without occasion or justification.

I beg you to understand that among those making attacks upon us will be organs established by us, but they will attack exclusively points that we have predetermined to alter. Not a single announcement will reach the public without our control. Even now, this is already being attained to such an extent that all news items are received by a few agencies, from whose offices they are focused on in all parts of the world. These agencies will then be already entirely ours and will give publicity only to what we dictate them to be.

Methods of organization like these, imperceptible to the public eye but absolutely are best calculated to succeed in bringing the attention and confidence of the public to the side of our government. Thanks to such methods, we shall be in a position as from time to time may be required, to excite or to tranquilize the public mind on political questions, to persuade or to confuse, presenting truth then lies, facts or their contradictions. We shall triumph over our opponents since they will not have at their disposal the press in which they can give full and final expression to their views. We shall not need to refute them except very superficially.

Protocol Number 13: Distractions

In order to distract people who may be too troublesome from discussions of questions of the political, we now put forward what we allege to be new questions of the political, namely questions of industry. In this field, let them discuss themselves silly! The masses have agreed to remain inactive, to take a rest from what they supposed to be political activity, only on the condition of being offered new employment, which we are prescribing to them as though it were the same political objective. In order that the masses may not guess what they are about, we further distract them with amusements, games, pastimes, passions, people's palaces.

Soon we shall begin through the press to propose competitions in art, in sport of all kinds: these interests will finally distract their minds from questions in which we should find ourselves compelled to oppose them. Growing more and more unaccustomed to reflect and form any opinions of their own, people will begin to talk in the same tone as we because we alone shall be offering them new directions of thought, of course through such persons who will not be suspected of solidarity with us.

Protocol Number 14: Assault on Religion
Destruction of all existing religions, especially Christianity, and the imposition of a singular world sovereign religion which will be forced upon everyone.

Protocol Number 15: Ruthless Suppression
When we at least definitely come into our kingdom by the aid of coups d'états prepared everywhere for one and the same day, no one shall with impunity lay a finger on the aura of our government's infallibility. We shall slay without mercy all who take arms in hand to oppose our coming into our kingdom. Every kind of new institution of anything like a secret society

will first be punished with death; those of them which are now in existence, known to us, serve us and have served us, we shall disband and send into exile to continents far removed from Europe. In this way we shall proceed with those goyim Masons who know too much; those who remain we shall constrain to discuss themselves into all sorts of observances and all kinds of service to the cause. We shall give them the fear of exile. We shall properly promulgate a law making all former members of secret societies liable to exile from Europe as the center of rule.

Protocol Number 16: Brainwashing

Emasculation of the universities and abolition of freedom of instruction. In order to affect the destruction of all collective forces except ours, we shall emasculate the first stage of collectivism — the universities — by reeducating them in a new direction. Their officials and professors will be prepared for their business by detailed secret programs of action from which they will not with immunity diverge, not by one iota. They will be treated with special precautions, and they will be so placed as to be wholly dependent on the Government.

We shall exclude from the course of instruction classical education, which has not the least practical use. Thereby, we shall cut down the young forces of thought by teaching them details and knowledge demanding servile labor, which does not allow the development of thought. Further, we shall not permit private lessons and everything that could convey direct knowledge to the young generation. Classicalism, as also any form of study of ancient history, in which there are more bad than good examples, will be replaced with the study of the program of the future. We shall erase from the memory of men all facts of previous centuries which are undesirable to us and leave only those which depict all the errors of the governments of the goyim. The study of practical life, of the obligations of order, of the relations of people one to another, of avoiding bad and selfish examples which spread the infection of evil, and similar questions of an educative nature, will stand in the forefront of the teaching program, which will be drawn up on a separate plan for each calling or state of life, in no wise generalizing the teaching. This treatment of the question has special importance.

Each state of life must be trained within strict limits corresponding to its destination and work in life. The occasional genius has always managed and always will manage to slip through into other states of life, but it is the exception that proves the rule. The genius who has highly developed thought, a man does not take to a lower calling, no matter in what difficulties he may be placed, but rises above them and captures the higher places, the more so since he has been trained for a high calling in the shadows of his ancestors by the conditions of his past life, and it is on them that his guide for the understanding of his position depends for the interpretation.

Protocol Number 17: Abuse of Authority

The practice of advocacy lends to making men cold, cruel, persistent, unprincipled, who in all cases take up an impersonal, purely legal standpoint. They have the inveterate habit to refer everything to its value for the defense and not to the public welfare of its results. They do not usually decline to undertake any defense whatever, they strive for an acquittal at all costs, caviling over every petty crux of jurisprudence and thereby they demoralize justice. For this reason, we shall set this profession into narrow frames which will keep it inside the sphere of executive public service. Advocates, equally with judges, will be deprived of the right of communication with litigants; they will receive business only from the court and will study it by notes of report and documents, defending their client after he has been interrogated in court on facts that have appeared. They will receive an honorarium without regard to the quality of the defense. This will render them mere reporters on business law in the interests of justice and as counterpoise to the proctor who will be the reporter in the interests of prosecution; this will shorten business before the courts. In this way will be established a practice of honest unprejudiced defense conducted not from personal interest but by conviction. This will also remove the present practice of corrupt bargaining between advocates to let that side decide which pays most.

Protocol Number 18: Arrest of Opponents

Measures of secret defense and undermining authority. When it becomes necessary for us to strengthen the strict measures of secret defense (the most fatal poison for the prestige of authority), we shall arrange a simulation of disorders or some manifestation of discontents finding expression through cooperation with good speakers. Round these speakers will assemble all who are sympathetic to his utterance. This will give us the pretext for domiciliary prerogatives and surveillance on the part of our servants from among the number of the goyim police.

Protocol Number 19: Rulers and People

As we do not permit any independent dabbling in the political, we shall on the other hand encourage every kind of report or petition with proposals for the government to examine into all kinds of projects for the amelioration of the condition of the people; this will reveal to us the defects or fantasies of our subjects, to which we shall respond either by accomplishing them or by a wise rebutment to prove the short-sightedness of one who judges wrongly. Sedition-mongering is nothing more than the yapping of a lapdog at an elephant. For a government well organized, not from the police but from the moment of its constitution, the lap-dog yaps at the elephant in entire unconsciousness of its strength and importance. It needs no more than to take a good example to show the relative importance of both and the lapdogs will cease to yap and will wag their tails the moment they set eyes on an elephant. To destroy the prestige of heroism for political crime we shall send it for trial in the category of thieving, murder, and every kind of abominable and filthy crime. Public opinion will then confuse in its conception of this category of crime with the disgrace attaching to every other and will brand it with the same contempt.

We have done our best, and I hope we have succeeded to obtain that the goyim should not arrive at this means of contending with sedition. It was for this reason that through the press and in speeches, indirectly—in cleverly compiled schoolbooks on history, we have advertised the martyrdom alleged to have been accredited by sedition-mongers for the idea of the commonweal. This advertisement has increased the contingent of liberals and has brought thousands of goyim into the ranks of our livestock cattle.

Protocol Number 20: Financial Program

When we come into our kingdom, our autocratic government, in principle of self-preservation, will avoid heavily burdening the masses with taxes, recognizing its role as father and protector. However, as state organization incurs costs, it is essential to secure the necessary funds. I will, therefore, carefully address the question of achieving equilibrium in this matter.

Our governance, wherein the king enjoys the legal fiction that everything in his state belongs to him, will enable the lawful confiscation of all sums for the regulation of their civilization within the state. Consequently, taxation will be most effectively implemented through a progressive tax on property. This method allows dues to be paid as a percentage of property value, without bankrupting anyone. The wealthy must understand their duty to allocate part of their surplus to the state, which, in turn, ensures the security of their remaining property.

Taxing the impoverished is a recipe for revolution and detriment to the state. Beyond this, attacks on capitalism, which diminishes wealth in private hands—where we have concentrated it as a counterbalance to the goyim's government strength and state finances—are counterproductive. Such measures will dissolve the poor man's resentment towards the rich, seeing in them necessary for financial support for the state and peace organizers, understanding it is the wealthy who provide the means for these achievements.

A reigning monarch will own no personal property, as all within the state represents his patrimony. Economic crises, inflicted upon the goyim by us through the withdrawal of money from circulation and the accumulation of vast capitals, forced states to seek loans from these same stagnant capitals. These loans burdened state finances with interest payments, enslaving them to capital. The concentration of industry in capitalist hands has sapped the vitality of the people and the states alike.

Protocol Number 21: Loans and Credit

By exploiting the corruption of administrations and the weakness of rulers, we have profited enormously by lending money to governments—money that was not needed. Could anyone else achieve such returns? Thus, my discussion will focus solely on the specifics of internal loans.

Upon ascending the world throne, any financial operations not aligning with our interests will be eradicated. Money markets, too, will be abolished, as we will not allow our power's prestige to be compromised by price fluctuations, which we alone shall determine through legislation, reflecting their true value without room for depreciation or appreciation. This strategy began with manipulating the goyim's values. We will establish monumental government credit institutions to dictate industrial values according to our perspective, enabling us to release or purchase vast amounts of industrial paper at will. Consequently, all industrial endeavors will depend on us, solidifying our immense power.

Protocol Number 22: Power of Gold

In our hands lies the day's greatest power: gold. Within two days, we can procure any quantity from our storehouses. Surely, no further proof is needed that our dominion is divinely ordained. With such wealth, we shall demonstrate that centuries of our committed evils were ultimately for the true well-being and order of the world. We will prove ourselves benefactors who, through order and the restoration of genuine freedom and dignity—albeit under strict observance of our laws—have mended a fractured world. We shall illustrate that true freedom is not about indulgence or unrestricted behavior, just as dignity and strength are not about promoting destructive principles under the guise of freedom of conscience or equality.

Our singular authority will be revered, guiding us without the chaos of contemporary leaders' cacophonous and meaningless principles. Our authority will symbolize order, encompassing total happiness. This mystic respect and awe for our governance will cement our unchallenged power, asserting rights not even God could dispute.

Protocol Number 23: Instilling Obedience

To habituate the populace to obedience, it is crucial to instill lessons of humility and limit the production of luxury goods, thus elevating moral standards debased by luxury emulation. We shall revive small-scale master production, vital for keeping manufacturers from inadvertently influencing mass sentiments against the government.

Small masters, unaffected by unemployment, remain loyal to the existing order. Laws will also prohibit drunkenness, punishable as a crime against man's nature, preventing alcohol-induced degeneration into bestiality.

The Supreme Lord, replacing all current rulers, must eradicate existing societies, even at the cost of his blood, to rebirth them as well-organized forces combatting any infection threatening the state's integrity.

Protocol Number 24: Qualities of the Ruler

Certain members of the seed of David will prepare the kings and their heirs, selected not by right of heritage but by their eminent capacities, and induct them into the secret mysteries of politics and schemes of government, ensuring, however, that none may come to the knowledge of the secrets. The purpose of this approach is to demonstrate that governance cannot be entrusted to those who have not been initiated into the arcane aspects of its art. The king's plan of action for the present and even more so for the future will remain undisclosed, even to those deemed his closest advisors. Only the king and the three sponsors will be privy to upcoming events.

No one will know the king's objectives with his dispositions, and hence, none will dare venture onto an uncharted path. It is understood that the intellectual reserve of the king must match the government plan it encompasses. For this reason, he will ascend to the throne only after his intellect has been scrutinized by the aforementioned learned elders, thereby placing the elders of the Sanhedrin above their puppet kings and controlling them.

This provides a brief overview of every Protocol known as the Protocols of the Learned Elders of Zion. They were authored in the late 16th century by the autocratic ruler of the new Dark Brotherhood known as the Black Pope, two centuries prior to the founding of the Luciferian last vehicle for world domination, the Illuminati. The Protocols were designed to outline the structure and framework for members of the new international order to devise their strategies for a global takeover.

The House of Rothschild and the Black Nobility of Europe have played crucial roles in implementing these Protocols, striving to convince the populace that they are descendants of the seed of David. The only monarch arising from the royal lineage of David to achieve kingship was King Arthur of the Courts of Wessex. Apart from King Arthur of the Courts of Wessex, a descendant of the early Carolingian dynasty, the Black Nobility traces its lineage back to the Babylonian Nimrod Esau lineage.

The Dark Brotherhood has consistently employed euphemistic terms to describe their orders and blueprints. For instance, Ignatius de Loyola named his order the Society of Jesus so that, if exposed, they would seem to be a benevolent entity, hence their name, Society of Jesus. In essence, they evolved into the modern core of the beast (Babylon), serving as a secret and powerful military branch of the covert government in contemporary times.

Similarly, when the Jesuits organized the modern-day Brotherhood of the Illuminati, they named it after the ancient order of the illuminated ones. By doing so, they aimed to confuse the masses into believing they were the original enlightened ones from antiquity. The next chapter will explore the history of the ancient Brotherhood of Light, known throughout esoteric history as the branches of the Great White Brotherhood of the Blue Lodge.

Chapter 8: THE BROTHERHOOD OF LIGHT

This ancient order was the authentic, original illuminated ones. As the original group of light-workers, they set themselves apart to become world servers, assisting the rest of mankind who had lost their spiritual connection due to the negative programming by the Dark Brotherhood since the days of Atlantis, and later, in Babylon. Nevertheless, the original ancient order of illuminated ones became the harbinger of higher spiritual knowledge in our world. They were known by various names, but one that came to significantly influence the Western world was the Ancient Order of Melchizedek.

In Egypt, the Brotherhood of Light created great orders of light that not only developed the higher education for this world's return to higher consciousness but also became the guardians of secret knowledge, protectors of truth, the Commonwealth, peace, and justice. Moreover, part of their task was to counteract every attempt at world domination made by the Dark Brotherhood as representatives of the forces of light on Earth. It is due to this great Brotherhood of Light that the world has been safeguarded from falling completely under the Luciferian manifesto, which is the empire exercised to its fullest degree. Besides their primary goal of battling the synagogue of Satan, they have also been the source providing the right education for enlightenment and exaltation, which is ascension into our divinity.

These sacred teachings were the central theme of the forgotten ancient wisdom of all ages, which is the original doctrine and central belief of the true spiritual association preserved by the original Brotherhood of Light, the Ancient Order of Melchizedek.

Zion, which literally meant the promised land before it was inverted by today's Dark Brotherhood, was part of the oral tradition of the ancient biblical Israelites associated with the Melchizedek order. Those who penetrated and deciphered the true meaning of the prophecies encoded in the Bible now know that Zion was, indeed, the established America. The United States of America was the promised land that the descendants of Abraham had been trying to implement for thousands of years, symbolically explained in the Bible as the land of milk and honey. Since our founding fathers planted the seeds of freedom in an attempt to bring the Commonwealth and abundance for all by establishing the constitutional Republic, it indicated that they were true descendants of Abraham. The original plan of this great nation was not only to enact this perfect utopian structure but to become a model for the rest of the world to follow. This nation was a prophecy fulfilled, the promised land of milk and honey, the true meaning of Zion, which used to be the land of abundance, freedom, and joy before it was inverted by today's Dark Brotherhood.

On the contrary, and as stated in the Protocols, the Dark Brotherhood used the term Zion as the opposite of its actual reality, the free world-based system known as the Commonwealth. The Dark Brotherhood, unfortunately, twisted and inverted the term Zion to describe their Kingdom of absolute power and control, which is the kingdom of Lucifer.

While the agenda of the Dark Brotherhood has been the oppression of humanity through the establishment of the

Luciferian agenda, the original Brotherhood of Light was more interested in the exaltation and ascension of humanity rather than the domination of them. The concept of our own Republic had been tightly preserved by the "forces of good" for over twenty-five thousand years. Many times, they attempted to manifest the Republic as a workable utopian system of government. However, because of the existing Luciferian Brotherhood, this resulted in a long battle between these two opposing secret society networks. The forces of darkness, unfortunately, tilt the scales of power to their side due to Marduk-Satan's temporary control of our planet. However, their time is limited, and it is coming to an end any day now.

It is good to know that today we have a special dispensation upon us like no other in the history of our world as we shift ages. This is one of restoration and balance, returning the Earth back to the original divine plan. These events are part of the prophecies held and preserved, along with the body of ancient knowledge, by the positive orders that have been repressed, ignored, or, at least, given a bad reputation by the victors of empires and those who have rewritten history. The truth is that the light has always been here on the planet to protect these original truths that have been manifested at different times under different orders and different names as the keepers of the flame of enlightenment.

The way the guardians of the Republic and enlightenment envisioned a positive future was by granting the people free will and choice, thus providing the grounds for spiritual evolution. The only way this could happen is by creating a perfect, workable system of government: a constitutional Republic based on the Commonwealth of the people and for the people. This workable system allows for an expression of full freedom and, at the same time, through exploring what makes people happy and igniting the spirit of cooperating with others, they would create peace, harmony, and balance among all members of their communities. This, of course, would be the result of proper education. Unfortunately, these periods, known as golden ages, were always rampaged by the hidden government of the Brotherhood of the Snake.

The benevolent orders of light have been the guardians of higher spiritual knowledge. Not only have they protected it, but they have also guarded the higher knowledge from falling into the hands of their enemy, the evil Dark Brotherhood, who have always sought to pervert, distort, and misuse it towards their advantage.

In the Bible, Abraham was counseled and initiated into the higher mysteries by Melchizedek, an important figure who, being a leading light bearer in the early days following the flood, was so righteous that even Abraham sought his wisdom and counsel. Many believe he was a celestial or could have been an archangel that gave mankind the true priesthood, preserved through the sons of Abraham, then later through the sons of David as the high priest of Zadok of the lineage of the Messianic bloodline. One of the strong tenets of this priesthood was that only men and women of righteousness, with good intentions, would receive initiation into it, for it was carefully guarded from the corrupt powers of the Babylonian brotherhood. With the inheritance of this priesthood came initiation into the higher knowledge of the sacred divine wisdom. Melchizedek was a pivotal figure, becoming the first king of righteousness who passed it on to Abraham, and Abraham unto his children, until it reached Moses and later King David.

In the records of the Brotherhood of Light, the order of Melchizedek existed even before the creation of this world. According to the Urantia material, this was the original order of sonship dispatched from the higher evolved worlds of subtle matter into the lower worlds of gross matter to serve as universal repairs of fallen worlds and systems, working under the direction of Christ Michael, who is the chief guardian and protector of the entire universe.

In the days of Abraham, the order of Melchizedek extended to the Earth the Melchizedek priesthood. In ancient Egypt, it was considered the high priesthood of the god-man partnership that existed before the creation of our world as a universal order overseen by Lord Michael, the original name of the Archangel Michael.

Before the Melchizedek priesthood descended upon the Earth, there were two other priesthoods in the ancient world that were total working vehicles of the Sanhedrin Luciferian brotherhood: the Thai priesthood and the Atep priesthood, governed by the dark arts of black magic and sorcery. These were the corrupt priesthoods that Akhenaton-Moses was attempting to overthrow as they emerged when the Fallen Angels took over the power of Earth during the times of Atlantis.

After the great deluge, knowledge was passed down by word of mouth from master to student or initiate, marking the beginning of the oral tradition. The oral tradition was implemented because of the nature and sacredness of this knowledge, which was guarded by the order of Melchizedek in the old world. These higher mysteries had become part of the esoteric tradition, given only to those initiates who were ready to know the higher sacred wisdom of all ages. During this time, Babylon had already spread a false sense of religious practices. This false system of religious idolatry could not mix with the purity practiced by the actual holders of the high priesthood of Melchizedek.

These two rivaling forms caused a split in the two streams that gave us the exoteric tradition, the lesser mysteries, which is the standard interpretation for the general populace, and the esoteric tradition, also known as the secret knowledge of the higher mysteries. The esoteric tradition was for a select few who proved worthy of receiving this higher knowledge. Therefore, it was necessary for the early holy order of Melchizedek to develop an initiatory pathway into the sacred for those who showed eligibility.

First, initiation into the mysteries served to guard the sacred divine knowledge of higher evolution from the profane, especially the Luciferians, who always sought to distort the great truths of God. Second, because the public was so embedded and hypnotized by the corrupt religions of the Babylonians, it became impossible to leap directly into divine knowledge that required a more refined understanding of our divine higher self.

In those days, humanity was ruled by fear, and it was believed that humankind was a rational animal that needed to be ruled over by the gods, who were the only entities of divine nature. Mankind had lost its own divine connection due to heavy indoctrination by this false doctrine.

Considering this, a precise initiatory pathway was set up by the Brotherhood of Light, who understood that mankind was more than a mere mortal and that we had fallen from a divine state into a lower condition. The understanding of the descent of mankind into a lower state of being marked the beginning of hidden knowledge preserved in mystery school teachings. Once men proved to be ready to ascend and come home to reunite with their divinity, this initiatory pathway would be available to all of them. However, according to prophecy, there would come a time when all of humanity would be ready to learn the sacred mysteries of the ancient knowledge of ageless wisdom, as the long-forgotten universal truths that would initiate the great awakening of all humanity.

The esoteric, therefore, flourished in secret for thousands of years and was only open to people who had proven themselves worthy and ready for more initiation into the higher knowledge of God, which had been entrusted into the hands of the benevolent orders of light. The orders of light became the pillars for the advancement of the kingdom of Heaven on Earth. They were representatives working on the side of light and life, acting as protectors and custodians of the living flame of God in the old world and in modern times. The Melchizedek order of light became known as the Great White Brotherhood in the ancient world. Central to their purpose was the completion of the work of all ages to bring to pass the immortality and eternal life of men, as stated in the Book of Moses.

The Brotherhood of Light brought the ancient mystery schools to Egypt during their first dynasties. In Egypt, it was they who established the ancient oracles, temples, and great academies of higher learning, which produced a beautiful classical golden era. They have also always guarded and protected the descendants of this ancient lineage, commonly known as the holy grail kings and queens, from extinction by the Dark Brotherhood, who has been trying to wipe out any trace of this lineage. This is why Pharaoh Akhenaten, also known as Moses, was heir to the throne of Egypt as a descendant of the original house of Israel before the infiltration of the Dark Brotherhood. In Egypt, this lineage was symbolized by the monolithic Sphinx, which has the body of a lion with a human face, indicating the tribe of the lion, which is the original Judah. However, this pattern of killing any descendant of the house of Judah, the lion, is seen again in the times of Herod when Jesus was born.

The higher knowledge is what gave Egypt the first group of healers known as Therapeutae, who developed a natural healing method by fusing spirituality with alchemy and using their developed gifts for good as the healers of Egypt. This type of healing became the harbinger of Reiki in today's modern world, as a form of spiritual holistic healing using etheric energy known as pranic or Chi in the East, in directing the spiritual energy of the universe into the chakra where the illness is manifested.

Other forms of healing were practiced through the use of natural herbs. These are among some of the spiritual sciences in the esoteric tradition used by these healers. Moreover, the central principle in the initiatory process of the secret tradition left behind by the Great White Brotherhood was that man was a great spiritual being expressed in human form. Therefore, the initiatory process provided mankind a way to rediscover that essence of the real self, also known as the higher self or, in Christian terms, the Christ within.

The objective was to integrate our spiritual essence, our true selves, with our physical form through spiritual exercises in a process known as ascension, merging spirit and matter once again, which marks the ultimate destiny for all of humanity. This aspect of ourselves has been hidden from us by the created illusionary and false realities originating in Babylon with the brotherhood of darkness. It is to this great truth that the forces of darkness have been working to suppress every form of knowledge that leads to the rediscovery of the Divine higher self, also known as the Christ consciousness, that therefore connects us to the higher spheres of reality in the spiritual realm.

If all mankind were to awaken to this hidden truth of discovering the God self or Christ within, and cultivate and develop it through appropriate spiritual practices, the kingdom of God would manifest for all of mankind to see and experience here on the Earth. This realization and manifestation are what the Great White Brotherhood and their custodians of spiritual knowledge have carefully been guarding as custodians of Truth and keepers of God's power on Earth.

For centuries, the lesser mysteries became the religion for the public, and the more esoteric tradition became known as the higher mysteries, which were a higher form of initiation for those that the priesthood of Melchizedek saw fit in becoming students of the way. The higher mysteries would only be open to those who became aspiring students and showed signs of humbleness. For the people that were heavily hypnotized by the corrupt priesthoods of the Luciferians were kept in the lesser mysteries, which was plain knowledge hidden in allegorical form.

As mentioned earlier, the wisdom and higher knowledge of the Egyptian Mystery Schools eventually spread to other regions as the lovers of truth and wisdom came from different lands to learn from the ancient Egyptians. This type of knowledge is what gave birth to the higher educational academy of Plato and the mystery schools of Greece. It is precisely this higher form of education that resulted in the beauty of their classical era, as Greece reached a height in the arts, music, philosophy, mathematics, and science, and through Solon of Athens, there was a period of the sovereign nation-state Republic that Plato wrote about in his treatise on the perfect state.

This is an example of how the outcome of a society is ultimately determined by the type of education it embraces. With appropriate learning, society can be created and flourished in a harmonious, beautiful, and peaceful manner in which true brotherhood and sisterhood would prevail. The creation of a universal brotherhood and sisterhood for all humanity has been the ultimate goal of the Great White Brotherhood. We would not have the Republic of the United States today if it wasn't preserved by these benevolent secret societies of the light.

It is important to know that within the priesthoods of light, they have always revered women and thought of them as equal to men. Therefore, women who proved to be righteous and ready would also become eligible for initiation and become high priestesses of the order. In this tradition, men and women were considered equal and taught that they were both children of the light. Therefore, every breathing soul, male or female, was eligible for initiation and exaltation after their initial screening into the mysteries of the celestial knowledge. It was the corrupt priesthoods of the Luciferians that placed women inferior to men.

The higher mysteries were practiced by men and women who were both aspirants of truth, universal awareness, and universal principles. It is to this mystery that Moses-Akhenaton wrote the Torah, known as the law, on different levels of understanding, with the literal composition being a continuation of the lesser mysteries, which later became distorted by the Dark Brotherhood, while maintaining the higher knowledge preserved in a sensitive composition that became known as the Kabbalah. As revealed, Moses was learned in the ways of higher knowledge, as there was substantial evidence that he was educated in the knowledge of the Egyptians, which is the same wisdom and knowledge of the mysteries of Melchizedek that Abraham received from him.

Melchizedek initiated Abraham, and later, Moses was initiated by the same priesthood. Perhaps this is why some researchers consider this the hereditary high priesthood of the original order of Melchizedek of the Great White Brotherhood and the reason why the program Israel began in ancient times. The Lesser priesthood, known as the Aaronic priesthood, also existed for beginners. The higher priesthood of Melchizedek was only for the initiation of the way. This initiatory process of secrecy needed to be established in order for the Brotherhood of Light to protect higher knowledge from falling into the wrong hands. For this reason, positive secret societies were created as branches of the Great White Brotherhood to safeguard this hidden tradition until the time was right for all to know the ageless wisdom and universal truths and attain gnosis, which is to have a direct connection with the source and the spiritual realms as a result of achieving a higher understanding by the raising of awareness. Ultimately, this leads to ascension or union with God and the integration infusing of spirit and body to spiritualize our physical body.

The seers of this knowledge were well aware that humanity used less than 10% of their full mental capacity. They believed that by raising awareness and consciousness, we would ascend degree by degree until we had integrated with our true divine self. Since the ultimate goal of all humanity is to eventually complete the ascension process, integrating spirit and matter, the secret tradition, which had begun in Egypt, was carefully guarded and passed down from generation to generation by the holy order of Melchizedek, to then manifest in the Judean community of Qumran, who became known as the Essenes. The Essenes were a benevolent secret society that had inherited the ancient mystery school teachings of Egypt and had practiced them in secret, isolating themselves from the rest of the world.

The Essenes were also known as the pure ones and had a very heightened level of consciousness. They had become masters of their thoughts, emotions, actions, and life. They were no longer victims of circumstances, for they learned to master the physical realm by becoming acquainted with the spiritual realm, which is never changing and is always eternal. They not only mastered themselves but had a deep understanding of gnosis, which is illumination, and as a result, developed many spiritual gifts such as telepathy, clairvoyance, levitation, and the art of healing, just like their Egyptian counterparts before them. Jesus, in this order, was even known as an alchemist, and he had the ability to transform the nature of physical substances, as in the case of turning water into wine at his own wedding to Mary Magdalene.

One of the most important cover-ups and threats to the Christian church has been that of Jesus's wedding to Mary Magdalene. The biblical story of the wedding that took place in Galilee, known as the wedding of Cana, was, in fact, the wedding of Jesus and Mary Magdalene. According to the principles of the Ancient Order of Melchizedek, all high priests and high priestesses of the order had to be wedded. Scholars who study the Kabbalah and sacred tradition know that this ancient truth was incorporated as the Cohenite right of marriage by the Ancient Order of Melchizedek for all male initiates who ascended into the level of high priesthood, as well as all women initiates who had become high priestesses, like Mary Magdalene.

In other words, marriage was a mandatory requirement and part of the covenant of the Melchizedek order. Jesus was made a high priest after the order of Melchizedek, as were Moses, Abraham, and their wives. However, this truth was deleted by the early church fathers, hiding over 700 books that were left out of the Bible.

Considering this, newly risen ancient Sea Scrolls, lost manuscripts that were translated in the middle of the 20th century and discovered in the mid-1900s, also reveal that Jesus and Magdalene had been married. This revelation came from unforgettable manuscripts that certain Essenes wrote and left behind, written by members of the order who had known the master Jesus personally. For example, some of the more esoteric gospel translations, like the gospels of the Apostles, the secret Gospel of Thomas, and the secret Gospel of Mark, and even John, all confirm that Jesus and Mary Magdalene were wedded.

Some of the scholars who penetrated the distorted truths in the gospels have also concluded that Jesus taught the masses in parables while concealing the more refined knowledge for his inner followers, demonstrating the rites of initiation. In fact, there is a Biblical passage that states this fact, and it goes to the effect of Jesus's words to them, "I speak in parables to the masses and riddles, but to you," talking to his inner circle, his Apostles and disciples, "I shall reveal the secret mysteries of the higher knowledge and the kingdom of God."

Jesus the Nazarene was the hierophant of the Essene and the master teacher at the ancient mystery school teachings of his time. After the crucifixion, the original teachings were corrupted by some of his followers. Therefore, the so-called father of Western Christianity became Paul of Tarsus, who was used by the Dark Brotherhood to distort the real message and teachings of Christ and those that were part of the followers of the way, what they used to call themselves. Paul's intervention is what evolved into the Christianity enforced by Constantine as an excuse to synchronize the old Roman religion, Sol Invictus and Saturnalia, under a new name.

New evidence shows that James the Just, the brother of Jesus, was a rivaling force to what became known as Pauline Christianity, the false branch of Christianity, which gave fuel to the beginning of the Holy Roman church. These facts regarding how Pauline Christianity conflicted with the authentic Christians, headed by James the Just, are found in a well-written book titled "Custodians of Truth" by Tim Wallace Murphy and Marilyn Hopkins. It has been revealed that the original followers of the way, headed by James the Just and St. John the Revelator, were, in fact, the real Christians whom Christ appointed to teach his message. This revelation contradicts the false deception that Christ led this responsibility to Peter. This was the greatest deception that the Dark Brotherhood maneuvered to continue the Luciferian manifesto at the collapse of the Roman Empire, as mentioned.

The situation may be that Paul, the so-called converted Christian, was possessed by the sorcerers of the synagogue of Satan and became a pawn for the Luciferian brotherhood. After all, Pauline Christianity gave the Dark Brotherhood even more fuel and disturbed the balance of the Godhead by wiping out the sacred feminine, thus giving rise to the patriarchal system of male domination ruled by the Papacy. The elimination of the matriarchal aspect of God has been something the Dark Brotherhood has been trying to accomplish in order to fulfill the Luciferian agenda. Even the name of Christ was slapped on by the Roman church, for his actual historical name was Esau Emmanuel, which meant "God be with us," or Joshua to the Greeks. Indeed, Esau Emmanuel became the absolute embodiment of Christ Consciousness on the Earth, who deserved the title of the anointed one by the Greeks.

After the erection of the Luciferian Roman church, most of the Essenes and several of the branches were killed. A few survived, Joseph of Arimathea, Mary Magdalene, Martha, and Bethany, and a few others that fled to safety, preserving the tradition of mystical knowledge and continuing the holy bloodline of the Davidic lineage in secret. This information is now coming forward, especially regarding the Holy Grail bloodline of Jesus and Mary Magdalene.

Evidently, the remaining Essenes were wiped out, with the exception of the few that survived by going into refuge. The remnant Essenes continued their work in absolute secrecy, which is why not all secret societies have been of evil intent. Several books have been written describing how the Essenes from Bethany, the family of Jesus, his half-brothers and relatives, and his spiritual brothers and sisters in the order, sailed to safety to the south of what we call today France. Other records indicate that some sailed eastward.

For about six centuries, the holy lineage, which manifested as twenty-four families according to the "Custodians of Truth," had resurfaced as the holy order of the Grail, which became the new name of the Ancient Order of Melchizedek that had reorganized in France. This new order of light flourished and continued its existence in secret through the Dark Ages, preserving the holy bloodline and the sacred knowledge. This is the true meaning behind the Priory of Sion in the unraveling saga of the Holy Grail. According to Tim Wallace Murphy and Marilyn Hopkins, the real descendants of Jesus Christ and Mary Magdalene became known as the Desposyni.

Overall, the Brotherhood of Light, under the new name the holy order of the Grail, continued in secret throughout the Dark Middle Ages, as righteousness became their motto. Some sources state that these were the Merovingians of the early Franks. Others say they were the Carolingians of the kingdom of Septimania of northern Spain. In either case, this bloodline has always been safely guarded by not only benevolent orders of light but by the angels, celestials that exist in the higher dimensions.

One example of the manifestation of the Holy bloodline is in the legends of King Arthur and the Round Table of the Twelve Knights. Conventional history had us believe that the story of Camelot was a myth because, after all, the forces of darkness, with their power and influence, rewrote history many times to suit their agenda while wiping out real historical events, especially regarding the existence of the Holy Grail lineage. In truth, the legend of King Arthur is a fact, not fiction, as we were taught. King Arthur's descendants were supposed to become the rightful rulers of the British crown as direct descendants of King David. The concept of the Round Table enacted by King Arthur was a perfect example of a commonwealth and a way to conduct a perfect democratic government and was also the manifestation of the true order of Melchizedek, as the Twelve Knights symbolized the twelve apostles. There is no doubt that if it wasn't for the Luciferians who secretly conspired and caused the fall of the dynasty of King Arthur and the Round Table courts, the age of darkness would not have happened, and the free world would have been born 1200 years earlier.

Other families that descended from the tribe of David also eventually rose to power in the world a few hundred years later during the Carolingian era. This was only possible because of the Brotherhood of Light that had planted their agents and infiltrated the Roman Church through figures like Bernard de Clairvaux, who managed to establish religious monasteries designed to help the Desposyni families of the Holy Grail in the 6th century AD. Just as the Luciferians infiltrated the good systems of the orders of light in the ancient world, so have the good guys also infiltrated the Dark Brotherhood's institutions as the battle between good and evil continued.

According to "Custodians of Truth," a book written by Wallace Murphy and Marilyn Hopkins, there was a time that the Grail families of Judah came to power and established the kingdom of Septimania, encompassing the northern region of Spain and Southern France. These families in the Middle Ages revived the ancient rites of initiation for people who showed signs of readiness to learn the higher mysteries of the esoteric tradition, the sacred knowledge.

For the most part, when the Mother Church thought they destroyed all records regarding the esoteric tradition, the holy order of the Grail and the 24 families had preserved it underground until the Carolingian Dynasty rose, which is when they were able to bring it back into the open world. In addition, another Essene Gnostic group known as the Sufis, who would have also been surviving branches of the Essene, became instrumental in the preservation and resurgence of ancient mystical knowledge that was brought through Spain under the Umayyad dynasty.

For example, one of the main branches of the sacred order of the Grail had been the medieval Stone Guild builders, the forerunners of modern-day Blue Lodge Freemasonry. These initiates had been selected by members of the Holy Order of the Grail to become the great architectural builders of Europe. Among some spiritual orders, they were called the Children of Solomon. For the Roman Church, they were poor Stone Guild builders, who the church saw as wandering men who would build most of the European buildings. They were the great architects, builders of temples, cathedrals, churches, and perhaps all the European monuments. Due to their humbleness and by making the church think they were on their side, the church didn't suspect that they had been working for the opposition, the Templars.

The Stone Guild traveler builders were the beginning of the resurgence against the growing power of the Roman church that could be traced all the way back to the Essenes and the original ancient Egyptians. It was this branch of Stone Guild builders that evolved into the Freemasons, who gave us our Constitutional Republic. They considered themselves men and women who were accepted and free in a world where suppression and oppression existed because of the Holy Roman tyranny that had centralized monopoly and control over education, religion, and knowledge. In a sense, freedom was a dream and a hope in the minds of the early Stone Guild masons, as they had learned about the golden ages of the past. It was within their private closed meetings that they and other orders of light, like the Rosicrucian, began formalizing ways in which the sovereign modern nation-state Republic would emerge again.

Now, to understand what led to the rise of the Knights Templars, it was important that the good orders play evil in their own game of infiltration. That is why it became important that certain members of the Holy Order of the Grail infiltrated the Roman Church by creating monastic orders like the Cistercians to gain influence within the Roman church. This move by the Order of the Brotherhood of Light was efficient for the Holy Grail to create their military vehicle of warrior monks that were designed for multiple benevolent reasons. These were the Poor Knights of Christ, which eventually evolved into the Knights Templar. Even though history states it was created to protect pilgrims who were traveling to and from the Holy Land, they were secretly created to act as the guardians and protectors of the continuation of the Ancient Order of Melchizedek, then known as the Holy Order of the Grail, the real Priory of Sion.

The "forces of good" were now playing the Luciferians in their own game. For the sacred order of the Grail, the White Brotherhood is the true Priory of Sion, that is, those that are going to bring about the free world or the Republic, as the benevolent Knights of the Temple, they were created to protect. From the time of the Essenes in Jerusalem, the Brotherhood of Light had foreknowledge of certain relics, treasures, and records hidden deep in the old ruins of Solomon's Temple. Upon creating the Knights Templar, which were fashioned after the Knights of King Arthur, they immediately began excavating the lost treasure and ancient texts of knowledge recorded by the Ancient Order of Melchizedek that was left by Solomon. The Knights Templar became the outer vehicle for the Brotherhood of Light in Dark

Age Middle Europe. It was Bernard de Clairvaux, a member of the Knights Templar, who infiltrated the Roman Church.

This needed to happen to infiltrate the Roman Church from within and protect the existing order of light. It is believed that the Templars were able to create the most spiritual cultures that ever rose during the Dark Ages that were left off the records. These were the Cathars of France. This community was based on righteous living, which maintained and practiced the principles of the originally suppressed Church of the followers of the way, going back to the Essenes. It was the Knights Templar that opened the channels of education to all people who sought it, not just the noble and rich. They brought forward methods of banking discovered in their excavations that would benefit everyone, not just the rich. They also acted as repositories of wealth by issuing notes so that people wouldn't be mugged as they traveled on dangerous roads during the Dark Ages. Their protection was directed towards the commoner and the least among us, providing that their actions were a direct reflection of the Christ principle.

The Knights Templar had become more than just protectors of the Holy Grail lineage. They stood for chivalry, truth, justice, and humanity, as they became great instruments of the Brotherhood of Light, endeavoring to bring Europe out of the Dark Ages while secretly opposing the behaviors and actions of the Luciferian-controlled Roman Church. The actions of this order of Knighthood gave the Dark Ages moments of light and freedom and prosperity for people with whom they came in contact. Their actions provided moments of literacy, which culminated in effective, prosperous living communities, as exemplified in the most European righteous communities that ever existed, like the Cathars of France and the Troubadours of Spain.

However, moments like this only lasted for a short period of time because eventually, the Luciferians would catch on to such moments of progress, as this stood in the way of a Luciferian Manifesto of absolute control. For how can you control a people who had become learned? The church had no other choice than to launch another papal crusade, for in their eyes, ignorance was their greatest weapon against humanity, and the community that became known as the Cathars had become very educated, therefore had become a threat to the Roman church. This unfortunate historical event became known as the Albigensian Crusade.

In this horrific event known as the Holy Roman Inquisition, the Pope massacred everyone in those communities, including their own Roman Catholics who lived side by side with the Cathars. It was revealed that the Papal Legates killed every living soul in that region, both Catholic and Cathar, with the attitude that God would know His own. This clearly reveals the nature of the Roman Church as the second beast of Babylonia.

The Albigensian Crusade destroyed all of the Catharian strongholds, beginning with the massacre of Beziers, as the Holy Inquisition continued with the fall and massacre in Carcassonne, and ended with the fall and massacre of Montsegur, the last of the strongholds of the Cathar community. To make things worse, after the Inquisition annihilated the Cathars, the Dark Brotherhood began to see that the Knights Templar had been leading agents behind such unconvertible communities who were living outside of Rome's jurisdiction and immediately turned against them. The Roman church planned their stooge, King Philip the Fair, who, in turn, planted his stooge, Pope Clement V, to break away from the influence of the Council of Bernard of Clairvaux, who was the mediator of the Templars and the Roman Church. This resulted in the suppression and execution of the Knights Templar, a horrible act because this order of Knighthood stood for good and justice.

On one note, some Knights Templar were able to escape with the Holy Order of the Grail to other regions of Northern Europe, like Scotland, and some even sailed across the Atlantic, becoming the first to reach the Americas before the agents of Rome did. This knowledge was preserved in the ancient writings of the Order of Melchizedek, who always knew the nature of our globe and that there existed a continent marked in the ancient text as La America, which was the destined promised land of milk and honey that would become the great Zion, the Republic.

Nevertheless, it had been documented that some of the high-ranking knights, like Jacques de Molay, who was the Grand Master of the order, were burned at the stake by the Holy Inquisition of the Luciferian Sanhedrin-controlled Roman Church. Since Babylonian times, all the prophets, seers, and good men of righteousness have been the victims of "The Hidden Hand", the synagogue of Satan, of the Luciferian Brotherhood.

The Knights Templar and the Holy Order of the Grail, the Brotherhood of Light, which was the inner core of the Templars, had carried and preserved the seeds and concept of the Commonwealth of the people, the great Republic of the Sovereign Nation-State Republic. The orders of light have always maintained and been extremely careful in guarding the principles of righteous government as depicted by Plato and his Republic, especially from eradication by the Dark

Brotherhood, who was using the Holy Roman Church to eradicate and erase all memory of this form of government. These right principles of government were preserved along with the ancient knowledge, as well as the true lineage of King David, which is why the secret Essene order needed to flee and go into hiding for many centuries after the crucifixion of Joshua, knowing that one day their descendants would excavate the records from the old ruin Temple of Solomon.

After the extermination of the Knights Templars in 1307, the surviving groups once again went into refuge and dissolved into different Orders of Knighthood throughout Europe to camouflage themselves from the brutal Inquisition that continued in all of Europe and lasted for another two centuries. The branch of the Knights Templar that sailed across the Atlantic under the direction of St. Clair of Scotland had arrived in the Americas before the agents of the Luciferian Brotherhood did. This happened as early as the late 1300s. The Knights of the Temple knew that this continent had other inhabitants and, therefore, established peace with them, creating a harmonious relationship with the Native Americans of the sacred land. They formed a relationship and began setting the stage, planting the seeds of freedom and righteousness that would eventually culminate in the great United States of America in 1776.

Around this time in Europe, the Knights Templar, under their various names, such as the Knights of Santiago, the Knights of the Order of Michael, the Knights of the Bath, and most importantly, the Knights of the Croissant, planted the seeds leading to what became known as the 15th-century Reformation and the Renaissance. The Brotherhood of Light knew that in order to weaken the Powerhouse of the Luciferian-dominated Roman Church, who was again in a position of dominating our world in a totalitarian way, they needed to create conditions in which the Mother Church would lose its grip on all the monarchs. This would be likening to the fall of Rome, as the 15th-century Reformation saved the world from once again falling under the Luciferian agenda.

The Roman Church's grip on monopoly over the Kings was due to the temporal and spiritual control they wielded since the days of Constantine. The Knights Templar, under different chivalric orders, had infiltrated their enemies once again by planting agents in the Roman Church, such as the bishop Martin Luther and Calvin, who rebelled by virtue of arguing that it is important for people to begin reading the Bible for themselves. This type of revolution was another rather gradual, silent one, for it was worked from within the church, as Luther became bishop. It was this protest about reading the Bible that precipitated into the Protestant Reformation. With the Protestant Reformation taking place, the Knights Templar knew that the time was right again for another enlightenment, but this time on a grander scale, encompassing all of Europe, not just the Catharian region in France.

This silent revolution in religion was made possible because the Protestant Reformation allowed the forces of light to strip the Roman Church of its absolute power over Europe. Each step was necessary; first, by stripping the Roman Church of its spiritual power, the Protestant Reformation also paved the way for the explosion of art, science, mathematics, and the revival of the classics of ancient Greece. This explosion of the arts and science helped launch the Renaissance, due to another infiltrator of light in the Roman Church, a figure by the name of Cardinal Nicholas of Cusa. In conjunction with Luther's Protestant Reformation, Nicholas of Cusa initiated the Great Ecumenical Council of Florence in Italy, which truly paved the way for the Renaissance. Other leading figures that helped spark the Renaissance were Cosimo de Medici and Rene de Anjou, who had been collecting a vast body of knowledge that resurfaced with the Sufis and the Knights Templar.

The Roman Church had, for the first time, lost absolute power over all of Europe, thanks to the Protestant Reformation and the Renaissance. This act by the forces of light took the world out of the long, fearful age of darkness. The time was right for the forces of light to begin their attempts at reforming absolutism in Europe into a democratic Commonwealth of the people and by the people. Unfortunately, this task would prove to be difficult in Europe because of the Dark Brotherhood's creation of the infamous Jesuit order that continued the Inquisition under the guise of a religious war against the liberal Protestants who sought reform in Europe.

Even though it was impossible to implement the Sovereign Nation-State Republic in Europe following the Reformation and Renaissance, the free world was finally made possible by the arrangements made by the good orders of light in America through our founding fathers. This was a brief description of the forces of light that have been waging battle against the forces of darkness throughout all of history. We owe a great deal of gratitude to the positive orders of light that have acted as protectors and, at times, martyrs for humanity. They are the men and women of honor who existed, been burned at the stake, and eventually gave the Earth the long-awaited Republic in 1776.

Even though the powers of darkness had mostly dominated and been the major powers of this world it is important to understand that the forces of Light have always been here playing their own game as positive secret societies securing and protecting the higher wisdom of the ages. They gave us the Republic, while balancing out the scales of power throughout history. The forces of Light have always attempted to uplift humanity from its fallen state. It is well known that many people are becoming enlightened and aware of certain universal principles that enable them to manifest anything they want in their life. However, while many people are empowering themselves, many are falling into subjection, allowing themselves to be controlled and manipulated by a corrupt system that continues to exist today.

Chapter 9: THE BATTLE CONTINUES

Another issue that was maneuvered by the machinations of the Luciferian Brotherhood to counteract the Renaissance was the nineteenth-century Enlightenment under the banner of Romanticism, led by their agent Joseph de Maistre. This move by the Dark Brotherhood was designed to counteract the explosion of knowledge and wisdom that resulted after the fifteenth-century Reformation, the Renaissance, and the scientific revolution. The Reformation led to many inaccuracies being corrected, such as the conversion of the geocentric model to the heliocentric model by Galileo Galilei.

Philosophical groups were springing forward; we had existentialism, empiricism, led by the followers of Francis Bacon who formed the basis of the scientific method on behalf of the positive brotherhood. We have the rationalists, who revived the works of Plato and Pythagoras, with the classics once again circulating in the West. Unfortunately, part of the Romanticist movement set forth by the Dark Brotherhood was to counteract such revivals, an attempt to destroy the real philosophers of Truth like Friedrich Schiller and his circle of friends. In this case, they educated, influenced, and sponsored their own philosophers like Frederick Hegel and Immanuel Kant, who continued philosophy in their favor. To our dismay, the Luciferian brotherhood became the instrumental forces in molding and creating philosophers of their own following the Renaissance.

Another figure who contributed to the totalitarian ideologies was Professor Carl Ritter, who laid the foundation of modern-day fascism. As is known, the Dark Brotherhood has always sought control through the manipulation of the educational curricula. They figured that if they controlled knowledge or, in the case of the Roman Church, suppress it all, they would control the way people think. That is why Professor Carl Ritter, a Jesuit, became instrumental for the Dark Brotherhood, for he was the true author of fascism by laying down the satanic principles of Nihilism. After his death, another infamous figure perfected it, Friedrich Nietzsche, who received all the credit and recognition for creating the fascist movement that led to Nietzscheism and later developed into National Socialism by the Nazis.

In truth, communism was taken out of its context to serve the absolute form of government instead of the commonwealth. Communism is a derivative of the term Commonwealth but used in a fascist system. It serves to maintain a perfect middle class without the boundaries of a Republic without any overly rich or poor, as in the case of feudalism. Communism has served as another form of oppressive regime where the state controls everyone into the Luciferian agenda.

In Edmond Paris' book titled, "The Secret History of the Jesuits," it is revealed how the Jesuits perfected this type of system in Paraguay in the 1600s. Ex-Jesuit priest Alberto Rivera confirms this information in his series Double Cross. Indeed, the Jesuits are the true authors of all fascist systems and why the Dark Brotherhood created communism to serve as a tool to bring the world to its final stage of world domination under a global fascist dictatorship. Bear in mind, this aligns perfectly with the exact blueprint of the Protocols of the Learned Elders of Zion.

All forms of political government fall under two types of systems: one being a centralized totalitarian system where the government controls everything by an established unelected oligarchy elite, which is the goal of the Luciferian agenda. This type of system controls all aspects of an individual and society, which is the type of system that the Luciferians are desperately trying to implement in pursuit of global domination. This is exactly the type of agenda that was set down thousands of years ago by Ham and his great-grandson Nimrod.

The other type of government or societal system is what Plato would consider the perfect Utopia: a society driving from the applicable concepts of democracy where power is not centralized but invested equally among all its citizens, where government is for the people and by the people. This is what a Republic would provide in an equilibrium of checks and balances where power is not concentrated in the hands of an unelected elite, nor in the hands of one person or a hereditary group of people, but in a body of legislation, judiciary, and executive branches whose politicians are selected by the people and for the people.

All other so-called political ideologies or forms of government are different aspects that derived from either totalitarianism or a Democratic Republic. In the context of communism as a form of government where all people are equally given the same amount of money by a state that controls and distributes everything with no one above or below anyone else, it is still a dictatorship under a different name. The problem with this type of communistic practice is that the state is acting as a totalitarian centralized body favoring the fascist model where its citizens are not active participants in their government and are instead subjects of their own state, thus implying that this type of communistic practice favors totalitarianism. This practice is another form of slavery where everyone works just to make a living with no livelihood or leisure that would otherwise provide an opportunity for personal, spiritual growth, and freedom which lie at the root of a perfect utopian system. This is the type of communistic system that the Dark Brotherhood under the guise of the Jesuits experimented with the Indians of South America in the 1600s. It was a system based on communes administered and controlled by the Jesuits.

During this experiment, the poor exploited Indians of Paraguay were reduced to outright slaves while the Jesuits figured out a way to apply it on a grander scale in the European Eastern hemisphere. After a couple of centuries, the Dark Brotherhood decided this was the pseudo-political ideology that they were going to set up in Russia to create a conflict between the new capitalist Western world that became the United States of America and their new communist bloc in the East. This type of world conflict would allow its creators, the Jesuit Illuminati, to usher in their ultimate solution of arriving at a totalitarian world government as stated in their Protocols.

Communism was created by the Dark Brotherhood to serve their agenda after the Jesuits perfected this type of system in Paraguay, and then they were ready to begin its development in Europe where it was born under another Jesuit-trained individual by the name of Karl Marx. This built the momentum needed to legitimately establish the tenets that allowed Bolsheviks like Trotsky, Lenin, and Stalin to overthrow the Czarist government of Russia a couple of hundred years later.

However, contrary to what communism was twisted to be, if applied in its original context as a tenet of the Commonwealth, it would provide perfect equality among a community of people who elect the representatives of their government and therefore are the power and voice behind their governments. In this regard, the representatives that were elected by the people would act as one voice with the people as one body, ensuring first that everyone in their respective society gets provided for and is given a chance to succeed and prosper. This includes making sure that all human beings have the proper housing, medical care, and most importantly, the right education. These are the three primary essentials in developing a perfect sovereign being that would be educated in ways that would allow each individual to discover their inner talents to contribute to the greater good. And since we are all made in the image of God, we all have something beautiful to contribute to the greater good. This would be the outcome of creating a perfect Commonwealth in a constitutional Republic.

This is exactly the argument posed by the real philosophers of truth, beauty, and goodness like Friedrich Schiller, Plato of ancient Greece, and many others. This model, as opposed to the fascist ideologies of Hegel, Nietzsche, Kant, and Marx and others, is considered the perfect community that is based on the Commonwealth, not communism or a centralized regime. Furthermore, there needs to be a middle ground between communes and capitalism. The real concept and meaning of communism as a derivative of the Commonwealth in an applicable system of a nation-state democracy where there is a balance between private ownership and egalitarianism, otherwise the elites would capitalize on the masses and that in turn creates a government by the rich.

As a result, capitalism becomes corrupt as communism did, and a plutocracy would result in a totalitarian government by the rich, who seek further riches to attain power as in the case of the top Illuminati families who are abusing the capitalist system of America through their Central banking system, private interest groups, and Multinational corporations. There needs to exist a balance where every individual is given an opportunity to prosper, not only a few. In essence, the concept of the Commonwealth ties into what true spirituality is all about. Equality does not have to mean a government that controls all assets of a nation. After all, equality is a key element which the government was founded under, implying that all men and women were made in the image of God.

This is normally the type of society that the Ancient Order of Melchizedek and the Holy Order of the Grail, the Brotherhood of Light, intended to implement and was the original purpose of America before the Dark Brotherhood infiltrated it. This is the original blueprint of the perfect Sovereign Nation-State Republic. This appropriate type of Commonwealth would also provide benefits worldwide, including health insurance and education for all the nations. This is the type of government that even Jesus would implement if he was governing the Earth.

It is only when all of mankind, or at least a great number of us, come to the great Universal understanding that we were made in the image of God will society begin to pick themselves up and begin forming perfect structures of living that would benefit the greater good and the greatest numbers. In short, in this idealistic type of utopian society, homelessness, hunger, and improper living conditions would cease to exist. Most importantly, education plays a major factor in the type of community it produces. If mankind received the highest form of education, beginning with the understanding of certain Universal important principles as simple as the laws of the universe, like the law of equilibrium, the law of resonance, and the Law of Attraction, we would all grow spiritually and eventually cooperate in a well-balanced society.

Only by properly educating all of mankind, regardless if they are wealthy, poor, black, or white, giving everyone a chance in becoming a doctor, an engineer, a scientist, or a president, etc., would we achieve Plato's original version of the utopian state of living. The other vital necessities in building up a perfect Commonwealth Utopia would be healthcare and roofing for all. Once all of these elements are firmly rooted and implemented in modern society, human beings can begin the process of developing into their optimal potential and become the greatest spiritual giants they were meant to be, as made in the image of God. This is the goal of all humanity and the greatest threat that has been standing in their way is the Dark Brotherhood.

This concept was preached and practiced by the real philosophers of freedom and truth. The real philosophers of the Enlightenment had become suppressed by the Romanticist movement led by Joseph De Maistre, who was used by the Dark Brotherhood to launch an attack against real philosophers like Friedrich Schiller and his circles of humanistic philosophers who were exponents of Freedom, attempting to pave the way for the Sovereign nation-state Republic in Europe in the eighteenth century.

Friedrich Schiller wrote great works like "The Robbers," a play geared toward anti-oligarchies, and "Thalia." The most important of his works was the "Wallenstein" trilogy, which focused on the historical period overshadowing Europe during the first Thirty Years' War from 1618 to 1648. The religion was perpetrated by the Luciferian Jesuits to maintain the power of the papacy in pursuance of the Council of Trent. It was Schiller's idea to use the theater as a tool in teaching mankind morals and ethics through plays to raise mankind's morality and education. This theater became known as the Reich Theater.

Schiller's greatest work culminated in his "Letters on the Aesthetic Education of Man," which attacked the fascist tyrannical philosophies of Immanuel Kant, a philosopher who had been promoted by the Jesuits to circulate further totalitarian ideologies. Unfortunately, the real humanistic philosophers were eventually suppressed by the Jesuits with the promotions of Friedrich Hegel, Friedrich Nietzsche, Immanuel Kant, and later Karl Marx.

Here is an example of the philosophies expanded by Schiller, opposing the totalitarian ideologies of Immanuel Kant and Friedrich Hegel. He argued that in the light to achieve political freedom, one must not agitate a population by appealing to its irrational and obsessions; rather, one must create within an individual a philosophical aesthetical state of mind, which is only accomplished by properly educating people. This would be in direct opposition to the Protocols of the Learned Elders of Zion.

According to Immanuel Kant, such a false axiomatic assumption about man's nature, which denies man's capacity for agape love and creative reason, is the basis for the argument in favor of fascist dictatorships as opposed to the possibility of governments based on political freedom. Schiller's solution is that morality could be achieved only by educating the emotions of man to bring them into harmony with reason.

Nevertheless, Schiller argued in favor of humanity and strongly believed that every man had a purely ideal man within and only needed the right type of education. Schiller also believed that this pure ideal man should always be represented by the state. He even refuted Aristotelian logic by arguing that man is capable of cognitive ability and that such things as eternal principles and ideas do exist and can be conceptualized and harnessed by a proper educational system. Aristotle believed that man is a rational animal and only capable of deductive reasoning, which places mankind as a subject for despotic control. Schiller, on the other hand, expresses the Platonic idea that all individuals are created in the image of God and therefore have within themselves the capacity for creative reason and agape universal love towards one another.

Schiller, like all other positive pro-human philosophers, based their philosophies on the grounds that man is a spiritual being made in the image of God and only needs the proper knowledge to unfold in the likeness of our creator. This is the same spiritual principles that Jesus taught and demonstrated to his disciples and followers of the way.

One of the best ways of showing Christ-like attributes is how well we serve and help others. It is this type of righteous philosophy propounded by the real philosophers known as the poet of Freedom, truth, and beauty, Friedrich Schiller. Furthermore, Schiller's "Letters on the Aesthetic Education of Man" is one of the greatest contributions to mankind, which is why he was attacked by the oligarchy and its philosophers who supported a system of control that regarded man as a savage animal, as expressed by Immanuel Kant, rather than a true spiritual being made in the image of God.

It is most unfortunate that the Dark Brotherhood suppressed the real positive thinkers of the Enlightenment era. The attack on the philosophers of truth and humanism was launched during the intellectual explosion known as the Age of Reason, following the Renaissance and the scientific revolution. The suppressed philosophers were Friedrich Schiller, Johann Wolfgang von Goethe, Christian Daniel Schubart, Wilhelm von Humboldt, and Heinrich Heine among others who revived the classics of the Greek philosophers like Plato, Socrates, Pythagoras, and Heraclitus, etc. It is this knowledge of the Greeks, which is really the knowledge of the ancient Egyptians that was preserved through the generations first by the sacred order of Melchizedek, then the Essenes during the time of Jesus, then finally by the sacred order of the Grail and the Knights Templar. The fight at a fundamental level has been a struggle of mankind in the image and similitude of God, which is the truth that the forces of Light have been endeavoring to teach.

Moreover, the Dark Brotherhood, the forces of evil which dominated our worldly institutions have fought endlessly to suppress such truth. This is why the Dark Brotherhood, the Jesuit Illuminati, launched their attacks during the eighteenth century against Schiller and his circle of friends who were pro-human. This is the same pattern that keeps lurking throughout history. In Greece, the Dark Brotherhood put Socrates to death. In Jerusalem, the Dark Brotherhood crucified Jesus for teaching mankind the truth, and in the modern European awakening revival, the real true philosophers were suppressed by the same Dark Brotherhood seeking control over the educational institutions by controlling the types of knowledge they wish to impart to the world.

It's a fact that the Jesuits have dominated most of the prominent European universities and have done so here in the West like Georgetown, Fordham, and Yale. It is now evident that throughout our entire history, this secret government of the snake and today, the final embodiment of them, the Jesuit

Illuminati have been dominating the halls of learning by keeping humanity at a very low level of knowledge.

Nonetheless, the Dark Brotherhood's control, or at least their intended manipulation of the educational system in Europe, enabled them to rewrite history to suit their desire and goals and have modeled and sponsored, the philosophers of their choice like Friedrich Hegel, Immanuel Kant, René Descartes, Friedrich Nietzsche, and Karl Marx.

It was primarily through Friedrich Hegel's philosophy that the Dark Brotherhood was able to continue their exercise of tyranny over humanity. René Descartes' philosophy kept mankind attached only to the world of sense perception, limiting us to that low level of thinking which Plato calls illusory reality, using his analogy of the shadows in the cave. Immanuel Kant further highlighted Hegel's ideology by his incorrect hypothesis of the categorical imperative that holds men as an irrational animal instead of a rational spiritual being made in the image of God, which is absolute truth.

Their favorite, most prosperous arrogant figure of all, who had no genuine talent whatsoever, continued and expanded the work of a Jesuit Illuminati Professor by the name of Carl Ritter, which further consolidated the works of Hegel and Kant and created the most totalitarian philosophy that has ever existed. This most favored negative philosopher was Friedrich Nietzsche, who gave the world Nietzscheism, which evolved into Nihilism.

These primary philosophies, which are utterly anti-humanistic, were influenced and sponsored by the Jesuits to pave the way for future dictators and allow the European oligarchy to continue their struggle for absolute control and power over

Europe and eventually the entire world. It was Hegel's philosophical bases that influenced political theorists like Thomas Hobbes and, to an extent, John Locke, who were instrumental in establishing the social contract theory along with Karl Marx. According to the Executive Intelligence Review, Schiller attacked John Locke for his ideas on slavery that didn't apply in a true ideal Commonwealth that goes against the fact that all men were made in the image of God. Therefore, under this truth, slavery would be a violation of the constitution. In either case, the Dark Brotherhood used the social contract theory to continue their form of totalitarianism while updating the practice of a monarchy.

Chapter 10 THE CONGRESS OF VIENNA

Since the beginning of our nation's establishment agents of the Dark Brotherhood have been sent to attempt to infiltrate our democratic sovereign nation state Republic. This was the result of the penetration that the Bavarian Illuminati executed over the lodges of Freemasonry. The Dark Brotherhood's endeavor was to create a secret society within an already secret society that had originally been designed to spread the concept of a free Republic. It was this practice of illuminism that British professor John Robinson of natural philosophy warned people about when he wrote, " Proof of a conspiracy to destroy all the religions and governments of the world." He published his book here in the states but by 1789 the Illuminati had already contaminated most of the Masonic lodges. Only a few remained loyal to the original Blue Lodge of the white Brotherhood while most became servants of the Black Pope and its new international banking plan.

For example, we can clearly see the battle between good and evil taking place in the beginning of our nation from the moment the two rivaling factions of the Masonic lodges battled it out in a political debate to see if the new Republic would act as a centralized form of government or not. This fascist idea was expanded by Alexander Hamilton, while his opponent, Thomas Jefferson believed in a government where power is invested in all the states honoring the constitution. Jefferson wanted to uphold a sovereign nation-state Republic as originally planned by the Blue Lodge faction who apparently had the upper hand.

We know any centralized form of government would ultimately lead to a dictatorship. On the other hand, inspired by the "forces of good", our founding fathers gave us a government for the people and by the people, thus becoming the model that gives birth to the commonwealth of the people or the commonwealth of nations, if applied on a global scale.

After the successful establishment of our world's second real Republic, it proved to be a better working system than any other existing form of government that had been ruling our world under the direction of the Luciferian brotherhood. The system of the Republic sovereign Nation state was designed to act as a model for the rest of the world to follow. However, this proved to be unrealistic in Europe because of the power and influence of the Jesuits. This would conflict with their attempt to implement the Luciferian agenda of absolute power and control, being the opposite system of the free world Republic as expanded upon by the Blue Lodge faction.

Other countries like France and Germany wanted a taste of freedom after seeing it established here in the west. Even the real philosophers like Schiller and his pro-human circle of friends were excited to know that the Republic was a success in America and eager to know that France was next in line for freedom. This was the original purpose that ignited what became known as the French revolution that had been the work of the existing Blue Lodge Masons particularly the Jacobins, who wanted to reform France from its oligarchic system into a Republic. On the other hand, the Jesuit Illuminati brotherhood quickly tried to put out the revolution by using Napoleon, who was trained and was financed by them.

During their suppression by the remaining good monarchs the Jesuits had been exiled through a region known as Corsica where they managed to train Napoleon Bonaparte who was also in Corsica during their stay. The Jesuits that became Napoleon's grand advisers, the ones who directed him all the way, were known as Abby Seyes. Of course, all the financing came from the house of Rothschild who saw this opportunity to begin financing both sides of every war to put countries in further debt to them as planned and stated in the Protocols.

Immediately the French Revolution that was to initiate Frances first Republic was put out by the Napoleonic wars that followed. Soon England jumped into the war as planned by the masterminds of the Jesuit Illuminati. The house of Rothschild used this opportunity to finance all nations in war to control their politics by first gaining control of their economy. As history states, England jumped into the war to defeat Napoleon's forces. However, history failed to reveal that the same people behind the Napoleonic wars were the same people behind England entering the war. For the record, the Jesuits, and the house of Rothschilds were behind the whole thing.

When the Rothschilds had England jump into the war through a different agent they started a rumor that enabled the house of Rothschilds to gain absolute control of England's economy. All secret government researchers know they did it by buying out all the stock in England at the price of a dollar when the stock market crashed due to a rumor that Napoleon was going to win the war. It turned out to be a false cry, and Napoleon was defeated as planned by the masterminds of the secret government.

The Jesuits, through the house of Rothschilds accomplished two things. First, they managed to stop the implementation of a Republic in France. Secondly, they managed to gain control of both England's and France's economy and were now ready to begin formulating a method in which they would revive the old Holy Roman Empire in Europe. This agenda, however, of resurrecting the Holy Roman Empire in Europe would be the first attempt to establish the League of Nations a century earlier.

This outcome gave the Dark Brotherhood secret control of England and France which resulted in the establishment of the Congress of Vienna which was totally controlled by the representatives of the Black Pope and his black nobility. This Event that led to the implementation of the fascist Congress of Vienna took about 35 years from the inception of the French Revolution to the end of the Napoleonic wars.

After the successful establishment of the Congress of Vienna, the Jesuit Illuminati thought the soil was fertile to establish the first League of Nations. History forgot to document this fact. This attempt at creating the first League of Nations would act as the secret government's first vehicle of bringing all of Europe back under one power control as a unified centralized European Union. This would revive the old Roman Empire or really the Babylonian empire as vowed by the descendants of Nimrod-Esau bloodline. If this attempt had been a success, the Jesuit Illuminati would wipe out all the rebel groups associated with the Blue Lodge faction who opposed the oligarch form of government.

As always is the case this attempt of reviving the Holy Roman Empire as the League of Nations a century earlier was blocked and thwarted by the Czars of Russia who knew the wicked intent of what could have been the first League of Nations in 1815. Imagine how our world would have been right now in the 21st century if the Dark Brotherhood had created the European Union 100 years earlier in1815. Thanks to the Czars of Russia the first attempt at unifying Europe failed at the beginning of the 1800s. In truth, the attempt at the Congress of Vienna in 1815 to impose a United Federal Europe was set to revive the Holy Roman Empire bringing all of Europe under one imperial feudal system of control.

Now comes the poisoning and infiltration of America that allowed the Dark Brotherhood to influence policy here in our country. After the Congress of Vienna, the Dark Brotherhood focused on creating a system with a shadow government in America that would secretly bring this country under their direction and control. Apparently, Europe wasn't enough; they needed to control what later proved to be the most powerful nation in the world, the United States. Their method of conquest was through infiltration, a tactic they have been employing since Babylonian times.

The establishment of America had been a major blow that proved to be a threat to the Dark Brotherhood's agenda of world domination. In their infiltration of the United States government, the cabal dispatched agents who would attempt to gain control of our government and economy. This move implemented a central banking system in the United States many times. After all it was the Rothschilds who believed that he who controls the economy of a Nation controls the nation. The Dark Brotherhood also decided to extend their power and control by infiltrating and gaining control of the educational systems in the United States.

By this time the Dark Brotherhood had established a global empire, a secret network of different secret societies all functioning and working together as one big interlocking web of conspirators. One of their extensions became known as the Knights of Malta that oversaw infiltrating isolated governments in order to break them from within and install their puppets in positions of power; another branch of the Dark Brotherhood was the Knights of Columbus which were associated and working for the Vatican. The Knights of Malta were also in control of the international crime family syndicate like the Godfather of Italy who was a member of the Knights of Malta. The Malta Knights were also known as the assassins of the Jesuits, executing all political opponents that stood in the way of the agenda of the resurrection of the Holy Roman empire.

After their infiltration of the American government, they went ahead and established a secret society after gaining control of the Yale educational curriculum. This was known as Skull and Bones. This was a secret organization set up as a vehicle to educate mold and train children of powerful families that were considered elite and carried the gene of power as descendants of the Babylonian bloodline. This explains the mysterious role of the Rockefellers, the Harriman, the Vanderbilts and Morgan's who became the elite of America rising to become powerful industrialist heads of new Industries banking and oil empires.

This element generated astronomical capital for the chosen few of the American elite. Today top independent researchers have discovered the apparent connection between these Elite families to the European nobility. In 1830, the newly organized financial beast system of the Jesuits under the direction of the House of Rothschilds were able to influence people like William Huntington Russell and Alfonso Taft who were educated in their universities to establish the black nobility branch in the United States also known as the secret establishment of America Skull and Bones as revealed by Anthony Sutton.

This maneuver allows the Dark Brotherhood not only to have influence in America but influence over prestigious universities like Yale, Georgetown, Harvard, and Fordham by creating a special course of education for the elite Bloodlines of the Western world. Other secret Elite groups were formed like skull and key and the Bohemian Grove along the lines of the Skull and Bones, but Skull and Bones became the primary one. The infiltration worked on many fronts. For instance, following the establishment of Skull and Bones, things began taking America into the great division that led to the separation of the North and the South as stated in their learned Protocols of Zion.

In the beginning the new Republic was unified, strong, and untouchable. The Dark Brotherhood knew that by applying their ancient technique of divide and conquer as highlighted by Hagel they would be able to overthrow the constitutional Republic of the United States government from within. They knew that after a major social cataclysm the division of the new nation would be able to overcome the new United Republic. On that note the initial plan and agenda was to begin the event that led to the separation of the North and the South here in the United States. All this took place under the direction and orders of the top elite families who were executing the overall command of the Black Pope, the supreme ruler of the secret government.

They manipulated events by using their control agents who succeeded in splitting our country leading to the separation of the Union and the Confederates. Now we have the Union to the North and the Confederates to the South as civil war broke out thanks to the manipulations of the secret government through Skull and Bones. To top it off and again what history books forgot to mention, is that the Dark Brotherhood arranged for the English and French armies to quietly close in on the states at the peak of the Civil war, so when the states were weakened the English, and the French armies would execute a military takeover of divided America. This event was properly left out of our history books. This shows how much influence the Dark Brotherhood has over what we learn in school.

The art of divide and conquer can be traced back to the fall of Greece. In Greece it was the Dark Brotherhood who acted as the masterminds that fomented the Spartans' wars through fascists Lycurgus, who like the confederate states were seeking to overthrow the unity of the Old Republic of Greece. Considering this, we can conclude that the Republic of Greece was destroyed by the same means that almost destroyed our American Republic during the civil war. The Dark Brotherhood was the intelligence behind the cold war plotting to destroy the Republic, the second Republic of our world.

As always, in the case of this attempt to revive the Holy Roman Empire as the League of Nations a century earlier, it was blocked and thwarted by the Czars of Russia, who knew the wicked intent of what could have been the first League of Nations in 1815. Imagine how our world would be right now in the 21st century if the Dark Brotherhood had created the European Union 100 years earlier, in 1815. Thanks to the Czars of Russia, the first attempt at unifying Europe failed at the beginning of the 1800s. In truth, the attempt at the Congress of Vienna in 1815 to impose a United Federal Europe was set to revive the Holy Roman Empire, bringing all of Europe under one imperial feudal system of control.

Now comes the poisoning and infiltration of America that allowed the Dark Brotherhood to influence policy here in our country. After the Congress of Vienna, the Dark Brotherhood focused on creating a system with a shadow government in America that would secretly bring this country under their direction and control. Apparently, Europe wasn't enough; they needed to control what later proved to be the most powerful nation in the world, the United States. Their method of conquest was through infiltration, a tactic they have been employing since Babylonian times.

The establishment of America had been a major blow that proved to be a threat to the Dark Brotherhood's agenda of world domination. In their infiltration of the United States government, the cabal dispatched agents who would attempt to gain control of our government and economy. This move implemented a central banking system in the United States many times. After all, it was the Rothschilds who believed that he who controls the economy of a Nation controls the nation. The Dark Brotherhood also decided to extend their power and control by infiltrating and gaining control of the educational systems in the United States.

By this time, the Dark Brotherhood had established a global empire, a secret network of different secret societies all functioning and working together as one big interlocking web of conspirators.

One of their extensions became known as the Knights of Malta, who oversaw infiltrating isolated governments to break them from within and install their puppets in positions of power; another branch of the Dark Brotherhood was the Knights of Columbus, which were associated and working for the Vatican. The Knights of Malta were also in control of the international crime family syndicate like the Godfather of Italy who was a member of the Knights of Malta. The Malta knights were also known as the assassins of the Jesuits, executing all political opponents that stood in the way of the agenda of the resurrection of the Holy Roman Empire.

This maneuver allows the Dark Brotherhood not only to have influence in America but influence over prestigious universities like Yale, Georgetown, Harvard, and Fordham by creating a special course of education for the elite Bloodlines of the Western world. Other secret Elite groups were formed like Skull and Key and the Bohemian Grove, but Skull and Bones became the primary one. The infiltration worked on many fronts. For instance, following the establishment of Skull and Bones, things began taking America into the great division that led to the separation of the North and the South as stated in their learned Protocols of Zion.

In the beginning, the new Republic was unified, strong, and untouchable. The Dark Brotherhood knew that by applying their ancient technique of divide and conquer as highlighted by Hagel they would be able to overthrow the constitutional Republic of the United States government from within. They knew that after a major social cataclysm the division of the new nation would be able to overcome the new United Republic. On that note, the initial plan and agenda were to begin the event that led to the separation of the North and the South here in the United States. All this took place under the direction and orders of the top elite families who were executing the overall command of the Black Pope, the supreme ruler of the secret government.

They manipulated events by using their control agents who succeeded in splitting our country leading to the separation of the Union and the Confederates. Now we have the Union to the North and the Confederates to the South as civil war broke out thanks to the manipulations of the secret government through Skull and Bones. To top it off and again what history books forgot to mention, is that the Dark Brotherhood arranged for the English and French armies to quietly close in on the states at the peak of the Civil war, so when the states were weakened the English and the French armies would execute a military takeover of divided America. This event was properly left out of our history books. This shows how much influence the Dark Brotherhood has over what we learn in school.

The art of divide and conquer can be traced back to the fall of Greece. In Greece, it was the Dark Brotherhood who acted as the masterminds that fomented the Spartans' wars through fascists Lycurgus, who like the confederate states were seeking to overthrow the unity of the Old Republic of Greece. Considering this, we can conclude that the Republic of Greece was destroyed by the same means that almost destroyed our American Republic during the Civil War. The Dark Brotherhood was the intelligence behind the Cold War plotting to destroy the Republic, the second Republic of our world.

As mentioned, during our Cold War, the English and French armies had been positioned in Canada and Mexico, making their entry easy after the states had weakened from battling it out. However, another act of God occurred when the Czars of Russia got hold of the plot, knowing that the British and French had stationed their armies and were going to overthrow the new Republic. The Czars created a blockade by sending over their armies to help defend and save the new Republic from the massive military invasion that was about to take place. The British and the French withdrew their men at the onset of the Czar's armies, and the union was preserved and fortified when the North defeated the South.

In the light of the age of information, and as we approach the end of the reign of the Dark Brotherhood, there is substantial evidence surfacing indicating that the split from the union was contrived and manipulated by the black nobility of the secret government under the direction of the Black Pope.

For example, according to new revelations coming to light by various researchers, it was Judah Benjamin, the acting chief advisor of Jefferson Davis, who was secretly acting under orders from Rothschild that manipulated Davis into conflict against the North. Contrary to what we learned in history class, this was the true reason why a Republic was divided. It was never about slavery or about the South not wanting to become industrialized; it was about the destruction of the Republic intelligently driven by the secret government so that more power could be invested in their effort to establish their Holy Roman Empire.

Another revelation that came to light was that the Jesuits created the Ku Klux Klan to purge the Jews and Protestants here in the United States pursuing the evil council of Trent. This makes sense when one considers that the Ku Klux Klan was only allowed to exist in the South, not in the North, and why they killed everyone but Roman Catholics. After the Civil War, agents of the Rothschilds infiltrated Lincoln's cabinet to have Lincoln sign a treaty that would allow the creation of a Central Banking system. He, of course, refused and was assassinated for it.

This mystery unfolds more when one considers the role played by the Skull and Bones which was established 20 years before the separation took place. Their establishment allowed the Jesuit Illuminati to put their man in positions of power to create the intended schism that led to the terrible split. Let it be known that the establishment of the Skull and Bones is also part of the Protocols of the Learned Elders of Zion designed to control education in top universities to mold leaders into positions of power just as the Jesuit Illuminati had done in Europe.

The secret government since the creation of the Jesuits under the direction of the Black Pope gave a set of instructions to infiltrate all educational systems as indicated in the Protocols of the Learned Elders of Zion. This continued with the Illuminati branch who immediately set out to fulfill this Luciferian Protocol of infiltration especially in the universities of the United States. The infiltration of the Dark Brotherhood created such Infamous secret societies like Skull and Bones that played and are still playing a significant role in the destruction of the United States.

Even though our Republic was saved during the Civil War, the Dark Brotherhood through Skull and Bones managed to establish a branch of the dark side here in our free world. According to researcher and author Anthony Sutton, the new secret order also became known as Chapter 322 from an earlier German secret society which was reinstated in the states to continue conversely the secret plan of destroying the new Republic. This, however, proved to be difficult because of the way our founding fathers structured our government, so it is incapable of being taken over by either an elite or by any dictator. Our founding fathers knew of the sinister behaviors of the dark forces that took control of Europe. If our founding fathers would not have safeguarded our Republic, the free world would have become yesterday's news just like the Cathars of France.

In today's world, the high-ranking Jesuits with their omnipotent autocratic ruler the Black Pope are the living core of the Luciferian conspiracy that originated in Babylon. After the Congress of Vienna, they extended their secret government worldwide by creating further secret societies that were to act as cloaks for the core levels of the new modern-day Sanhedrin. By the end of the 19th century, the Dark Brotherhood maneuvered the round table groups through their Illuminati stooge by the name of Cecil Rhodes, who was a criminal that became instrumental in stealing all the diamond reserves in Africa leaving the country in an impoverished state that through the years has only worsened. His partner in the crime was documented to be Joseph Ratzinger. We can conclude that the reason why Africa is still in a state of impoverished living conditions as a third-world nation is because of the machinations and exploitations of the Jesuits and the Illuminati deliberately causing these conditions in Africa.

In closing, the company of the international military order of the Jesuits has been infiltrating every nation in the world. This information is confirmed in the secret history of the Jesuits by Edmund Paris. The control of our country's economy was the first and foremost important step in gradually subduing our Republic and eradicating our constitutional rights.

Chapter 11: THE SUCCESSFUL INFILTRATION OF AMERICA

For the revelation of the further infiltration of our country, I would like to expose the suppressed research gathered by none other than Mr. Myron Fagen, a true patriotic figure who fought for freedom as he exposed the evil one-world government plot in his work. In the early twentieth century, Mr. Fagen became a successful playwright who was involved in the Hollywood scene from its beginning.

Mr. Fagen wrote great classics like "The White House," "Two Strangers From Nowhere," "Miss Mates," "The Fascinated Devil," "The Little Spitfire," "The Great Power," "Indiscretion," "Nancy's Private Affair," and "Peter Files High," to name a few. Mr. Fagen also proved to be a great intellectual and activist in human rights. He served as the dramatic editor for the Associated Press and worked with the New York Globe and various newspapers. In 1916, he took a sabbatical from the theater and served as a director of public relations for Charles Evans Hughes, then the Republican candidate for the presidency. Mr. Fagen's career included not only the theater but also journalism and national politics.

Mr. Fagen came into knowledge of the Luciferian agenda and its conspirators in 1932 when he attended a meeting in Washington, D.C., upon an urgent request from John T. Flynn, the famous author of "The Roosevelt Myth" and "The True Story of Pearl Harbor."

In this meeting, Mr. Fagen was shown a set of microfilms and recordings of the secret meetings that took place on an island called Yalta, privately owned by J.P. Morgan. He was not only exposed to the agenda of how a handful of powerful figures laid out their plot to deliver the Balkans to the Bolsheviks, thereby imposing communism in Russia, but was also informed of the true purpose and agenda of the creation of the United Nations, which was designed as the One World Government covert vehicle umbrella.

As a result of that meeting, Mr. Fagen wrote two plays designed to reveal such evil plots. One of them was known as "Red Rainbow," and the other was "Thieves Paradise." Mr. Fagen launched a one-man crusade to unmask what he termed the red conspiracy in Hollywood as well. Apparently, the secret government was going to utilize film to aid the idea of a one-world government. Out of this came the Cinema Educational Guild (CEIG), organized by Mr. Fagen in 1947. Next came the Congressional hearings that busted 300 of Hollywood's leading figures, directors, actors, and writers from both TV and radio as the chief activists of the red conspiracy.

This event is what became known as the Hollywood infamous ten. However, thanks to the works of Mr. Fagen, they were sent to prison. Note we could see here the infiltration of Hollywood in its earliest years by the Jesuit Illuminati who initially planned to use film to aid the concept of the one-world government. How intelligently driven are these thugs knowing that film and plays have a way of influencing people's minds? Mr. Fagen is no longer with us, but his research gave us enough light to shed how the real conspiracy penetrated the United States.

Mr. Fagen deciphered that the conspirators took advantage of America following the Civil War because America was in a state of explosion regarding massive industrialization and modernization. This is the type of opportunity that the Dark

Brotherhood used to succeed in their diabolic endeavors. The House of Rothschilds wasted no time and wanted to be the core of all the financing that would take place to produce the railroads, commerce, steel, oil companies, and banking following the Civil War. Their hidden agenda was to seize control of our money system by establishing a central banking system, an objective that became the issue between the battle of good and evil here in America. The central banking system was already prevalent in Europe. The Dark Brotherhood needed to do the same here in the States because they had already failed twice.

Under the direction of the supreme autocratic ruler, the Black Pope, the House of Rothschild, the Knights of Malta, and the chief head of the Illuminati agent sent Jacob Schiff over to the States. In Europe, Schiff proved to be a potential money genius, trained by the Rothschilds, who saw in him the Machiavellian qualities qualifying him as their secret weapon that poisoned America.

According to Mr. Fagen, after a brief training in the Rothschild London bank, Jacob left for the States with instructions to buy into a banking house which would be the tool to obtain control of the money system in the United States. Besides the ultimate treason of establishing a central banking system in the States, the Rothschilds also left Schiff with three other secondary duties to carry out as specific assignments to further weaken the Republic.

Mr. Fagen revealed that there were four directives in the takedown of America. The primary and important one was to acquire control of America's money system. Another one was to fit a desirable man who for a price would be willing to serve as agents furthering the idea of the One World Government and promote them in high places in our federal government, Congress, Supreme Court, and other federal agencies. This assignment corresponds to the biblical passage reminding us that the love of money is the root of all evil as men became corrupt for a prize. The second directive given to Schiff was to create minority strife throughout the nation, especially between the whites and the blacks. This corresponds to the ADL, the Anti-Defamation League, which was created and used by the secret government to create more schism in the States and to destroy our unity. The last directive given to Schiff was to create movements that would disintegrate religion in America, especially Christianity. Bear in mind that these are the implications of the Protocols of the Learned Elders of Zion in conjunction with the Vatican's Council of Trent.

Unfortunately, Jacob Schiff established every single directive given to him by the Jesuit Illuminati in Europe. As we know, the House of Rothschild and Jesuits had agents planted here from the beginning of our country, managing to establish the secret society of Skull and Bones in 1830 and succeeding thereafter in splitting the sovereignty of the Republic into a north and south.

The steps Jacob Schiff took to accomplish these directives were maneuvered and masterminded by the Jesuit Illuminati from the top level down and are the Protocols in action to infiltrate the state of the goyim. According to Mr. Fagan, when Schiff arrived in the States, he quietly set out to look for the perfect firm to buy into, which he did when he found Kuhn and Loeb, who like Schiff, were all immigrants from Germany. Kuhn and Loeb had come to the United States in the mid-1840s. In the 1850s, they pooled their interest and set up a merchandise store in Lafayette, Indiana, under the firm name

Kuhn and Loeb, and eventually expanded to Cincinnati and St. Louis.

Adding pawnbroking money lending proved to be a major step for them. Upon Schiff's arrival from Europe, they were already well-established as a private banking firm. Even though Mr. Fagan didn't document any possible connection to the Rothschilds, chances are that they could have secretly been working in coalition with the Black Nobility of Europe. Nevertheless, Schiff bought into the private firm as planned and even went on to marry Loeb's daughter, Teresa. At this point, Schiff bought out their partner Kuhn and moved to New York, where they became known as Loeb and Company. Thus, the first organization of international bankers was born in America, with the House of Rothschild at the core and headed through Jacob Schiff. This was the beginning of what Mr. Lyndon LaRoche considers the international synarchy banking cartel.

The consolidation of private bankers needed to come into play. Mr. Myran Fagan further documented that in those days, it was J.P. Morgan who had also been a Rothschild agent from the beginning, coming for the primary reason of gaining control of the banking house in America. There were other bankers like the Drexel's and Biddle's of Philadelphia; however, all these men were dancing to the tune of J.P. Morgan, who was considered the Rothschild in America. It was at this point that major financing was needed to begin the industrialization programs that built modern America. Schiff banded all the financiers together to finance all the major industrializations that began to take place.

The House of Rothschild, through Jacob Schiff, became the chief central financier of powerful industrialists like John D.

Rockefeller, who was also sent here under Rothschild orders. There were others like Edward R. Harriman and Andrew Carnegie. The Rockefellers became the kingpins of the American oil companies. For Edward Harriman, the railroad empire was financed, and for Andrew Carnegie, the steel empire was financed. Now there was a tight unit among the infiltrated United States government. In truth, they became the international clan of bankers, industrialists, and powerful interest groups that have been influencing our country ever since.

It is no coincidence that these three figures received their special education through Skull and Bones. In a grander sense, they had been molded to become industrialist giants and moneymakers. In addition, Jacob Schiff had become the overall director and super boss of these powerful American giants, thus beginning the hierarchy of command for the Jesuit Illuminati agency in America. Ever since then, the Rockefellers entered the game and gradually influenced American politics from behind the scenes to a greater degree because of Skull and Bones. The American elite were getting ready to achieve the first major coup of quiet control of our money system. However, under constitutional law, all control of our money system was designed to be vested solely in Congress, thanks to the intelligence of our founding fathers. Schiff's next move was to seduce Congress or plant obedient puppets who, for a price, would be willing to commit treason by establishing another central banking system.

Remember the warnings of our own Thomas Jefferson regarding the central banking system being a bigger threat than standing armies to the free world. The success came when Schiff began infiltrating stooges into both the House of Representatives and Congress. Stooges who were not only powerful enough but loyal enough to the dictates of Schiff and his Illuminati gangsters to railroad Congress into passing it as legislation. The most important part of the conspiracy was finding a perfect puppet to plant in the White House to serve as a president who would immediately sign the legislation into law. To accomplish that, Schiff's secret gang needed to get control of either the Republican or the Democratic Party. The Democratic Party was the most vulnerable one, as revealed by Mr. Fagan; it was the hungriest party of the two. Apparently, the Democrats had been incapable of putting anyone in the presidency prior to the Civil War.

The financial problem was not the worst, though. It was not having enough voters, so the Illuminati created the problems themselves as the end justifies the means. Since they needed more Democratic voters, they set out to create conditions to give them sufficient voters. The method was ruthless and murderous, but it worked for them. In 1980, they engineered a series of nationwide programs in Russia that included Poland, Romania, and Bulgaria. Under these programs, many thousands of innocent Jews were slaughtered by groups of people known as the Cossacks. Again, the Jews became the number one target, what a coincidence.

Even though the Cossacks were reported as peasants executing the massacres, they could have been secret members of the Jesuit Illuminati or at least trained by them to appear as peasants but were really trained assassins. What we do know is that this massive slaughter was absolutely masterminded and fomented by some Rothschild agents in Europe following the blueprint of the Protocols of the learned Elders of Zion.

Bear in mind that this is the Hegelian Dialect as the conspirator created the problem which is slaughter, and the reaction was followed by a solution. In this case, the solution resulted in hundreds of thousands of targeted people seeking refuge and heading here to the United States as planned by the masterminds of the secret government. Note this slaughter convinces us that even through the financial interest groups of the secret government considering themselves to be Jews they are not, for they are Babylonians descendants of Nimrod-Esau and are willing to sacrifice anyone they consider human cattle. They repeated this sacrifice again in World War II for they are bent on making sure that if there are any descendants left of King David that they are to be exterminated.

These refugees first arrived in New York and, through the fake humanitarian effort by Schiff and his game here in America, they were shuffled into other parts of the states like Boston, Philadelphia, Chicago, Los Angeles, and Detroit. They quickly became naturalized citizens and were educated to register as Democrats, as planned by the masterminds of the Luciferian conspiracy. Now the conspirators have solid Democratic voters in our country. This was one of the methods employed by Schiff to plant politicians like Nelson Aldrich in our Senate as the senator who railroaded the legislation of the Federal Reserve into Congress.

By 1908, Schiff was ready to seize control of America's financial system; he had his lieutenant and number one key player, Colonel Edward Mandel House, a powerful figure connected to the money men of New York-powered interest groups. Mr. Fagan documented that Mr. House was Jacob Schiff's number one chief executive and courier in the states for the execution of the central banking system. The secret meetings took place on the private island owned by J.P. Morgan. This was known as Jekyll Island Hunt Club in Jekyll Island, Georgia.

Others who were present and also active members of the conspiracy were John D. Rockefeller, Senator Aldrich, Vandalip of New York National City Bank, Jay Seligman, Eugene Meyer, Herbert Leman, Paul Warburg, and his brother Felix, all molded as part of the international banking cartel headed by the House of Rothschild orchestrating what became the biggest act of treason that Thomas Jefferson warned us about.

The conspirators emerged with what they called the Federal Reserve System, a central banking system legislated by Aldrich through Congress. By no later than 1913, this illegal institution was established, posing as a national federal bank. Since the new Democratic Party had been revived, the secret government managed to plant their White House puppet who would sign the treasonous act. This was Woodrow Wilson, who became their puppet.

Two nights before Christmas when most of Congress had gone home except for a select few that illegally maneuvered and passed the bill into law establishing the long-dreaded central banking system known as the Federal Reserve. This was an evil and successful plot by the Dark Brotherhood who had been trying to implement a central banking cartel since the beginning of the nation.

With this in place, Jacob Schiff had accomplished his first and most important directive. Now the United States of America's money system had fallen into the hands of the secret government, the financial arm of the embodiment of the Jesuit Illuminati. Since then, our country has begun to be influenced by powerful interest groups.

Along with the treason of the Federal Reserve, the secret government masterminds maneuvered the illegal ratification of the 16th Amendment, also known to most researchers as I.R.S. cancer. Do you remember that our founding fathers forbade the establishment of any taxation, another reason we liberated ourselves from the tyranny of Europe and it didn't exist until the beginning of the 20th century? The Dark Brotherhood used the coming second Thirty Years War which was executed from 1915 to 1945 as an excuse to implement taxes in America.

Now that the most important goal by the secret government had been accomplished in the United States, the rest of Jacob Schiff's assignments were a piece of cake. In 1913, the same year of the treasonous act, Schiff and his conspirators were able to organize the Anti-Defamation League (ADL) to serve as the Gestapo for the Luciferian conspiracy. It was reported by Mr. Fagan and confirmed by others that today the sinister ADL maintains over 2,000 agencies in all parts of our country, and they advise and completely control every action of the NAACP and other organizations. Originally, the secret government's intention was to create racial strife as ordered by the Rothschilds. Eventually, great leaders like Martin Luther King, who had originally been financed through another Illuminati group like the NAACP to help create dichotomy among whites and blacks, became a disappointment to the Illuminati because Mr. King was a good man and did not go the way they wanted him to.

That is why he was assassinated by the secret government corrupt FBI branch. Bear in mind that the secret government's original intentions were to create racial tensions as ordered by the Rothschilds. However, thanks to Dr. Martin Luther King, the plans backfired as more equal rights flourished for the minority groups.

The ADL's job was also to acquire absolute control of the mass media so that the secret government could slant, falsify, and fabricate news to incite tension. However, this directive didn't take effect until after the First World War.

Even though Schiff managed to get control of our money system and plant many agents into various key government positions, he failed to create racial tension as well as destroying Christianity in America as given to him in his third assignment. It was revealed that the attempt was made when the Rockefellers financed a wolf in sheep's clothing by the name of Harry F. Ward. Dr. Harry Ward passed as a reverent and was even a professor at the Union Theological Seminary, teaching religion at the beginning of the 20th century. According to ex-Jesuit priest Alberto Rivera, some Jesuits post as Christian ministers to destroy heretical Protestantism. Considering this, Mr. Ward could have been one of many Jesuits trained to destroy Protestantism in America.

Mr. Fagan reported that Harry Ward was financed by Rockefeller in 1907 to set up the Methodist Foundation of Social Services. His assignment was to teach young men who wanted to become preachers, ministers, and pastors that the story of Christ was a myth. Those he found worthy of such Luciferian indoctrination were placed as pastors in certain congregations. The Rockefellers and Mr. Ward were utterly brainwashing as many people as possible, and those students that were unable to be brainwashed were rooted out of the Methodist Foundation Seminary.

Mr. Fagan further revealed that the Methodist Foundation of Social Services became known as America's first Communist front organization, which later changed its name to the Federal Council of Churches. By 1950, it had become suspect, so they changed their name again to the National Council of Churches. From then on, this satanic organization camouflaged itself as a Christian institution and infiltrated many Protestant organizations to attempt an indoctrination that would lead many Christians into the power of a global universal religion controlled by the secret government.

In addition, Mr. Harry F. Ward was documented by Mr. Fagan to be one of the founders of the American Civil Liberties Union, a notorious pro-communist organization. He was its head from 1920 to 1940. He also became the co-founder of the American League against War and Fascism, which under Browder became the leading agent in the establishment of the secret communist party in the United States. Ward's entire background was evil as it was controlled by the secret government and was also identified to be a part of the Communist party and ideology that was also created by the secret government through Carl Marx. Eventually, Dr. Ward, the man that John D. Rockefeller helped and financed by orders of Rothschild and Jacob Schiff to destroy Christianity in America, died. Nonetheless, he served as a great tool for the Luciferian agenda as today the National Council of Churches is an active organization in conjunction with Rome's Global Ecumenical Movement.

Chapter 12: THE ORCHESTRATION OF WAR

During the middle of the 19th century, the Jesuit Illuminati were preparing to launch our world into another Thirty Years War. This time, however, the war proved to be more deadly with more lives destroyed because of the new, superior technology that was employed.

By now, you should have discovered that the Dark Brotherhood's agenda was planned as a long-term strategy rather than aiming for immediate success. This was due to the establishment of the free world, the American constitutional Republic, which was the Dark Brotherhood's only objective in overtly imposing global fascism.

In the orchestration of the second Thirty Years War, the Dark Brotherhood first intended to overtly impose universal despotism in Europe through the alliances of the central empire. However, in their failed attempt, they also maneuvered a second solution wherein by applying the Hegelian dialectic, they would arrive at a covert dictatorship. This would take time, but it would ensure the ultimate arrival of a global central empire, a one-world government.

By taking the covert dictatorship method, which history referred to as World War One and Two, the second Thirty Years War would allow them to impose their covert first League of Nations, which would evolve into the United Nations. After the Second World War, and through the third and final World War, known as the third and final social cataclysm, according to the military blueprint of Albert Pike, they would arrive at imposing the one-world government. This is the Luciferian agenda in covert action, which they failed to implement a century earlier.

Considering this, we can conclude that all the wars that are taking place in the 21st century have all been orchestrated by the secret government of the Black Pope. That includes the Iraq wars, the Israel-Lebanon wars, and all others have been intelligently and deliberately orchestrated to ignite the third and final social cataclysm and throw our world into the absolute tyranny of the Dark Brotherhood's government coup. After all, the orchestration of these wars falls in line with Protocol Number 3 in creating worldwide wars and revolutions to arrive at a totalitarian world government.

However, before we can understand the second Thirty Years War from 1914 to 1945 as planned by them, we must first understand the previous conflicts that pervaded Europe in the middle and late 19th century. As mentioned, the Dark Brotherhood's plot to resurrect the first League of Nations in the Congress of Vienna in 1815 failed thanks to the intervention of the Czars of Russia. This move not only interfered with the plans to establish the Holy Roman Empire but also allowed for various revolutionary activities to be conducted by the Masonic brothers of the original Blue Lodge. The Blue Lodge Masons were also active in Russia through the Czars and were the source behind the spreading ideologies of freedom in Europe.

Again, the battle for French independence, which resulted in the French Revolution, was the first attempt at establishing the First National Republic of France. This coup failed because the Jesuits, through Napoleon, thwarted the Jacobins who were trying to give France her first taste of freedom. Thanks to the Czars, the Blue Lodge Masons were able to gradually restore the Republican France, since the first Republic failed; this became known as the second Republic of France.

The establishment of the Second Republic of France through Léon Gambetta proved a success, thanks to the Blue Lodge faction of the Masonic brothers in the geopolitical arena. Unfortunately, this Republic did not last very long because of the continuing subversive acts conducted by the Jesuits and their Illuminati gangsters. The subversive acts led to the massive infiltration by the Jesuits who, after penetrating their agents which took over two decades, took the French Republic from within. This was proven when the Jesuits managed to rig the elections by voting Louis-Napoleon the third as president of the Republic. At this point, the French Republic was transformed into the Second Empire of France, as revealed in the secret history of the Jesuits by Edmund Paris. This was the same tactic of infiltration employed by the Sith in the movie "Star Wars: Revenge of the Sith."

Under the rule of Napoleon III, the Jesuits maneuvered into play the Falloux Law, which gave the Jesuits absolute control of the educational curriculum in France. France had lost her liberty, and now the Jesuit Illuminati were ready to make good use of her by using her army to expand the central empire of the Habsburgs. The engineering of more wars by the secret government, who were eager to put nations further in debt. With France under the control of the Dark Brotherhood, the Crimean War was in full swing as the French, backed by Austria and Hungary, the Jesuits set out to consolidate central power in Europe. What started as the Crimean War became the Franco-German war and eventually evolved into the Franco-Prussian War, which ended the expanding Second Empire that was overtly trying to bring all of Europe under one single central empire.

The aim of these wars was to increase the power of the Holy Roman Empire of the Habsburgs and their allies, the absolutists of Europe. As in the Treaty of Westphalia, the expansion of the Second Holy Roman Empire was thwarted by the all-powerful Prussian Army, who vanquished the French, who were extremely exhausted after two centuries of war. This was Orthodox Prussia, backed by Russia, who were not in line with the Vatican's plan of restoring pontifical universal power over all of Europe.

Under their own volition, the French implanted their Third Republic, and once again, France was free. The years continued, and eventually, independent European nations like France, Prussia, and Russia had formed their own alliances from the growing power of what later became known as the Triple Alliance empire. The pact between France and Russia became known as the Franco-Russian Alliance, and it infuriated the Jesuits who had lost control over France once again. It was the turn of the new century, and the Holy Roman Empire ceased expansion because of the sovereignty of nations who wanted their independence. To the Papacy and the secret government behind them, it was a measure for further war. So, under the direction of the Jesuits, the secret government began formulating their plans to plunge Europe into an even bigger war. Under the control of the Jesuits, the central powers of the Holy Roman Empire Alliance, the Habsburgs, and Austrian Emperor Joseph François Ferdinand were to continue their plot for universal domination of Europe.

Since the secret government is, by some accounts, a hundred years or more advanced in technology than the public, it had been using radio as a form of communication before Marconi was credited with its invention—or, more accurately, its rediscovery. The secret scientists of the Jesuits and the Illuminati were already employing such technologies for communicating with their agents worldwide and in secret, right before the onset of the events leading to the Second Thirty Years War.

Ivan Fraser suggests that this technological advantage enabled intelligence officers to understand apparently unrelated incidents, such as the assassination of the Austrian Archduke Ferdinand, and other simultaneous events that precipitated the First World War. According to Edmund Paris, the Jesuit Superior General, known as the Black Pope—Count Halke von Ledochowski at the time—was the chief commander of the entire secret worldwide government and had issued the orders for the orchestration of what we now call the First and later the Second World War.

With the orchestration of the Second Thirty Years War (1915 to 1945), the Jesuit Illuminati implemented all the political ideologies they had developed and inspired through their chosen philosophers, like Friedrich Hegel, Karl Marx, and Friedrich Nietzsche, earlier in the Romanticism period. They were ready to begin the agitation that would lead to a full-scale war. The assassination of Franz Ferdinand ignited the Central Powers of the Triple Alliance—Austria-Hungary and Germany—into declaring war against Serbia and Russia.

However, what the Central Powers didn't realize is that, according to the Protocols of the Learned Elders of Zion, the masterminds of the Illuminati Jesuits had arranged for the assassination of their own servant, taking any measure necessary to justify their ends. Austria-Hungary and Germany, predominantly Roman Catholic nations, under the secret control of the Jesuits, had become the secular arm of the Vatican in pursuit of the evil Council of Trent's objectives. In this light, the First World War served as another camouflage for a modern-day Inquisition.

The First World War

The First World War was fought for multiple reasons. The Roman Church, under Jesuit control, saw this war as a modern-day Inquisition to purge the unconverted Orthodox Christians in the Balkans, Croatia, and Serbia, due to the independence of the Russian Orthodox Church, from not merging with the universal power of the Papacy. In the eyes of the Vatican, the Russian Orthodox religion had been considered heretical since 1540 and therefore condemned by the Council of Trent.

This war would also serve as retribution against France for reclaiming her independence and freedom from the power of the Papacy. The Jesuits sought revenge, and for England, predominantly Protestant, this was a bonus in conducting this overt inquisition. The war also aimed to eliminate the Czars who had protected Russia for centuries. These were the authentic reasons why the Dark Brotherhood decided to foment the Second Thirty Years War, repeating the same battle repeatedly throughout history.

The Second Thirty Years War was devised as a two-way plan. The first was to use the overt method of expanding the central empire, forcing it on all of Europe. When this overt method did not always prove successful, the masterminds of the secret government also arranged for a covert method, resulting in the implementation of the League of Nations, which would act as a covert vehicle to gradually bring all of Europe under their absolute control, as seen in today's European Union.

However, this method would take time, and the secret government would eventually revive the Holy Roman Babylonian Empire by either overt or covert methods. This move would bring the world stage closer to fulfilling the ancient agenda of world domination, initiated by ancient Babylon over four thousand years ago. Despite the First World War being orchestrated by agents of the Black Pope, if it weren't for the intervention of the United States government, the Dark Brotherhood might have had the upper hand, allowing the Holy Roman Central Powers to expand until power rested in their hands.

The Second World War

Similarly, the Second World War was designed by the masterminds of the Jesuit Illuminati as a backup plan in case the First World War did not meet their criteria. After the First World War, the secret government immediately began molding their perfect Manchurian candidates, who would serve and implement what became known as totalitarian conservatism or fascism. For the Jesuits and the Vatican, the immediate orchestration of the Second World War was another attempt to overtly bring Europe under their absolute control. For the Illuminati, it continued to serve the covert agenda by financing all the nations involved, which would put them further in debt to the international bankers.

Most Illuminati researchers are aware that after the Third World War, power became concentrated in fewer hands as nations became more indebted to the international cartel. Today's discoveries provide evidence that the international bankers—the Rothschilds, the Warburg's, the Rockefellers, the Morgans, the Harriman's, even Henry Ford—were all members of the modern-day political Zionist movement that financed the Nazi war machine as well as the First World War.

To support this, political economist and activist Lyndon LaRouche reported in the Executive Intelligence Review that the international bankers were the ones who placed Hitler in power. Just as they had earlier fomented programs of slaughter in Russia, the international bankers, under the direction of their supreme boss, the Black Pope, initiated the brutal Holocaust, targeting not only Jews but also Protestants, liberals, and Republicans through Hitler, as another attempt to eliminate anyone who sought freedom and lived under a Republic.

With the dictatorships of Mussolini and Franco in place, the Jesuits were ready to overthrow the Weimar Republic of Germany. Everything proceeded as planned by the secret government, according to the Executive Intelligence Review; even the bombing of the Reichstag was planned to serve the imposition of the Nazi regime. Under Hitler, the central power of the Austria-Hungary Alliance was once again ready to continue the plot. Following the Vatican-Nazi Concordat, Hitler received his blessing from Pope Pius XII, as had Napoleon III before him, and now the secret government had all their fascist nations geared up to force the Holy Roman Empire upon the world.

The Second World War ignited

Even though the secret government of the Jesuit Illuminati failed through their overt method, they succeeded with the covert one by establishing their first global vehicle to gradually bring about the one-world government. That is why Albert Pike outlined three major social cataclysms that would lead the world into a one-world government solution.

The arrival of the United Nations and its covert takeover was maneuvered by employing the Hegelian dialectic as Europe cried out for a solution following the First and Second World Wars.

This time, there were no Czars to interfere, for they had been overthrown by the Bolshevik Revolution, another tactic employed by the secret government. Nevertheless, both the First and Second World Wars were fought to further the plans of the global secret government of the Luciferian agenda, whether through overt, immediate solutions or long-term covert ones. The Second Thirty Years War eliminated three enemies standing in the way of the Holy Roman Empire: France, the Czars of Russia, and it brought down the Second Republic of Germany and Spain, not to mention the Eastern European bloc.

Despite the promises Hitler made with the Vatican, the outcome was controlled by the international bankers, the true global Nazi fascist machine, also known as the political Zionist international bankers, who established the Treaty of Balfour and the modern state of Israel.

World War 3 would be the final World War, as outlined by Albert Pike and the plan Protocols of the Learned Elders of Zion. World War III was designed to bring about the final solution for world government through the United Nations, evolving into the World Union, aka one-world government.

The steps taken to achieve World War 3 include the buildup of international communism until its strength equals that of

Western capitalism and using their differences to create conflict. This was the real reason behind the Cold War and what Albert Pike considered the final social cataclysm that would make people cry out for a global solution, a world government.

Considering this, economist and insider, the author of the Executive Intelligence Review, Lyndon LaRouche, reported that following the Second World War, the international cartel manipulated the U.S. government into launching a preemptive nuclear strike against the Soviet Union. Somehow, the Soviets developed thermonuclear weapons in the nick of time, so this coup, intended to impose world government, failed. This was none other than the third and final social cataclysm proposed by Albert Pike a century earlier, as the coup that would foment a devastating final.

Third World War

It is also believed that the secret government had a second plot as a backup to achieve the final outcome of world domination through a third world war. The second plot was to use the controversies between Islamic nations and Western Christian nations. As we know, this hasn't yet happened, and that is why this book is being written: to expose the true nature of the secret government.

The forces of Light have also been prolonging World War 3 as they currently hold off the forces of darkness and their agenda to plunge our world into a nuclear war as we approach the end of the era. It is a relief to know that the Dark Brotherhood's agenda is being delayed and will not come to fruition because this world is under a Divine blueprint.

In light of the information revealed in this material, we can safely conclude that the secret world government of the Jesuit Illuminati has orchestrated all the conflicts ongoing in the Middle East so that the third and final social cataclysm would usher in World War III. This agenda has been engineered because the first plot failed due to the collapse of the Soviet Union. After all, creating worldwide wars and revolutions is Protocol Number 2 and the true reason for the conflict ongoing in the Middle East today. In the words of the international bankers, the enemy of humanity, as reported in the Executive Intelligence Review in August 2005, was trying to plunge the world into another age of darkness by initiating World War 3.

Communism: A Tool Designed by the International Bankers

Communism was purportedly created by the Jesuits as early as the 17th century in Paraguay if we recall. It was presented to our world through the Jesuit-trained political analyst Karl Marx in 1848 and later financed by the international bankers in New York, the capital of the international bankers and the establishment of the Federal Reserve. According to the research of Myron Fagan, the plot began in the 1850s when the Illuminati international cabal held a series of secret meetings in New York, which were addressed by a British illusionist named Wright. Those in attendance were told that the Illuminati was organizing to unite the nihilist and atheist groups with all other subversive groups into one, to be known as the Communists.

This was when the term "communism" came into being, as revealed by Mr. Fagan. This false political ideology, driven by the Jesuits in Paraguay two centuries earlier, was intended to be the supreme weapon or scare word that would terrorize the whole world and eventually drive the terrified people into the one-world scheme. Communism was a scheme used to enable the Jesuit Illuminati to foment the third world war necessary to help bring about the one-world government.

In the words attributed to Albert Pike, "We shall unleash the nihilists and the atheists, and we shall provoke a great social cataclysm which in all its forms will show clearly to all nations the effect of absolute atheism, the origins of savagery, and of the bloodiest turmoil. Then, everywhere, the citizens will be forced to defend themselves against the world minority of revolutionaries and will exterminate those destroyers of civilization. And the multitude, disillusioned with Christianity, whose spirits will from that moment be without compass or direction, anxious for an ideal but without knowledge of where to render their adoration, will receive the true light through the universal manifestation of the pure doctrine of Lucifer, brought finally out into public view, a manifestation which will result from the general reactionary movement which will follow the destruction of Christianity and atheism, both conquered and exterminated at the same time."

The final stage of the conspiracy laid down by the Illuminati One World Government will consist of a king dictator, the head of the United Nations, or the Global Union, with a few billionaires, scientists, and economists who have proven their loyalty to the Illuminati. The rest of humanity would be integrated into a vast conglomerate of slaves.

This narrative resembles the Protocols of the Learned Elders of Zion. While World War One broke out, the secret government arranged for the planned assassination of the Austrian Archduke by a Serbian secret society that was connected to and controlled by the Black Pope. During this time, the banking cartel in New York organized what would be known as the Bolshevik Revolution. The Bolsheviks were to be their instruments to remove the Czars from Russia and implement the Communist Manifesto as their boogeyman trap, setting forth the final social cataclysm that would lead into World War Three.

The chosen and trained Bolsheviks were Nikolai Lenin, Leon Trotsky, and later Joseph Stalin, who, like Napoleon and Hitler, were pupils of Albert Pike and all active members of the dark faction of the Masonic Illuminati Lodge that was totally controlled by the Black Pope under the Illuminati banking clan.

According to Mr. Fagan, their headquarters were on the lower east side of New York, which was largely inhabited by Russian Jewish refugees. Neither of these puppets had an occupation, yet they appeared to be always well-equipped with money. The answer to this mystery is that all their funding was coming from the Rothschilds via Jacob Schiff. The plan for the Bolshevik takeover was orchestrated in the lower east end of New York, providing a preliminary training ground for all the men who were going to participate in the Bolshevik Revolution's takeover of Russia.

After their training and reorganization, Trotsky and 300 of his men were sent off to Europe towards Switzerland, where Lenin and his group were waiting for their arrival. Mr. Fagan also revealed that Trotsky had more than just men on his ship; they had financing of $20 million in gold that had been given to them by their master, Jacob Schiff.

In anticipation of Trotsky's arrival, Lenin prepared a special welcoming party in his Switzerland hideaway, which was also provided by the international bankers. For the record, the entire Illuminati gang of international bankers participated in financing the secret operation. By 1917, the war was well underway. England, France, and Russia, the Allies, were fighting against the Axis powers, Austria-Hungary, and Germany. To our surprise, men in very high places in all these nations, both from the Allies and Axis powers, attended the party and meetings in Switzerland. Attendees included American elitists like Colonel Edward Mandell House, the advisor and mentor of President Woodrow Wilson, who was considered Jacob Schiff's confidential messenger. Other guests were Paul and Felix Warburg from the banking clan of Germany, who were not only part of the Illuminati but were initially financed and trained by the House of Rothschild to finance Wilhelm Kaiser of Germany.

To further demonstrate the power and network of the secret government, Mr. Fagan documented an episode when the Bolshevik ship almost became intercepted by a British warship. Immediately, the secret government, through Colonel Edward Mandell House, made the necessary adjustments to release the ship and continue the plot. Schiff immediately rushed orders to Colonel House, who in turn ordered Wilson to order the British to release the ship. Wilson, acting as the puppet he was, ordered the British to release the ship with Trotsky, the gold, and his associates by threatening not to have the United States enter the war if they did not comply. The United States had arranged to enter the war in April of that year, revealed Mr. Fagan.

Unfortunately, Trotsky and his soldiers arrived in Switzerland, and Lenin's party went off as scheduled. The Warburg's, who were the secret police of Germany, assisted the Bolsheviks by loading them into freight cars and made all the necessary arrangements for their secret entry into Russia. This is how the Bolshevik Revolution took place, with members of the secret government all playing their part in immediately overthrowing the Romanov family and the Czars, the last protectors of the Orthodox Eastern establishment.

According to Lyndon LaRouche, it was reported that the English monarch King Edward had incited conflict between his nephews, Wilhelm Kaiser of Germany and Alexander of Russia, the head of the Czars. This aligns with the notion that the House of Rothschild had absolute control over the English and French monarchies but not over Germany, and the Czars were on their death list for thwarting their League of Nations at Vienna a century earlier. King Edward's loyalty and allegiance were to the Rothschilds and served to initiate the First World War.

Nonetheless, Russia was part of the Allies and, after fighting a lengthy war, had become exhausted. This is another example of the divide and conquer method, the same method that the Dark Brotherhood has implemented since ancient times as a supreme tactic, also known as one of the most famous strategies in "The Art of War". These events were engineered and fomented by the same masterminds that maneuvered the illegal Federal Reserve System into existence. In a similar manner, the secret government also used the war as an excuse for the implementation of the I.R.S. Federal Income Tax and the 16th amendment. According to our Constitution, the privately owned Federal Reserve and the I.R.S. are unconstitutional.

The income tax was designed to tax the earnest income of the American people, while the massive wealth of American international financiers had been converted into trust endowment foundations, becoming tax-free foundations. This maneuver by the secret government's international financiers affected everyone in America, apart from the powerful and wealthy who are secretly aligned with the European financial oligarchy and the Black Nobility, in the dissolution of our Constitution.

By converting their wealth into tax-free foundations, the American Illuminati were able to evade all taxes. Their foundations, like the Rockefeller Foundation, the Carnegie and Ford Foundations, the Mellon Foundation, and hundreds more, were all tax-exempt. This cover-up was disguised by the false humanitarian fronts these foundations posed as.

After the First World War, it was also revealed that the Treaty of Versailles was hosted by Baron de Rothschild, Lloyd George, and Alfred Milner, who, with Cecil Rhodes, helped establish the Round Table groups in 1891. From America, Woodrow Wilson attended, as well as Colonel Mandell House and the Dulles Brothers—John Foster Dulles and Avery Dulles, his brother—who were both Jesuits and major secret government manipulators in the United States. Other international bankers who attended the treaty were Max and Paul Warburg and J.P. Morgan. This treaty gave us the League of Nations in 1918, the long-awaited vehicle for the resurgence of the Holy Roman Empire, today known as the European Union.

Two factors prevented the U.S. from joining the first League of Nations. The first was that while Jacob Schiff and his associates were busy trying to implement the Federal Reserve System and fomenting the Bolshevik Revolution, they had forgotten to fully accomplish one of the directives given, which was the entrapment and control of all mass communications media, press, etc. Mr. Fagan believes this was the reason why the cabal failed to manipulate America into joining the League of Nations. The second, and perhaps most important reason, was Henry Cabot Lodge, another hero who was righteous, respected, and trusted by the members of the House of Representatives and the Senate, saw through the cabal's scheme, unmasked Wilson, and helped keep the United States out of the League of Nations.

Chapter 13: THE SECRET SOCIETIES AND THE TRUTH BEHIND THE U.N.

As the final attempt to establish the Holy Roman Empire two years later, before the onset of World War II, the Jesuit Illuminati masterminds maneuvered more extensions to aid their Luciferian agenda. In Europe, the secret government established a semi-secret organization in 1920 by the name of the Royal Institute of International Affairs (RIIA), which was based at Chatham House in London. This secret organization was manipulated into being by the same people who gave us the Round Table groups. They were set up by the Rothschilds to help coordinate events that not only led to the Second thirty-Year War but, the European Union as well.

The Royal Institute of International Affairs became the offspring of the Round Table groups, with Queen Elizabeth II appointed as Patron. It was also revealed that Queen Elizabeth II of England was involved with the Knights of Malta in Europe, answering to the Jesuits. This confirms the Queen's involvement in the secret government of the Black Pope. In either case, the Royal Institute of International Affairs was designed not only as a think tank but as a semi-secret organization created to dictate British policy and, through the League of Nations, to dictate European policy with its aim at consolidating Europe into one monetary unit. This was accomplished through the European Economic Community, which in turn was designed to eventually evolve into the European Union.

It has been confirmed that the powers associated with an active role in the Royal Institute of International Affairs have mostly been members of the Black Nobility, the European organized financial elite. For instance, Ivan Fraser discovered that the presidents of this subset secret organization, the Royal Institute of International Affairs, have been prominent European elitists such as Lord Carrington. Lord Carrington served as a former foreign secretary and prime minister. There was also Lord Roy Jenkins who was a former Chancellor of the Exchequer and president of the European Commission.

A year later, the Jesuit Illuminati secret government manipulated the branch of the Royal Institute of International Affairs in America known as the Council on Foreign Relations. It was revealed that it was this organization that hurled us into joining the United Nations. The traitors who had become instrumental to this also had been playing the game for a while. The 20th-century Benedict Arnold was none other than Edward Colonel House. Edward Colonel House was the chief advisor to President Woodrow Wilson and Bernard Baruch.

Jacob Schiff was getting old and on the verge of retiring, and he appointed Colonel House and Bernard Baruch with proper instructions from the Rothschilds to continue the conspiracy of centralizing world government. The Council on Foreign Relations was established through their efforts, becoming the controlled institution of the secret government here in the United States.

It has also been revealed that the members of the Council on Foreign Relations had changed their family name to acquire American names. For instance, we had Dillon, who served as Secretary of the Treasury for the United States, whose true name was Liposky. Another example was Pauley, the head of the CBS TV channel, whose name was Polinsky. It was estimated that membership in the CFR reached about a thousand. Their members penetrated not only positions of influence and power but also planted their puppets in key positions in press and media outlets as well.

The CFR is considered the sister organization of the Royal Institute of International Affairs and was a brainchild of the secretive Round Table groups commissioned in 1891. With the creation of the CFR, the Jesuit Illuminati secret government established a policymaking organization here in the states. This enabled them to throw the US into the United Nations.

It was believed that the Luciferian Babylonian secret brotherhood, as descendants of the original Babylonian networks, have always known and kept records of who was part of the Nimrod-Esau bloodline. It makes perfect sense why someone like Adolf Hitler was specially groomed and molded by negative secret societies like the Thule or Vril Society, a Luciferian secret society in Germany. In a similar manner, Napoleon Bonaparte, Adam Weishaupt, Hegel, Marx, and Nietzsche were all indoctrinated by the Dark Brotherhood to keep the torch of world domination alive and moving forward into the 20th century.

Even Napoleon was part of a secret society; therefore, most influential figures have been involved in secret societies whether they serve the Luciferian agenda or the agenda of the Brotherhood of Light. Some researchers propose that Hitler could have been closer to the Rothschilds by blood. His ability to play the role of Antichrist could have been attributed to a heavy concentration of the gene of power in him, which is why he was able to hypnotize people during his speeches. His rise to power was financed and launched by the same forces that have been trying to rule our world since ancient times.

The International Military Society of the Jesuits had a strong connection to the Thule Society, whose members had been a variety of black nobility, black magicians in Europe. It turns out that the Black Pope, through a different instrument, developed the Vril and Thule Societies to control the black arts of sorcery and black magic, making them available only to those of their bloodline. For example, it is well known that Hitler, just like Goring, Rudolph Hess, and Himmler, were all part of the Thule Society and were initiated into the arts of magic. Considering this, we can conclude that Hitler was indoctrinated into the world of occultism, sorcery, and black magic from his adolescent years, and likewise, so were the Rothschilds and the 13 bloodline families running the worldwide secret government.

After two major world wars, the people of the Earth were compelled to seek a solution. The United Nations was a solution as planned by the secret world government a century earlier. In truth, the United Nations became the housing umbrella of the creeping One World Government, and NATO became the forerunner of its covert world army police force. Even though most of the people working for the United Nations have been known to genuinely seek world peace, the real powers behind the United Nations are globalists and affiliates of the Council and Foreign Relations, the Royal Institute of International Affairs, serving the Jesuit Illuminati world government networks. It was documented by both Myron Fagan and Ivan Fraser that all its U.N. Secretary Generals have promoted the New World Agenda. The United Nations Population Fund, the United Nations Environmental Program, and UNESCO, despite their names, have been actual proponents serving and working towards the opposite of what they claim to be.

Since the establishment of the United Nations, the spread of communism and fascism has escalated as confirmed by Mr. Fagan. Despite the foundational aims of the United Nations, the continuation of wars has been evident since its inception. Mr. Fagan highlighted that the United Nations has never passed a resolution condemning communism in Russia.

For instance, when Communist Russian Mongolian troops occupied Hungary, the United Nations failed to act, which facilitated the Communist Russians' extermination of the Hungarians.

Nearly every war, including the Korean War and Vietnam War, has seen a predominant involvement of American soldiers, despite the United Nations comprising about 60 nations. Mr. Fagan documented that approximately 95% of all wars since 1945 have involved American soldiers. In his words, "Where was the U.N. when all those poor Hungarian Freedom Fighters were slaughtered by the Russians? The United Nations did nothing when China invaded Laos and Vietnam. Likewise, when Nkrumah invaded Goa and other Portuguese territories, the U.N. did nothing."

Mr. Fagan also revealed that the so-called peace force of the United Nations was used to oppress, assault, and kill anti-communists in Katanga. Furthermore, the United Nations passed a law to disarm all Americans, which infringes upon the Second Amendment of our Constitution. Article 47, paragraph 3 of The United Nations Charter states, "The Military Staff Committee of the United Nations shall be responsible through the Secretary Council for the strategic direction of all armed forces placed at the disposal of the United Nations Security Council," implying that if all our armed forces were transferred to the United Nations, American soldiers would be compelled to serve and perish under the United Nations command worldwide. This act is considered treasonous.

When the United Nations attempted to manipulate Congress into passing such a treasonous act, a commendable congressman by the name of James B. Utt, who was not affiliated with the Council on Foreign Relations or any secret government tentacle, thwarted the transfer of America's armed forces to the United Nations world police force, NATO. About 50 congressmen had supported such a treasonous act, indicating the influence of the Council on Foreign Relations.

Through the CFR, the Jesuit Illuminati have successfully placed their puppets in the cabinets of the White House, Congress, Senate, and House of Representatives. The CFR has a membership of about 1,000 people. This includes the heads of every industrial empire in America, such as Blough, president of the US Steel Corporation; Rockefeller, the kingpin of the oil empire; and Henry Ford II, the founder of Ford Motors.

These individuals have been provided with substantial funds to influence the elections of Presidents, Senators, Congressmen, Secretaries of State, and of the treasury. CFR members have influenced every important federal agency. Regrettably, in the 21st century, most of our United States government consists of individuals planted by the CFR. For example, the United States Presidents known to be CFR members include Truman, Hoover, Nixon, and the Bushes to name a few.

Other major secret government manipulators affiliated with the CFR include John Foster Dulles and his brother Alan Dulles, who were also connected to the international military order of the Jesuits. They control the affairs of Fordham

University, Georgetown, and Yale. The Jesuits, as major university manipulators in both Europe and the United States, have been covertly manipulating the U.S. government through international bankers. It is highly unfortunate that the Council on Foreign Relations, controlled by the Jesuit Illuminati, has been infiltrating and indirectly controlling the U.S. government since its inception in the 1920s.

The Bilderbergers

By 1954, the secret government had established another semi-secret instrument known as the Bilderberg group. The figurehead used to create this organization was Jozef Retinger, known as a Polish socialist and a major advocate behind the European movement, and Prince Bernhard of the House of Orange and the Netherlands, who, according to Ivan Fraser, was known to be an SS spy for the Nazis and was later appointed chairman of Shell Oil by David Rockefeller.

This organization was intended to serve as a collective of leading politicians, advisors, executives from media, banking, and multinational corporations, educationalists, and military leaders. The members of this group met in secret to discuss the global future and address matters of importance without public awareness or interference from other politicians. This group has been documented to hold meetings in secrecy with no information leaked to the public.

According to Ivan Fraser, an independent researcher who has uncovered extensive information regarding the networks of the shadow government, the leaders of this group form an unelected steering committee, with chairmen selected from various aristocratic houses. For instance, Lord Carrington has been chairman since 1991, and since its creation, only powerful figures have been part of its inner circle of influence. This indicates that the black nobility is running this group as another instrument of the worldwide secret government of the Black Pope.

The Trilateral Commission

Twenty years later, the secret government maneuvered another vehicle designed to further consolidate economic power. This vehicle, known as the Trilateral Commission, is considered the offspring of the Bilderberg group. Its creation is attributed to David Rockefeller and Zbigniew Brzezinski. This instrument of the Dark Brotherhood was established at the end of 1972 to overtly consolidate the policies of the United States through NAFTA, Asia through APEC (the Asia-Pacific Economic Plan). This organization was also created to aid and serve the Council on Foreign Relations to seize absolute control of the American government. For instance, President Jimmy Carter, whose personal National Security Advisor was Zbigniew Brzezinski, the first director of the Trilateral Commission, was the first president to direct policies for the Trilateral Commission.

Chapter 14: THE CARTEL AND THE RATLINES

Another important issue is that before and during the Second World War, the international banker set up a chemical company by the name of I.G. Farben, whose purpose was manifold according to various researchers. According to investigations, this company became the biggest chemical manufacturing industry in the world, financed by the international bankers, during the building up of Germany made enormous amounts of money for the international secret government before enduring the Second World War. According to Ivan Fraser, the international bankers allowed this company to enable Germany to become self-sufficient in rubber, petroleum oil, and explosives. It has also been discovered that this company used the inmates of Auschwitz as slave labor at their chemical plants. Estimates prove that the Nazis had worked at least 25,000 Jews to death, while others were killed in the drug testing programs.

The concentration camps of Nazi Germany had been more than just a Nazi extermination of the Jews. It was a major secret government experiment on a larger scale. The Nazis' rule was to act as sole perpetrators to cast all the blame on them. Concealing the true perpetrators, who are the Jesuit Illuminati of this Satanic act of Nazi war crimes. To understand the horrid inhuman exploitation that took place in those concentration camps, one must understand the implications involved in the overall agenda of the modern-day Luciferian brotherhood. While reading this, please keep in mind the Protocols of the Learned Elders of Zion that were written by the great Sanhedrin himself, the Black Pope.

In the late 19th century, a figure by the name of Wilhelm Wundt who was recorded to be the founder of all psychiatric treatment in theory, and as a result, all mental development such as shock therapy, were coming into use. It is important to know that Wilhelm Wundt had been an ardent student of both Hegel, Darwin, and Nietzsche and had developed an erroneous understanding based on non-humanitarian principles, believing that humans were irrational animals and needed to be fixed.

Wilhelm Wundt believed that by altering the chemical processes in the brain by using certain chemicals, such as man-made drugs manufactured by them, the mental hygiene of men would become more rational, safe, and a better subject to the state. His theory was later expanded and developed through his students and successor, another Luciferian indoctrinated figure by the name of Emil Kraepelin, who came up with the chemicals needed to make the brain adjustments in what they considered the goyim human cattle.

Emil Kraepelin gathered and collaborated with another mad-man chemist who was already educated in the Jesuit-run institutions. They mixed chemicals and developed various synthetic drugs. At the turn of the 20th century, this secret expenditure by the Jesuits and their molded and appointed mental hygienist came up with various chemical mixtures that would in fact affect the human brain. However, they didn't know which one would prove lethal and which ones were not lethal, but they would work to alter the chemicals in the brain, perhaps rendering the subjects more dependent on the states without killing them.

They were now ready to appoint their mental hygienist to begin the experimentation of these man-made drugs on human beings, so they waited until Hitler came to power and, through another Jesuit Illuminati figure, Ernest Rudin, who was appointed as one of Hitler's primary doctors, began administering these chemical lethal injections to the Jews in Germany, beginning the awful experimentations in the concentration camps.

The experiments ranged from putting hundreds of Jews in gas chambers with chemicals to prove to be deadly, massacring them by the thousands. They also injected them with every possible man-made fluid that the secret government Auschwitz doctors created to see which chemicals were lethal and which were not. Not only the Jews, but the freedom fighters and the Protestants of Germany became guinea pigs in these atrocious experiments. It is now obvious that these murderers that were administering these lethal injections and experiments upon the freedom fighters and Jews in Germany were none other than people that were appointed by the Jesuit Illuminati syndicate.

For instance, the concentration camp experiments were also secretly financed by the international bankers who are controlled by the high Knights of Malta and the Rothschilds. The Jesuit Illuminati world secret government were the real criminals behind the Nazi war machine, as it is obvious that they were covertly behind all the inhuman acts performed in these camps. Apparently, the Nazis served as a good cover-up, concealing the real perpetrators, the secret government of the Black Pope.

These wicked experiments served various causes for the secret government. First, it gave them an ability to do away with any possible remnants that they thought were of the lineage of King David or the "Holy Blood Holy Grail", something that the Vatican failed to do during the dark ages and medieval times. Remember, since Babylonian times, the original Israelites that are part of the Davidic bloodline have been targets of the Babylonian networks, and so it is just history repeating itself under different names. The second reason that they conducted these awful experiments in Germany was to also covertly begin the programs known as the Eugenics movement that led to the creation of what today we call the pharmaceutical cartel.

Therefore, we could now state that all these drugs that are being distributed to the Americans from the pharmaceutical cartel evolved out of these mental hygiene programs that began with Wilhelm Wundt, Emil Kraepelin, and Ernest Rudin. Along with manufacturing synthetic drugs, the scientists working for the secret world government developed and were responsible for creating all the viruses known to mankind. The world eugenic program continues in secret as stated in the Protocols of the Learned Elders of Zion.

This explains why entire continents have been victimized by these programs, like Africa, where there are many diseases and many illnesses that have been wiping out the people of Africa. This is a fact only a few have been able to uncover in a world of cover-ups and conspiracies. The lethal drugs experimented and modified in the concentration camps became the forerunners of today's pharmaceutical empire, which, next to the oil industry, is the largest money generator for the self-proclaimed elite of the worldwide secret government of the Black Pope.

Here's the proof, The Dark Brotherhood through the International Bankers, particularly the Rockefellers, created the AMA, the American Medical Association, and the APA in America from the research gathered and experimented upon by the secret scientists of the Nazi Regime. Their overall purpose was to cover up all the natural remedies that have been in practice for thousands of years by the healers of the Brotherhood of Light. Therefore, the world secret government suppressed the real remedies to only administer their chemical drugs. For example, it is well known that the ancients and Aboriginals have always known that the cure lies in everything within the avenues of holistic and natural medicine, but for the secret government, they don't like people to be healthy, and so they completely suppressed these natural remedies in order to offer their created synthetic chemicals that would ensure more sickness and more money for the elites.

The synthetic drugs act as suppressants of illnesses, like colds and flus, which keep manifesting over and over without curing it from its roots. On the other hand, the real cure that the ancients have practiced and preserved through the benevolent orders, such as the therapeutic schools of healers in ancient Egypt, the Essenes of Judea, who were herbalists, and the Cathars of France, who were also natural healers, have been suppressed. But because there is a great awakening, people are waking up to the truth and are resorting back to these natural remedies.

The pharmaceutical industry was created by the powers that rule this world. It is well known by most researchers that today's medications are nothing more than chemicals that only numb or temporarily suspend illnesses while at the same time perpetuating more illnesses as side effects. People will continue consuming these drugs as long as they are in a rcpeated cycle of illness. Unfortunately, all we have available in every grocery store are these man-made drugs, suppressing the real natural remedies that have been proven more effective for thousands of years, that cure all illnesses and diseases known to man.

Throughout all of history, the suppression of the real natural cures has been a major cover-up by the secret government of Babylon, who only seeks the domination, the enslavement and sickness of humanity. This movement of giving people chemical drugs is also part of the Eugenics programs of the population and aligned with the Protocols of the Learned Elders of Zion, as they consider humans human cattle.

According to the investigations of Ivan Fraser, in 1939 the drug trust alliance was formed by the Rockefeller Empire and I.G. Farben, Martin Bormann, Hitler's second in command for the Nazis, was working with the Anglo-American industrialist to continue the cartel of the chemical giant. I.G. Farben, who evolved into the pharmaceutical industry here in the states. Other companies that eventually became integrated into American culture were ICI, Borden, Carnation, General Mills, MW Kellogg Company, Nestle, Pet Milk, Squibb, Sons, Bristol Myers, Whitehall Laboratories, Procter, Gamble, Roche, and Hoechst and Bayer and Company. It was even believed that during the Nazi Vatican ratlines, Operation Paperclip, which will be revealed shortly, two extended pharmaceutical companies even employed convicted war criminals like Friedrich Jahne and Fritzter Meer as board chairman.

Another fact to consider in the implementation of the pharmaceutical cartel is that the Rockefeller Empire, in conjunction with Chase Manhattan Bank, who now owns half of the U.S. pharmaceutical interest, is the largest drug manufacturing company in the world. Overall, since the second thirty-year war, from 1915 to 1945, also known as the First and the Second World War in our history books, the drug industry has become the second biggest manufacturing industry in the world.

In fact, healthcare, as inspired by the pharmaceutical cartel today, is a multi-billion-dollar industry worldwide, and the big corporation companies that sponsor it control most of the healthcare and set the standards for the practice of medicine worldwide. Doctors are not able to choose their own form of practice or anything alternative other than the rigid and imposed man-made drugs of the pharmacy. All their finances come from Wall Street, the central haven of the international bankers.

The pharmaceutical companies rely upon sick people and perpetual illness for big business to survive and reap their profits; they are no different than the tobacco industry, who lie about everything for gain. No drug company will ever invest in curing illnesses and diseases, just like tobacco companies will never stop lying about the truth behind smoking tobacco. One thing these companies have in common is that they are financed and controlled by the same people, the secret government. Another fact covered by Ivan Fraser was that in the U.S. in 1978, 1.5 million people were hospitalized due to medication side effects alone. In 1991 in the US, 73,000 people were killed due to these chemicals that the doctors prescribed. Facts: 24,000 died victims of firearm shootings, which makes doctors nearly three times more lethal than guns.

Here's the heart of the cover-up: the collective effort of both Ivan Fraser and Mark Beeston discovered that indeed exist cures for all diseases, including cancer and A.I.D.S., through alternative natural means. One known cure for cancer is Essiac, which has been in use since at least 1922, revealed Ivan Fraser. This cure has been known to have no side effects as it is made by nature. Even though it has come close to becoming a public cure, it has always been available through underground outlets. It has also come to light that the secret government has been hoarding these cures for themselves for over a century.

It has also been revealed that in the 1930s, a man by the name of Royal Raymond Rife developed a very high-powered microscope which apparently could detect organisms which cause diseases such as infections and cancers at the early stage of development. By using this new alternative apparatus known as Rife technology, these organisms are bombarded by frequencies and are restored and cured without any side effects. Mr. Rife demonstrated that it was possible to create and destroy cancer at will and succeeded in curing otherwise terminal patients of this disease as well as others such as polio and typhus in almost 100% of cases.

Ivan Fraser also discovered that there exists another effective cure for A.I.D.S. and cancer that has been employed successfully in clinical practices all over the world for at least 50 years. This alternative care, effective for all known germs and diseases, is known as oxygen-ozone therapy. Of course, it is being suppressed because of its threat to the pharmaceutical cartel that is controlled by the secret government. Since oxygen is one of the most fundamental elements, oxygen-ozone therapy works by flooding the bloodstream with enough oxygen to kill any abnormal organism that might have affected the human body.

Among the multiple diseases that this natural remedy cures are all forms of viruses and bacteria from Blood Hepatitis, Arthritis, Mononucleosis, Cancer, Cirrhosis of the Liver, Cardiovascular Disease, Herpes, Lymphomas, High Cholesterol, cancerous tumors, Leukemia, allergies, and A.I.D.S.

These revelations were provided by the testimonies of certain international MDs who assembled at the May 1983 Six World Ozone Therapy Conference in Washington, D.C. It appears that oxygen-ozone therapy is a natural cure for most, if not all, ailments. On the contrary, there have also been suppressed reports and substantial evidence revealing that the medications that come from the pharmacy have been proven to be more harmful than alleviating. The following is a list of the side effects of the medications prescribed by conventional medicine:

• Eraldin, prescribed for heart disease, with side effects causing corneal damage, including blindness.
• Paracetamol, given as a painkiller, has been reported to have hospitalized 1,500 people in Great Britain in 1971.
• Orabilex, has been known to cause kidney damage with fatal outcomes and, when given as an anti-hypertensive, has been known to cause cataracts.
• Methaqualone, used for hypnotic inducements, has caused severe psychic disturbance leading to at least 366 deaths, mainly through murder and suicide.
• Thalidomide, a tranquilizer, has led to 10,000 malformed children.
• Isoproterenol, given for asthma, caused 3,500 deaths in the '60s.
• Stilboestrol, given for prostate cancer, has been known to cause canccr in young women.

- Trilergan, given as an anti-allergenic, has been known to cause viral hepatitis.
- Flamamil, given for rheumatism, has been known to cause loss of consciousness.
- Phenformin, given for diabetes, had cost 1,000 deaths annually until withdrawn.
- Atromid S, which is given for cholesterol, caused deaths from cancer, liver, gallbladder, and intestinal diseases.
- Valium, given as a tranquilizer, has been proven to become another addictive sedative drug.
- Preludin and Maxiton are diet pills which have been known to cause severe damage to the heart and the nervous system.
- Nembutal, given for insomnia, causes even more insomnia.
- Pronap and Plaxin, used as tranquilizers, have been known to have killed many babies.
- Phenacetin, used as a painkiller, has been known to cause severe damage to kidneys and red blood corpuscles.
- Aminopyrine, another painkiller, also causes blood disease.
- Marzine, used for nausea, has been reported to be damaging for kids.
- Reserpine, used as an anti-hypertensive, increases the risk of cancer of the brain, pancreas, uterus, ovaries, skin, and women's breasts.
- Methotrexate, given for leukemia, is reported to cause intestinal hemorrhage and severe anemia.
- Urethane, given for leukemia, has been known to also cause cancer of the liver, lungs, and bone marrow.
- Mitotane, also given for leukemia, has been known to cause kidney damage.
- Cyclophosphamide, given for cancer, also causes liver and lung damage.

- Isoniazid, given for tuberculosis, is known to cause liver destruction.
- Kanamycin, also given for tuberculosis, is known to cause deafness and kidney destruction.
- Chloromycetin, given for thyroid, is known to cause leukemia and cardiovascular collapse in death.
- Clioquinol, given for diarrhea, is also known to cause blindness, paralysis, and death.
- D.E.S., used for preventing miscarriages, is also known to cause birth defects and cancer.
- Debendox, given for nausea, is also known to cause birth defects.
- Accutane, given for acne, is known to cause deafness and kidney destruction.

These medications are but a few that have been known to cause more damage than good. When they seem to help one illness, it appears that they manifest another illness. In general, society at large is in the dark regarding the truth behind the pharmaceutical cartel as lethal. Furthermore, this cover-up goes well in hand with the genetically modified processed foods we have all been given through the fast-food chain empire, which was also designed to keep the pharmaceutical cartel in business. There is no coincidence that the fast-food industry emerged as soon as the pharmaceutical industry emerged at the same time.

The reality highlighted in the movie "Supersize Me" demonstrates a troubling cycle: excessive consumption of fast-food leads to illness, which in turn drives people to pharmacies to purchase man-made drugs provided by the secret government, as outlined in the Protocols of the Learned Elders of Zion. This leaves us in a loop where the offered solutions only suspend or suppress sickness, ultimately exacerbating health issues.

The time has come for an awakening, to recognize the forces aiming to dominate and potentially annihilate humanity. Armed with knowledge, we can choose alternative paths like homeopathic, herbal remedies, and holistic medicine, which aim to cure rather than merely suppress or cause additional illnesses. By rejecting the secret government's monopoly and prioritizing organic, healthy food intake, we can start taking our health seriously.

Genetically modified foods, chemtrails, and consumer products ranging from toothpaste to makeup are designed with harmful intentions, stripping nutrients from our food and exposing us to toxins. Embracing organic farming and consuming organic foods, including vegetables, fruits, grass-fed meats, and eggs, can provide the essential nutrients our bodies need.

Maintaining a healthy body involves proper nutrition, but also incorporating exercise, sunlight exposure, and healthy water intake. Exploring suppressed holistic and alternative medicines can further enhance our wellbeing.

Evidence points to the Nazi experiments as foundational to modern conventional medicine. They used individuals as test subjects for drugs ranging from cough syrups to vaccines. I.G. Farben played a critical role in establishing the pharmaceutical cartel, revealing the deep-seated involvement of the secret government in the health and medical industries.

Understanding the secret government's intent to dominate and enslave through the suppression of beneficial goods and services is crucial. Recognizing this not as mere conspiracy theory but as manipulative control stretching from ancient Babylon to the present can motivate us to disengage from supporting their industries, companies, and institutions.

The existence of bacteriological warfare and the creation of viruses underscore a silent war against humanity's health, waged covertly by those in power. However, as secrets are unveiled and the Kingdom of Light approaches, there's hope that awareness and action can lead to positive change.

The Nazi regime's contribution to the pharmaceutical industry was just the beginning. The transfer of top scientists and doctors to the U.S. through operation Sunrise and Paperclip allowed for continued secret government projects, from anti-gravity aircraft to mind control technologies, demonstrating a profound and ongoing impact on global health and policy.

This transfer not only advanced technological development in the U.S. but also laid the groundwork for manipulative practices, including mind control via electromagnetic frequencies, with projects originating in Germany and perfected in America.

The establishment of intelligence agencies like the C.I.A. by Reinhard Gehlen, a top Nazi spy, and the collaboration between Nazis and extremist groups highlight the extensive influence and manipulation exerted by these forces over global affairs, aligning with the ominous foresight of the Protocols of the Learned Elders of Zion.

In addition, Martin Bormann, a leading Nazi, arranged for all the Nazi gold, silver, and wealth taken from the Jews to be secretly sent to countries like Spain, Italy, and Argentina to rest in the hands of the secret government. This operation, known as Eagle Flight, was documented by Mr. Hertz. Other Nazis, such as Heinrich Müller, the head of the Gestapo in Germany, and Walter Rauff, head of the S.S. in Milan and inventor of mobile gas used to exterminate approximately 250,000 Jews, also escaped into the USA to work with Reinhard Gehlen in the C.I.A.'s corrupt corps that later became known as the counterintelligence unit, as described by the Executive Intelligence Review.

Project Paperclip and Operation Sunrise reveal a shocking reality. It can be surmised that the creators of the C.I.A., among other agencies within the United States, have been covertly working for the Knights of Malta. There is significant evidence to suggest that the C.I.A., at its highest levels, became a vehicle for the Jesuit Illuminati's secret world government. Furthermore, the Knights of Malta, acting as the Jesuits' most brutal extension, are ruthless mercenaries who also helped establish the British M.I.5 and M.I.6, the Russian K.G.B., and the Israeli Mossad, as well as supporting the Shah of Iran. These agencies were reportedly modeled after the original Gestapo of Germany. Today, sufficient evidence credits Reinhard Gehlen as the instructor and official trainer of these intelligence communities, which, at the highest levels, have been working secretly for the Black Knights of the secret government and their leader, the Black Pope.

This aligns perfectly with a covert dictatorship approach that is gradually steering our world toward a centralized World Empire, akin to a resurrected Holy Roman Empire. This assertion is supported by various sources now coming to light, such as Eric John Phelps' book "Vatican Assassins," which reveals the truth behind the international intelligence apparatus.

This strategy also aligns with the Protocols, as the secret world government aimed to create an entire community of intelligence agencies to serve the covert Luciferian agenda of establishing world domination. The secret government has managed to use these ostensibly unconnected opposing entities to covertly work together at the highest level to erode the freedoms and democracies developing in our world, while secretly imposing a more centralized fascist system worldwide, known as communism. The plan suggests that once most of the world's nations have been covertly taken over, there will be less resistance at the onset of imposing a New World Order, One World Government, or Holy Roman Empire.

Victor Marchetti's book about the C.I.A. and the cult of intelligence offers an alternative view of the C.I.A. that the powers and rulers of this world prefer to keep hidden. Additionally, a vast number of well-researched papers, like Steven Kangas's work, have compiled data on corruption at the highest levels of our own C.I.A.

Stephen Kangas's paper, "The Timeline of C.I.A. Atrocities," exposes how the C.I.A. and its counterintelligence corps have been covertly collaborating with other intelligence agencies in coups to overthrow all Republican presidents in the name of fighting communism, only to replace them with right-wing fascist dictators. These clandestine operations, particularly prevalent in Latin American continents, demonstrate the real masters behind the C.I.A. at the highest levels. Kangas details all the coups executed by the C.I.A. since its inception, showing how escaped Nazis were employed by the C.I.A. to teach and train others in tactics such as interrogation, torture, blackmail, and election sabotage, not to mention economic sabotage. This report also corroborates William Hurt's paper titled "The Nazi Ratlines."

Furthermore, Kangas exposes the C.I.A.'s role in igniting the Korean War and the Vietnam War, revealing how the United Nations has been secretly operating contrary to its stated goals, in conjunction with the corrupt actions of the C.I.A. and the Counterintelligence Corp. Lyndon LaRouche's Executive Intelligence Review supports this by revealing how Henry Kissinger was a key figure in igniting the Vietnam War.

Kangas's investigation uncovered the C.I.A.'s dirty tricks, from the overthrow of the Republic government in Iran in 1953 to the placement of Fidel Castro in power in Cuba in 1961, as well as the sabotages in Haiti and the overthrowing of the Australian Democratic Republican government of Prime Minister Edward Whitlam. These cover-ups are among many clandestine operations known as Black Ops, conducted by the highest levels of the C.I.A. under the guise of fighting communism, when in reality, the intelligence community has been used by the secret government to oppose the concepts of freedom and the commonwealth of nations.

These operations align perfectly with the Protocols of the Learned Elders of Zion, as the Hegelian dialectic proves to be successful again for them. As mentioned earlier, the constitutional Republic of the United States of America, thanks to our founding fathers, remains the only significant obstacle in the way of the secret government's ability to enslave the entire world into a totalitarian global fascist system.

Chapter 15: THE WORLD

In light of the truth, another revelation and suppressed fact involve the real murders of our late President John F. Kennedy. I remember sitting in high school, learning about J.F.K.'s assassination, trying to figure out who really killed our president as our teacher played the J.F.K. tapes over and over. After this long journey of truth-seeking and discovery, and the realization of the secret government and their quest for world domination, it is now plain and simple who killed J.F.K.

The real assassins of our president were the Jesuit Illuminati, the secret government. They had various reasons for ending his life. Initially, President John F. Kennedy was supposed to help further the global one-world government programs as he was part of the Council on Foreign Relations.

However, in the end, we also know that he changed sides. What we do know is that his father, Joseph Kennedy, had been a key player in the secret government for the International Military Order of the Jesuits and the Knights of Malta, who had arranged for his successful election. When Kennedy became president, he had no idea what he was getting into. J.F.K. had no clue that his father was connected to the cabal through the Knights of Malta and the Knights of Columbus.

Some researchers believe that when Kennedy was informed of his duties and expectations by his secret government advisors, he was disgusted and decided to do what was right. Kennedy was expected to disarm the American people, which violates the Second Amendment. Instead, Kennedy decided not to comply. The real problems arose when Kennedy figured out that his entire cabinet had been planned with Council Foreign Relation agents who were not aligned or respectful of the Constitution. To top things off, things exploded when Kennedy found out that the war in Vietnam had been a planned intervention and a phony war designed for other purposes than what he was told.

Things really hit the fan when he discovered that our own C.I.A. was also being used to assist in these evil operations. Not to mention he was shocked to know that the Federal Reserve had been a central banking system, putting our nation in enormous debt to the private interest groups, the international bankers.

With all of these discoveries, Kennedy, as the good man, decided to play the hero by implementing a U.S. treasury backed by precious metals. In addition, after learning about the corruption of the C.I.A., the Counter Intelligence Corps, and connections to the phony Wars in Vietnam, he quickly set out to end this phony war and even attempted to end the reign of the C.I.A.'s Counter Intelligence Corp.

Apparently acting out of the goodness of his heart, he turned against his father's wishes and against the plans that his father had expected of him. Boy, did he piss off the secret government and saw him as a threat to their globalization programs, and the order was issued immediately from the Black Pope, the most powerful man in the world who controls the entire secret government syndicate, to end his life. As stated in the "Protocols of The Learned Elders of Zion," they would take out presidents if they needed to in order to ensure their plans as a means to justify the ends. The major key players involved in taking him out were many, but the commander in charge was Cardinal Francis Spellman, known as the American Vicar and chief leader of the Knights of Malta in America.

Cardinal Spellman, a superior in the secret government, called all the shots in the planned assassination of J.F.K., which is why his own father, Joseph Kennedy, couldn't do anything as he was superior to him. Another key figure involved was William F. Buckley, a top C.I.A. agent; John McCone, who had been the director of the C.I.A. during the time of the J.F.K. assassination; Henry Luce, a CFR member and the force behind Life Magazine did his part; McGeorge Bundy, a Knight of Malta, and most of the infamous CFR agents of the Black Pope were all involved in executing the plot against Kennedy. Moreover, the third in command in the FBI, Cartha DeLoach, was also a key figure in the assassination. Even the mafia was playing a part in this. Of course, Lee Harvey Oswald acted as the Patsy to cast the blame on someone. Many believe that Lee Harvey Oswald was mind-controlled by the C.I.A. Unfortunately, Kennedy's assassination was perfectly masterminded and covered up.

It has been revealed that Oswald had been tied in with the Knights of Malta as a trained assassin. This is correct in view of how the secret government, "The Hidden Hand", has always had trained assassins since the times of Babylon. Various sources have also revealed that the mafia played a role in the assassination of President Kennedy. It's no coincidence that Cardinal Francis Spellman had arranged for the release of mafioso Lucky Luciano around the same time that the entire secret government coordinated the coup against him.

On behalf of "The Hidden Hand", Kennedy's own father warned him prior to his son's actions not to do anything contrary to what he was told to do. Joe Kennedy was a strict soldier of the Black Pope under Cardinal Spellman; as part of their brotherhood, he had no choice but to allow the assassination of his own blood. This was a case of brotherhood over family. After all, money is a major force and tool behind the authoritarian structure holding together the pyramid power control system that runs our world.

A century earlier, this same fate of assassination was also attributed to President Abraham Lincoln, who wrote a letter to his good friend and ex-Jesuit priest by the name of Charles Chiniquy, "The Jesuits are so expert in those deeds of blood that even Henry IV could not escape them, and so he became their victim, though he did everything he could to protect himself. My escape from their hands, since the letter of the Pope to Jefferson Davis, has been to sharpen a million daggers to pierce my breast; it would be more than a miracle."

Unveiling the truth behind the secret government of the Jesuit Illuminati syndicate, we can safely conclude that Abraham Lincoln was also assassinated by the Black Pope and his chain of command. According to Myron Fagan's research, Lincoln's entire cabinet had been infiltrated by agents of the Rothschilds.

In Mr. Myron Fagan's research titled "The CFR and the Illuminati World Government," Lincoln was asked to form a pact with the House of Rothschilds by establishing a central banking system. Of course, he refused. Instead, he decided to issue our own United States note and a U.S. Treasury, and that is the reason why they killed Lincoln. Lincoln kept the Republic alive and strong, preserving the Republic. There is also ample evidence pointing out that John Wilkes Booth, the patsy in Lincoln's assassination was part of a conspiratorial group and was trained to be Lincoln's lone assassin, those covering up the true perpetrators of "The Hidden Hand".

We can also attribute the assassinations of President James Garfield and President John McKinley at the hands of the Jesuit Illuminati syndicate. Garfield was eliminated for monetary issues, as well as McKinley. Unlike the traitorous Woodrow Wilson, these presidents defied the central banking system and their private banking cartels. Another president whose life was ended by the secret government was President Franklin D. Roosevelt for attempting to implement the Bretton Woods economic system based on the principles of the Commonwealth, where all the world's nations would participate in a good neighbor policy. This perhaps has been "The Hidden Hand"'s most perfect cover-up, for they made everyone believe he died of natural causes.

Furthermore, in the Executive Intelligence Review, Roosevelt's policy opposed the international banking cartel, that is, the Jesuit Illuminati Syndicate that became known as the Bank of International Settlements launched back in the 1920s. This bank is the type of movement that set the stage for the international financing of the Hitler War machine.

In contrast, the Bretton Woods system, as promoted and resurrected by Roosevelt, was to counteract the Bank of International Settlements by replacing it with an American constitutional model opposing the banking cartel of the Anglo-Dutch Central oligarchical banking system. It was precisely this opposition to the agenda of the Dark Brotherhood by F.D.R. that covertly ended his life. There were other reports indicating that there might have been a few attempts at his life prior to his assassination and a coup d'état to overrun him, set up by the secret government, but God preserved him so that he would end the reign of Hitler's Nazis, as explained in the Executive Intelligence Review by Lyndon LaRouche.

All evidence expresses that the Jesuit Illuminati syndicate has been behind every assassination of every figure that has been trying to implement and preserve the concepts of freedom and the practices and structures associated with the sovereign Nation-State Republic.

In the fight for the free world, not only have U.S. presidents been victims, but others have as well. In Europe, a figure fighting for the establishment of the sovereign Nation-State Republic and a free-world advocate by the name of Leon Gambetta was assassinated. Mr. Gambetta knew of the Jesuits' intriguing actions, and after they controlled France for thirty years through Napoleon III, Gambetta expelled them out of France for the last time, giving France her Third Republic in 1880.

All this makes perfect sense when one considers that the creators of the Bavarian Illuminati are Jesuits and have been behind every assassination since the Counter-Reformation Coup. Henry IV, who was one of the first who tried to institute the Sovereign Nation-State Republic, was also victimized, along with his follower King Louis XV, who was also assassinated.

In truth, for the last 500 years, all good men who have dared to fight for the implementation of freedom, justice, and the Commonwealth of Nations have fallen prey to the Jesuits since 1540, and through their Illuminati Financial Enterprise, which is controlled through the Jesuit Knights of Malta, have continued their secret warfare against the free world. The "synagogue of Satan," as Jesus referred to them, does away with anyone who stands in their way of their goal of implementing the Luciferian agenda. As is known by now, this is the same Brotherhood of the Luciferians that descended from the ancient world and will not rest until our world is put under a universal totalitarian fascist system controlled by the descendants of the Nimrod-Esau bloodline.

In truth, the real war is not being waged against communism, for this was a Dark Brotherhood trap employed by the Hegelian dialectic and executing the Protocols of the Learned Elders of Zion. The real war was waged by the secret world government against the free world. "The Hidden Hand", secret world government, are the authors and sponsors of national socialism, communism, and all terrorism. Therefore, the conspiracy is against the free world and the freedom of humanity. Since the adversary temporally rules the foundations of this world, almost everything has become a cover-up.

The truth and final war that is to usher in the Luciferian agenda failed in its first design. However, the second plot of pitting Western Christianity against Eastern Islam is currently being waged as another secret government plot to initiate a final and last social cataclysm, as explained by Albert Pike. Only after a major social cataclysm would a secret world government arrive at instituting their long-awaited One World Government, which is no other than the resurrected Holy Roman Empire.

In fact, we can further conclude that all coups, wars, and revolutions following the Second World War have been and are being conducted covertly by the secret government's corrupt intelligence agencies known as the Counterintelligence Corps (C.I.C.), which encompasses the cooperation of not only our C.I.A. but the entire world's intelligence agencies including the K.G.B., the British M.I.6., the Israeli Mossad, the Ayatollah, etc. All these agencies are being manipulated and controlled at the highest level by the Black Pope, International banking clan, the Illuminati syndicate.

The Knights of Malta are the true controllers of all the world's intelligence agencies and communities conducting clandestine military coups worldwide to install their puppet dictators, such as Castro, Pinochet, Mao Zedong, to name a few.

Another important issue regarding the extensions and arms of the secret government in controlling the world's economies and fostering all the mayhem around the world is the world groups of organized crime families. First, let us remember that there is a powerful truth in the Scriptures that clearly states that the love of money became the root of all evil existing in today's world. Considering that, when one studies and investigates the origins of these organized crime families like the Mafia, one discovers an inevitable connection between the entire system of the Mafia gangsters to the secret government through the existence of the global black markets, which is all part of the system of Babylon.

Mafias fit in perfectly with the Protocols of the Learned Elders of Zion when they stated that they would create organized terrorist groups and organizations that would victimize the world. In light of this, we could say that the mafia are extensions of the real mafiosi, who are the secret government. What would happen if the people of this world found out that the leading world crime organizations are all being executed from the highest levels by the Knights of Malta?

The mafias became an extension to the secret government to the Black Pope, establishing a worldwide network of trafficking and the worldwide black market. The black market not only involves the worldwide sales of illegal drugs and weapons but also involves the sales of humans as sex slaves. There wouldn't be a black market if it wasn't for the activities of the Dark Brotherhood, for the black market is also controlled by the secret government of the Black Pope.

Having an established network of illegal sales enables the system of the beast to be above all constitutional law, running a worldwide enterprise of gun and weapon exchange as well as the illegal drug empire.

The mafias have been designed to run the show as the lone organization of illegal operations in the existing international black market, concealing the real masterminds and harbingers of the dark world. This creates a smokescreen in the eyes of the public, casting the blame on mafias as the only world crime organizations and concealing the real perpetrators and the real mafiosos who operate above all governments and all mafias.

Just as in wars, it is the secret government who benefits the most in the black-market trade of the world. Anybody who knows the truth about mafias knows that the mafias always must pay their cut to the corrupt government in their jurisdiction. For instance, if the Colombian Mafia is trafficking the drug trade out of Colombia, they must give a cut to the government every time they run an operation. In this way, the powers of the corrupt Colombian government ensure that such operations run smoothly without any interruptions. This allows everyone involved to make a large amount of money while keeping it secret from the general public.

On the other hand, in case a certain mafia transaction decides to exclude their corrupt government from their share, which has been known to happen, the people in that mafia who decide to bend the rules by not cooperating get taken out as an example to the rest of the organized crime families that such behavior is not tolerated by the preceding corrupt government. This type of ordeal exists in every country that the secret government has its antennas in, including the United States of America, which at the highest level is run by the Council on Foreign Relations and the Skull and Bones.

The first notorious mafia commission in the world began in Italy as a result of the fallen Italian aristocracy who wanted to maintain power. They decided to go clandestine and wreak havoc, not only for the new aristocracy but for anybody that stood in their way, including the innocent people of Italy. The notorious fallen aristocratic family that started it all was the Comorras of Sicily. They never gave up their struggle for wealth and power in Italy, and by going to Sicily, they organized the first network of criminal bandits, assassins, and agitators against those that they saw as a threat to their organization. It is also no accident or coincidence that the structure of this organization was fashioned as a military dictatorial structure, resembling the more infamous killers and their superiors, the Jesuits.

For instance, starting with the Godfather acting as the sovereign master and dictator of the families, in like fashion, the Black Pope is the supreme ruler of the entire Jesuit Illuminati syndicate. Then we have the bosses, who act as lesser Godfathers, each controlling his own gang and associated families, just as the professed provincials of the Jesuits and the Knights of Malta, who control and oversee the secret government in various regions of the world. Then comes the underbosses, who are appointed by the boss Godfathers and would be second in command in case the boss Godfather is in prison or dies. In the same manner, the Black Pope has chosen a successor in case something happens to him. Then comes the consigliere, who acts as the mafia's advisor. The Jesuit General has advisors in the form of his inner counsel, consigliore.

Then we have the capo regime, also known as the captains, who are in charge of running a particular crew in the mafia, and like the Jesuits, have their captains running things all over the world like the Knights of Malta. Finally, there are soldiers of the mafia, who are the representatives of the bosses when a drug deal is taking place. The Jesuits also have soldiers representing them in their huge covert operations and world cartels, like the High Shriner Freemasons working for the Illuminati. Finally, there are the associates at the bottom of the mafia, who are useful for running errands, representing the bosses in drug transactions. The Jesuits also have their lower soldiers, as in the case of John Wilkes Booth in the assassination of Lincoln and Lee Harvey Oswald in the assassination of Kennedy.

The Italian mafia originated in Sicily and became known as the Cosa Nostra Commission. The Godfather was established as the supreme boss controlling the entire worldwide commission. In the beginning, it was strictly in Italy, but later the Godfather, in an act of expanding the Cosa Nostra Commission, began sending his first band of mafiosos into the States, beginning with Giuseppe Esposito and his Sicilian associates who had been known to murder prominent wealthy landowners in Italy.

According to the Wikipedia World Encyclopedia, they were later arrested in New Orleans. Nevertheless, more waves of mafiosos came to the States and established several more branches. Their chosen region of arrival and central haven became New York, but later expanded into major cities such as Chicago, New Orleans, and Los Angeles. The first major families became the Bonannos, the Colombos, Gambinos, the Genoveses, and the Luccheses. Together they composed the entire Cosa Nostra Commission in the States.

Here's the connection between the Italian Mafia and the Jesuit Illuminati syndicate: The Italian Godfather, who acts as the absolute sovereign of the Commission, is under oath and under the direction of the Black Pope himself. Just like Hitler was part of a German secret society, the Thule, so is the Godfather part of a secret society known as the Knights of Malta.

Considering this, the Godfather further answers to a higher, more secretive power: the Black Pope. The evidence lies in the research of John Eric Phelps, who discovered that the entire Mafia Commission is controlled by the Supreme Jesuit General through the Knights of Malta.

An example of the Mafia secret government connection is how they work together in the distribution of drugs in America during and after the Vietnam War. Evidence now proves that the Black Pope's secret government engineered the Vietnam War through their puppet, Henry Kissinger, as an effort to control the drug explosion in China and Vietnam, as well as in other Asian countries that were producing massive amounts of heroin and opiates. This phony war enabled the secret government to have control of that region, allowing them to have absolute control over the entire international drug apparatus.

This information is shown in greater detail in "Vatican Assassins," a book written by Eric John Phelps. John Phelps's extensive research provides a link that shows how the Jesuits facilitated the wars in Vietnam to gain control of their agricultural drug reservoirs. He also reports the C.I.A. Counterintelligence Corps were used to transfer all of the heroin and opiates to the states for distribution by the Mafia families, like the Santos family and the Gambinos.

In addition, Mr. Phelps also informs that the high Mafia in the states was intimate with Joe Kennedy, who was the Knight of Malta, the father of John F. Kennedy. The American Mafia dons are also intimate and overseen by the Cardinal of New York in St. Patrick's Cathedral Square, Cardinal Edward Egan, who, like his successor Cardinal O'Connor and Francis Spellman, have been making sure that the truth behind the Kennedy assassination remains covered. Phelps has also revealed that the Cardinal of New York controls all of the military orders such as the Knights of Malta in the states as well as the Cosa Nostra Commission, which is all controlled by the secret government. This Cardinal oversees and directs all the black operations from St. Patrick Cathedral and answers directly to the Black Popes in accountants.

Another revelation comes from a hero who put his name on the line, Alberto Rivera, who was an ex-Jesuit priest providing the link between the Jesuits and the Cosa Nostra Commission. Mr. Rivera is no longer with us, for he was assassinated by the secret government. Mr. Rivera was a practicing Jesuit until he converted to Christianity and left the order. He wrote a series of magazines that revealed the real workings of the Vatican and the Jesuit masters. After his conversion to the light, Alberto Rivera became a great man of God, dedicating his whole life to the exposure of the Antichrist as the horror of the Earth Revelation 17 and 18. His insider role as a Jesuit priest provided definite proof connecting the Illuminati of today with the Jesuits.

We can decipher that the Italian Mafia wasn't the only criminal organization created by the secret government; there are hundreds of other mafias plaguing our role, including the notorious Russian mob and the Triads of China, as well as the Irish Mafia, the Mexican Mafia, the Colombian Mafia, etc. Almost every country in the world in which the secret government of the Black Pope has spread its beastly tentacles has created a mafia of their own. This fits in with the Protocols of the Learned Elders of Zion as they create the necessary chaos needed to bring death and destruction to as many goyim (human cattle) as possible.

Chapter 16: THE REAL WORLD TERRORISTS

In addition to implementing Protocol Number 2, the method of conquest, and Protocol Number 7, creating worldwide wars, here are other disturbing revelations that need to be uncovered. One of those is how the secret government uses all the resources and power to further consolidate their agenda over the world by creating international terrorist networks. It is known by many independent researchers and inside ex-intelligence officers that the radical Islamic terrorist academy was financed, sponsored, and directed from behind the scenes by the Jesuit Illuminati secret world government. For instance, there is substantial evidence that indicates that the Taliban, Al-Qaeda, as well as ISIS, were all creatures of their own C.I.A. particularly the Counterintelligence Corps.

As early as the 1970s, it was reported that the Bin Ladens were financed by the (CIC) to fight against the Soviets, as they wanted us to believe. However, this was another cover-up and never the case because, later, at the collapse of the Soviet Union, it was reported that he continued receiving money and support from our own C.I.A.

For instance, a well-researched paper titled "The Hidden Face of Terrorism" by Paul David Collins has provided irrefutable data connecting the creation of radical Islamic networks to the Illuminati Jesuit syndicate. Paul Collins also exposes Operation Northwoods, which is the Black Ops that allowed Castro to gain power in Cuba, which was also facilitated by the initiates of the C.I.A. serving the secret policy of the Council of Foreign Relations. Mr. Collins' shocking revelations provide documented data that proves that our own C.I.A. under the manipulation of the Illuminati, created the Mujahideen, a terrorist group in Afghanistan that was supposed to work against the Soviets in the 1980s.

He reveals that during the Cold War, the United States spent millions of dollars supplying Afghan children with textbooks filled with violent images and militant Islamic teachings under the assumptions of fighting communism. These are no other than the workings of the secret government who, through the Council on Foreign Relations, has been manipulating policy in the United States.

He goes on to expose how the Bush family had connections to Bin Laden and further reveals how they mutually owned a mega energy oil company known as Arbusto Energy Oil Company, implying that the Saudi royal families and the Bushes have been business partners all this time. Connected to this revelation was another book that revealed the same information from a source affiliated with the elite families. The book was titled "The Good Son" and it only lived on the shelves for two weeks because it was suppressed. This book disappeared and mysteriously so did the author, who had apparently been working with the elite families but had a change of heart and decided to expose the truth.

In light of this, we can conclude that Bin Laden and the entire Islamic terrorist networks have been deliberate creations of the secret government for various reasons. The primary one is to ignite the conflict needed between Western Christianity and Eastern Islam, as stated in the words of Albert Pike and the Protocols. This conflict is the second plot that is to foment World War 3 since the first one failed in order to usher in their world government.

This second plot highlights the overall agenda to use Islamic terrorism as a way to ignite another phony war to jump-start the third and final social cataclysm, as in the case of the prolonged Iraq war. One can now understand how the Sanhedrin's hidden hand engineered the differences that led to the never-ending schism between Israel and Palestine, thus providing "The Hidden Hand" indirect power over both. Another reason was to consolidate more power over the oil reserves in the Middle East. After all, the secret government wants to own all the resources before implementing their New World Order one-world government.

What is happening today is none other than the backup plan that was designed two centuries ago by the masterminds of the Jesuit Illuminati Syndicate. As revealed earlier, the first coup to impose world government following the Second World War in 1946 backfired. The secret government plotted a coup utilizing the Hegelian method on a large scale during the onset of the Cold War when Truman, under the direction of his superiors, launched a preemptive strike against the Soviet Union.

Bin Laden and his terrorist networks were used to create the terrorism needed as an excuse to pass more totalitarian laws and erode freedoms. The secret government needed a major attack that would give the executive branch absolute power over, thus overriding the Constitution in declaring martial law in the name of a national emergency. To this insanity, the Patriot Act was born, which marks the beginning stages of Big Brother in America. However, the Council on Foreign Relations did not have all the support of the Senate, and that is why this coup failed as well, thanks to the good people in power that later revealed themselves as the White Knights.

The real terrorists are not foreigners but those unseen powers that are the movers and shakers controlling the ranks of the entire secret world government. They function from behind the scenes in Washington as the executive order of the Council on Foreign Relations, the CFR, the secret government branch that controls the United States. Bin Laden was only one of many pawns working secretly for the Black Pope and his entire secret society network. Bin Laden's financing came from the Western American Anglo cartel. He is under payroll and has been revealed by John Phelps since 1970 because he had been working for the C.I.A., explaining why the C.I.A. never captured him. In fact, he and his family have been protected by the C.I.A., and the person that they lied about that they caught was an imposter. The real Bin Laden still lives.

Furthermore, it has been revealed that the monarchies of the entire Middle East, particularly the Arab nations, have been placed in power by the secret government of the Western elite in order to control the people and cause all-out wars, fulfilling the directives of the House of Rothschilds. These Saudis were planted as loyal puppets in those areas that are rich with oil so that the secret government could have indirect control of those regions. The consolidation of the world's oil companies has been in progress and part of the agenda for years.

New information shows that there was an intricate connection between the Western powerful families like the Rockefellers, Harriman's, and the Bushes to the Arab powerful royal families. All these families are playing their roles as puppets of the Black Pope to the tune of billions of dollars, which come directly from the international bankers who are under the direction of the House of Rothschild. Researchers have uncovered that while most pawns in the secret government play their role for the love of money, only a few have been aware of the true sinister plot that the secret government is trying to implement.

Also to note is that the dark forces within the Masonic branch grew to include many men from many nations as they became agents of the Jesuit Illuminati and were dispatched everywhere. For instance, Saddam Hussein and the high leaders of the Muslim nations, the Ayatollahs, were active members as Shriner Masons. Saddam Hussein decided to rebel against the Brotherhood, and they quickly turned the tables on him, which is why he was taken out. This is the international function of Masons who are controlled by the Knights of Malta and the Bavarian Illuminati after they have infiltrated the original Blue Lodge. It is believed that this dark Masonic Branch, known as the high Shriners, includes Arab nations and many other countries in the world.

Perhaps, on a more subliminal level, right-wing radical Islam, along with Western fundamental right-wing Christianity, are really instruments of the Dark Brotherhoods as they have always been fighting one another. Those are the Protocols in action. In fact, modern-day political Zionists have been controlling Israel and are puppets of the House of Rothschild, doing their part in the perpetuation of wars in the Middle East.

In truth, the secret government has always been coordinating all of these conflicts until a full-scale war has been achieved, as people continue to remain unaware of humanity's true enemy.

In light of all of this, there is ample evidence that reveals that the order on the attacks of the World Trade Center was obviously issued by the Black Pope, who went by the name of Count Hans Kolvenbach. He carried out and coordinated the entire network of the secret world government involving all the corrupt agencies that are working for the Black Pope. It is believed that in the pyramidal structure of this secret world government, all levels that are involved from the bottom up only answer to the levels right above them in a compartmentalized structure.

In this way, the top levels of the secret government can send a chain reaction that would mobilize thousands of men into action, who, for the love of money, are ignorantly serving the dictates of the Black Pope.

This explains why certain high-level C.I.A. players directed the whole thing in September 2001. Of course, they blamed it on their Islamic puppets who were even willing to sacrifice their life. Others suspected that the Muslim terrorists never boarded the airlines involved in the 9/11 attacks and that it was done through holographic advanced tech and planned demolition.

This attack could have been prevented, as evidence now reveals. The corrupt agencies under the direction of the Council on Foreign Relations and its puppets were directly responsible as they enabled and conspired to execute this act of treason. Some reports indicate that our own president had foreknowledge of the attacks. Pope John Paul II visited with President Bush two weeks prior to the attacks to warn Bush that the attacks were scheduled for the second week of September. The Bush Administration did nothing because they, unfortunately, are all silenced by the real secret government that controls them. The Executive Intelligence Review called this Administration a fascist one.

Those in the Bush administration, like Dick Cheney, as well as Rumsfeld and Rice, were all lackeys who had been placed in positions of power by powerful interest groups who had knowledge of the plot.

The 9/11 Cover-Up

Here are important facts providing that 9/11 was the deliberate workings of the secret government. This information was gathered by many independent researchers. According to Dr. Garth Nicholson, a foremost researcher of the Gulf War Syndrome, investigations revealed Pentagon officials confirmed intelligence indicating that on September 11, 2001, a terrorist strike against the Pentagon would take place. This warning was passed on to Condoleezza Rice but was ignored by the Bush administration. Another doctor, Leonard Horowitz, an award-winning author of several books, also alerted the government of the intended attacks, and he was also ignored.

Mr. Phelps advised that on Sunday, September 17, 2001, a CBS Television report entitled "60 Minutes" revealed that President Bush's close associates suddenly sold all their airline stock just a few days before the terrorist attacks. This story, like all other stories that exposed the truth, was buried as soon as the Council on Foreign Relations-controlled press got a hold of it. In addition, Mr. Phelps discovered that Osama Bin Laden and his terrorist team would not have pulled it off without the help of certain C.I.A. operatives who were under the direction of George Tenet, the C.I.A. director during the 9/11 attacks and a major CFR member and player in the red conspiracy.

In addition, Milt Bearden, who was hired by the C.I.A. as an advisor to Bin Laden, came clean in an interview with Dan Rather on September 12th. When Mr. Rather asked Milt about the culpability of Bin Laden, he answered that if they didn't have Osama Bin Laden, they would invent one.

On October 30, 2001, the French daily "Le Figaro" reported that Osama Bin Laden had met with a high-level C.I.A. official in July 2000. This was the time Bin Laden was being charged for the U.S. Embassy bombing as well as the U.S.S. Cole attacks. The meeting was held in Bin Laden's private suites in the plush Dubai hospital built by American construction companies for the care of the orders of Masonic royal Muslim families running the Islamic community and terrorist network on behalf of the C.I.A.

It is now apparent that the secret government, through the (CIC), controls all the Islamic networks in Pakistan, Iraq, Iran, Jordan, Syria, Lebanon, Egypt, Libya, and Turkey. These facts correspond to the words of Taliban leader Mullah Muhammad Omar, who stated in an interview on page 34 in a November issue of free America, "America controls the governments of Islamic countries," he was really referring to the secret government operating within the U.S. government. Furthermore, according to Aaron Swirski, one of the architects of the World Trade Center, stated that those towers were designed to withstand airplane collisions. He said, "I designed it for a 707 hit." The collapse of the buildings came as a complete shock to him and his colleagues. In support of this, Van Romero, a demolition expert and former member of the Energetic Materials Research and Testing Center and vice president for research at New Mexico Institute of Mining and Technology, stated that the manner in which the twin towers collapsed resembled those of controlled implosions used for planned demolition. According to Mr. Romero's observation and Mr. Swirski's revelations and a woman's testimony, there was the sound of a loud blast as she and others were exiting the building.

These are among a few facts that indicate the massive intelligence engineering and plotting that went behind the orchestration of 9/11. In truth, 9/11 was the Dark Brotherhood's last resource to override our Constitution, imposing martial law and arriving at a world centralized government. Even after 9/11, the secret government worked endlessly to undo our Constitution, but to no success. It has been reported by Mr. Lyndon LaRouche that on May 23, 2005, the Bush administration attempted to dissolve our Constitution by undoing the other two branches of government, giving the executive branch full power over all government. However, that coup was blocked. This goes to show that no matter how much the secret government attempts to achieve totalitarianism, they are unable to do so because of the good men that later became known as the White Knights.

The 9/11 atrocity served many purposes for the secret government. Considering the Jesuit Illuminati method of creating the problem, people reacting to it, and then offering their solution, the American people would never support an overt dictatorship. In evidence of this, there is no doubt that all the conflicts in the Middle East have been maneuvered by the members of the secret government in order to ignite the Third World War as their third and final social cataclysm. Therefore, in light of this, the Iraq War has been fraudulently driven by the same secret agenda that only those in the high ranks of the secret government know about. There was no doubt that the secret government was attempting to foment World War Three in order to impose their One World Government, the resurrected Holy Roman Empire.

Another important and very vital reason why the secret government chose the destruction of the Twin Towers was that the North Tower, particularly the 22nd, 23rd, and 24th floors, contained massive documents unveiling the corruption of the Council on Foreign Relations, the Counterintelligence Corps, secret government scandals, and all of the evidence needed to bring down this secret government cabal. These documents had been accumulated over time by the White Knights in government, who have remained loyal to the original Blue Lodge that gave us our Constitutional Republic. Over time, even though they have kept their existence private, there will come a day where they would reveal themselves to the world as the White Knights who have been fighting the secret government from behind the scenes.

These documents, which had been gathered by the White Knights, had been investigated by the good sanctions of the F.B.I., revealing massive evidence against James Clifton, the CEO of the CFR in 2000, and a major key tool for the secret government. Imagine the type of reformation that could have occurred if these high-level treasonous scandals had been exposed and dealt with in 2001. There is no doubt that this hidden group known as the White Knights had enough evidence to bring down the corruption of the secret government and remove all illegal institutions such as the Federal Reserve, the I.R.S., and the entire CFR embodiment, which is a branch of the Jesuit Illuminati syndicate.

Despite the fact that the rulers of this world have been serving the Luciferian cause and have had the upper hand, the forces of light have always been counteracting them and balancing the scales of power, preserving the concepts of freedom and protecting humanity until the restoration.

Chapter 17: THE NESARA

It is important to understand that the forces of darkness were only given temporary rule of our planet and that their time would come to an end. That time has come in our present day for the last cabal of the old guard that has ruled our planet for thousands of years is finally going to be defeated and exposed, by the guardians of our constitution, the resurfaced White Knights that signed the NESARA law and who have been blocking every attempt at dissolving our constitution, from the Dark Brotherhood.

The forces of light have never forsaken us and have waged an endless battle against the forces of darkness. We have seen this throughout all of history as the original descendants of the Holy Grail and the Knights Templars who secretly carried the torch of freedom throughout the Middle Ages. It is important to understand that the forces of light also operate on many levels and they were and are always steps ahead of the Dark Brotherhood. Touching on another important subject is the fact that there are angelic realms that exist in higher dimensions or densities that are also assisting us from behind the higher realms. In the lower Heavens, we have the Earth angels who never left the Earth round even after ascending and completing their program here on the Earth.

In mystical esoteric studies, these individuals became known as the ascended masters of light. As a result of mastering the Earth plane, they were transformed into immortals and have been guiding the evolutionary process of our planet from behind the scenes. It is believed in esoteric knowledge that from a higher perspective, even mortality was mandatory for the growth and expansion of all souls in the universe.

Despite the many mysteries shrouding the great Initiates of light, the ascended masters and those White Knights that are the surviving Templars and original Blue Lodge members of the positive secret societies, have never left the scene.

Let's face it, there were always two brotherhoods, the brotherhood of darkness as directed by the Fallen Angels and the Brotherhood of Light who are directed by the angels of light. As mentioned earlier in Chapter 8, the Brotherhood of light has never left the scene; they have always operated from behind the scenes and this explains why the Dark Brotherhood has never been fully successful in their attempt to implement their Luciferian agenda.

In light of this, there is an opposite agenda that the White Brotherhood has been trying to execute for millennia and that is known as the Great Work of All Ages. In esoteric studies, the Great Work of All Ages is about restoring the Earth back to the Golden Age. In light of this, let me reveal that there have always been two parts within the networks of light from a higher dimension: we have the ascended masters and ladies of light that have guided the spiritual evolution from behind the scenes. On a more third-dimensional level of reality, we have had their third-dimensional counterparts which are the man and woman that have always been associated with the positive secret societies that can be traced back to Jesus and Mary Magdalene as mentioned earlier.

All throughout history, we have seen the effects of the ascended masters and the networks of light throughout our planet. Their influence has been experienced in several moments of light and prosperity and even the creation of America was maneuvered into place by some of these ascended masters of the planetary spiritual hierarchy who have been guiding their third-dimensional instruments that became our founding fathers. For example, it was ascended master St. Germain the adept of the flame of freedom and holder of the transmuting 7th Violet ray who was the mastermind of America. Ascended Master Saint Germain has been known to be the force behind the Russian order of light and the harbinger of the Blue Lodge Masonic network. Some even claim he would have been the higher self of George Washington.

In fact, right before the final signing of the Declaration of Independence, certain men were hesitant to sign the declaration because of their repeated failed attempts. Under British policy, they knew if they hatched another revolt that they would all be hanged. However, a mysterious stranger appeared at the signing and encouraged all to sign in a speech arousing and igniting the desire for freedom in them once again. They all signed the declaration and as they turned back to see if the inspiring figure was there, he had vanished into thin air. This mysterious figure was none other than Saint Germain, who is an ascended being and holder of the Violet transmuting flame of freedom.

Throughout history, the ascended masters (Earth Angels) have been guiding humanity as the planetary spiritual hierarchy that has been revealed in esoteric literature. They are the creators and facilitators of the Brotherhood of Light and have worked with great seers, prophets, and mystics all throughout the ages. The mysterious Melchizedek of Salem who initiated and bestowed the high priesthood of Melchizedek to Abraham was an ascended being and part of the Brotherhood of Light.

As mentioned earlier, Enoch was the first grandmaster who became known as the great initiator of light in our ancient past, beginning the work of the Great White Brotherhood in our world. The contributions of Enoch became the forerunner of the Blue Lodge in modern times that used to also exist in the ancient world establishing the procedures of gradual knowledge or grades of attainment into divinity or in esoteric terms reaching oneness atonement with God. This process of initiation continued through the Melchizedek order Abraham and Moses who were all high initiates of this Brotherhood and adepts of the sacred knowledge.

The Brotherhood of Light in the east has also contributed to the preservation of ancient knowledge including cosmology, metaphysics, and all aspects of ageless wisdom. Just like the Brotherhood of Light in the west form an initiatory system based on grades of ascent, so has the Brotherhood of Light in the east continuing their traditions in secret and guarding their knowledge away from the profane and wicked men who are always seeking to invert and corrupt the knowledge.

There exists a different type of government that is more of a spiritual nature than the governments we have witnessed on our Earth plane. This type of spiritual government is constituted by ascended beings also known as Earth angels that have ascended in the past. As the Great White Brotherhood and through their correspondence here on Earth, the positive secret societies have always opposed and counteracted the efforts of the Luciferian brotherhood even up until modern times. As mentioned earlier, they were the force behind the Reformation, the Renaissance, and the Scientific Revolution, and also the forces in modern times that restored the Sovereign Nation-State Republic.

These positive networks on Earth have always realized that the Great Work of All Ages originated within the mind of God and have carried it forward by the people that are aligned with what is good. It is believed, as revealed in my next upcoming book, "Our Cosmic Origin," that they have been closely working together with celestial non-terrestrial intelligences in order to liberate this planet from the dark force that extends beyond our planetary sphere.

Since we do live in a universe that is inhabited by many worlds and many realms, dimensions, it is important to state that the war against evil originated when Archangel Michael began to cleanse the higher Heavens from the fallen legions that eventually contaminated the lower levels of reality. Therefore, it is important to understand that due to the rise of a new era, the time for the forces of darkness is up, and the good people of the Earth will bring about a change that will transform the political, social, economic structures, and restore our planet back to a golden era.

This procedure is being carried forward through a law known as NESARA that would eventually include the entire planet under GESARA. For example, in the political arena, the Guardians of our Republic, those that were associated with the Blue Lodge, now known as the White Knights, have issued a massive Reformation to dismantle all of the tentacles of the secret government. This Reformation has been bestowed to us by God through the White Knights. This dispensation will begin with the implementation of a law known as NESARA, which stands for the National Economic Security and Reformation Act, also known as the National Economic Stabilization and Recovery Act.

This Reformation will remove all systems of oppression by reinstating them with balanced, workable systems of global prosperity. It will influence the way we conduct science and education, opening the doors to a higher understanding of where spirituality and science become one once again. NESARA/GESARA is an eclectic program for the fullness of time.

Going back to the 9/11 coup, part of the records destroyed in the 22nd level and 23rd floors of the World Trade Center were the NESARA programs, which, in conjunction with the massive criminal evidence, would serve to immediately implement the necessary reforms first in the United States and hence the reformation worldwide. This would eliminate the Jesuit Illuminati globalization programs of the fascist One World Government and dissolve them.

It is believed that the reason why the creatures of Jekyll Island have failed in totally subduing the constitutional Republic of the United States government is because the White Knights, those that remained loyal to the Blue Lodge, survived and worked in secret two steps ahead of the secret government to protect the constitutional Republic of the United States and the freedoms of the world. Therefore, NESARA/GESARA is to be more than just a mere political and economic reformation; it is the uprooting and dismantling of the entire worldwide structure of the Jesuit Illuminati syndicate group.

NESARA began with investigations conducted by U.S. Supreme Court judges after many farmers lost their farms in the Midwest due to illegal banking foreclosures. The fraudulent operations were illegally performed by certain banks in conjunction with corrupt government officials from the Council on Foreign Relations. It was also discovered that the

Federal Reserve System, along with the I.R.S., was never properly ratified, as stated in the NESARA files.

In 1993, Supreme Court judges ruled in favor of the farmers on all major issues, including that the Federal Reserve System and the I.R.S. were unconstitutional and that the U.S. government had been operating outside of the Constitution since 1933.

The judges decided that major reformation of government and banking systems were required, and remedies needed to be provided for all the financial losses suffered by the United States and its citizens. It was reported that due to the extraordinary nature of the reformation, the court sealed all court records and placed all the people directly involved under non-disclosure agreements, known as gag orders. This tells us who controls most of the Supreme Court judges, apparently. These orders would stand until the reformation was publicly and officially announced. The NESARA Announcement and Reformation were going to be announced on September 11th, 2001, a few hours before the 9/11 attacks. Along with the NESARA records were records revealing all of the Council on Foreign Relation criminal activity against the U.S. Constitution and the free world.

The court had a duty to implement the Reformation due to a massive amount of injustice and corruption. The good judges not affiliated with the Council on Foreign Relations recruited experts from fields of economics, banking, and constitutional law to work on the case with task force groups in order to proceed in the development of the reformation. Here we see the White Knights of the Brotherhood of Light at work.

After two years of working on the case, the experts developed irrefutable proof providing that the 16th amendment, the I.R.S., was never ratified, and therefore the judges had no choice but to include the abolishment of income taxes along with the abolishment of the Federal Reserve. In addition, it was also discovered that federal administrations and Congress had been ignoring the Constitution and its laws since 1933. This was largely accomplished by Council and Foreign Relation members Jacob Schiff, Bernard Baruch, and Colonel Mandel House, placed in top government positions since the Dark Brotherhood established the Council on Foreign Relations in 1921.

Technically, according to all this, the U.S. began operating outside its constitutional boundaries when Woodrow Wilson signed the Federal Reserve into existence as early as 1913. Experts working on the government Reformation determined that to end the pattern of blatant disregard by ignoring our constitutional laws, it would be necessary for the current Administration in U.S. Congress, which is polluted with Council and Foreign Relation puppets, to all resign immediately following the NESARA announcement.

That would probably be over 50% of Congress, including members in both the House of Representatives and the Senate. These reformations were signed by Bill Clinton in 1999. The National Economic Security and Reformation Act would provide worldwide benefits.

The first and foremost is that it restores constitutional law in America the way the founding fathers wanted it to be as a system based on the commonwealth of the people and for the people. Secondly, it would require the current Administration to resign their positions to allow a fresh start at the national level by installing a constitutionally accepted NESARA President and Vice President who have absolutely no ties to the agenda of the secret government. Since the Council on Foreign Relations holds major control over Congress, new candidates would have to be voted in.

This would rid the American government of all agents planted in power by the Council of Foreign Relations and their Jesuit Illuminati overlords. In addition to the implementation of this Reformation, there would also be immediate peace, ending all of the current wars in the world which had been maneuvered by the secret government. It would also resolve the current global economic crisis that the world has been thrown into by replacing it with a New Bretton Woods system based on the good neighbor policy that would benefit all of humanity.

Furthermore, as a partial remedy for the 100 years of government and banking fraud, credit card balances would zero out, and debt would be remedied from all bank loans, including mortgage, auto, education, and business loans, because all the financing was coming from the Federal Reserve. Most importantly, it would rectify the astronomical debt incurred on our country by the Federal Reserve private banking cartel, and all the citizens would be debt-free. The Federal Reserve would be abolished and replaced by a U.S. treasury.

This law is also to include the Global Reformation and Security Act that would restore the economic infrastructures of all the countries that have been affected by the secret government. In addition, this would also dissolve the Trilateral Commission, the Bilderbergers, and all of those secret societies that have been working with the international cartel. It is obvious that if it wasn't for the 9/11 atrocities, this law would have been implemented in 2001, and the world would have been a better place.

Today there still remains a gag order on the NESARA, preventing its announcement, which is soon going to be dissolved as the powers of the secret government become dismantled and removed from our world. It has been reported that our country is facing the worst crisis of its history because of the legal economic injustices. Most Americans had faced unemployment and had been drowning in debt. The poverty rate is increasing, especially since General Motors and other companies have crashed due to the secret government's intent to collapse our economic infrastructure.

We've lost many men in battle because of this secret government that is and has been trying to dominate our world. The truth is that even our elections revolve around lies, bribery, and betrayals. The forces that control elected officials and our government are the high unseen powers and secret societies that have been working for the Black Pope since 1501. Jacob Schiff, as revealed earlier, was the main person that gained absolute control of the press and media and has been spreading false indoctrinations and false information to the American people regarding the truth since the 1930s.

Therefore, we won't hear the truth in the mainstream news and only lies and misinformation as planned by the Learned Elders of Zion. The media has been covering up everything for decades and is working to serve their secret masters. Perhaps many people in the media don't have any inclination of the extent of the secret government control. However, it is at the highest level of the media that is being manipulated by the secret government of the Council and Foreign Relations.

Moreover, these unseen powers have been poisoning humanity and the free world and have achieved major accomplishments in their quest for absolute power. Let me remind us of the words of one of our greatest American heroes, Abraham Lincoln: "We the people are the rightful masters of both Congress and the Senate, not to overthrow the Constitution but to overthrow the men who pervert the Constitution." Thomas Paine said, "The cause of America is in a great measure the cause of all humanity." It is true; as America goes, so does the world. This great nation affects all of mankind, as Mr. Paine states, it is this great nation that is ultimately hampering the secret government from succeeding and accomplishing their age-long agenda of world domination.

The necessary Reformation is to take place first in America, and then the entire world would follow. The second part of the NESARA programs is to release the prosperity programs the White Knights have been working diligently to secure from the elites. The White Knights have been the instruments working towards redirecting all of the consolidated wealth that has concentrated in the hands of the few, distributing it back to the people of the world as it was meant to be. The prosperity programs are part of NESARA law as confirmed in biblical prophecy that the power and wealth of the world is to return to the people of Earth, who are the true heirs of divinity and abundance as children of the one God.

It is a responsibility as Americans to follow in the same footsteps as our founding fathers and restore our country back. We must petition our government to announce and implement the new law that will preserve the free world and the Republic. The NESARA website reported that the World Court ruled on August 22nd, 2002, the justice removed many gag orders, and that radio and television talk show hosts across the country began broadcasting this information to the public for the first time.

In November of 2003, activities moved to a different front with individuals and groups taking a role in the presentation for the golden age. It was also reported in that same year that the supreme autocratic leader of the secret government, the Black Pope, was removed from our Earth by the forces of light and is now facing charges for his crimes against humanity. Congruent with cosmic shifts, the month of November in that year also marks what most spiritual people call the Harmonic Concordance.

This means that there was a major shift in energy that tilted the planetary energy field toward the light of higher frequency. Apparently, our energy field has been mostly dark and gloomy due to the negative energy that has accumulated for centuries or perhaps thousands of years under the control of the dark forces. For those of you who understand the functions and workings of energy fields, this makes a lot of sense. For those of you who don't, I will elaborate more about this in the next few paragraphs. However, more information on energy transmissions, shifts, planetary cycles, and cosmic cycles will be shared in the next book to come, "Our Cosmic Origin," which will be a continuation of this material.

Other revelations were also reported; for instance, in 2005, things began to boil up when the Jesuit Illuminati Syndicate attempted to derail the announcements by using nuclear hydrogen explosions to destroy the whole planet while the secret government and their elites hid away in underground caverns. The Dark Brotherhood will not go without a bang, meaning that in the event that they get taken out, they want to take out humanity with them. Luckily for the people of the

Earth, the nuclear reactors became neutralized, and nothing detonated, thanks to the White Knights and the forces behind them.

In conclusion, the announcement and implementation of NESARA since its inception has been central to the ongoing struggle between good and evil in our world. The Bible predicts the last battle of Armageddon will occur on this planet, symbolizing a time when Archangel Michael and the Heavenly hosts complete the purification of higher realms, indicating a parallel need to address the turmoil on Earth. The unveiling of the secret government allows us to understand the forces that have, for millennia, maneuvered global events from the shadows, often referred to as the representatives of Lucifer.

Does Evil Have a Purpose? A Final Warning to the Dark Brotherhood.

The truths revealed, tracing the lineage and intent of the Dark Brotherhood from post-diluvian times through the eras to the secretive Luciferian societies of Babylon, elucidate an age-old agenda for global domination under a despotic regime. This narrative underscores that history is not a series of random events but a deliberate orchestration by clandestine societies wielding significant influence. This book posits that the universe operates on deliberate intelligence, negating the notion of coincidence; every cause produces an effect, adhering to universal laws.

In the cosmic scheme, truth invariably emerges victorious, affirming the existence of a Supreme Being orchestrating creation, fully aware of every nuance. This grand cosmic play of polarity integration serves a divine purpose: it fosters the evolution of consciousness across all realms, propelled by the inherent dynamism of the Divine.

The presence of the Dark Brotherhood, or the principle of duality, is indispensable for souls to experience the full spectrum of existence, thereby ensuring the universe's perpetual expansion and perfection. Without duality, the universe would stagnate, contradicting the observed cosmic expansion. The ultimate triumph of light over darkness is assured by the governance of a Supreme Being, positing evil as merely a deviation from light, remediable through love and compassion.

This narrative suggests that if the Divine had intended to eliminate evil at its inception, it would have been feasible. However, the existence of free will in the universe mandates that all occurrences serve a higher purpose, contributing to growth through the learning derived from choices and their repercussions. This process underpins the cosmic law of karma or the metaphysical principle of reciprocity.

From a broader perspective, the cycle of creation, involution, and evolution provides souls with comprehensive existential experiences, facilitating their ascent to higher consciousness. This journey allows each soul, as a divine spark, to achieve unity with the totality of existence.

Understanding darkness as a necessary counterbalance to light and goodness contextualizes evil as a transient yet essential element in the grand cosmic design. Those who currently align with darker forces, playing their designated roles, are, in essence, our kin, having once belonged to the grand celestial family of light. We are all manifestations of the same divine essence, evolving at varying degrees within the vast spectrum of the singular, all-encompassing light.

A Message to the Dark Side

I extend an invitation to those within the cabal to willingly embrace change towards goodness and light, as the time of significant transition, often referred to as the great harvest, is imminent, in alignment with ancient prophecies. The removal of your leader, the Black Pope, along with numerous sorcerers, warlocks, and black magicians, was a necessary step due to their central role in the Luciferian agenda. For those who continue to engage in darkness independently, be warned: the repercussions of your actions, your karma, will surpass any harm you have inflicted on others. The clock is ticking for those still enacting roles of darkness; a significant cleansing is approaching, poised to eradicate such forces. As we near the conclusion of various cycles, it is time for you to relinquish your control and join the broader community of light.

Consider this perhaps your final warning, as events are rapidly unfolding. Relinquish your dominion over humanity and unite with us to partake in the forthcoming era of peace and prosperity, symbolized by the millennium or Golden Age, and the bountiful tree of eternal life and glory promised in the Age of Aquarius.

The era of malevolence is concluding; the extensive experiment with duality is drawing to a close, and the universe's natural state of oneness, disrupted by what is termed 'the fall' in Christian doctrine, is being restored.

Echoing the "Chronicles of Narnia", Aslan's spirit is rekindled through the many volunteers present today, signaling the transition from a prolonged period of darkness to an imminent Age of Enlightenment, heralded by the enactment of NESARA/GESARA laws.

This serves as a stark warning to adherents of darkness: abandon your agendas or face inevitable removal, experiencing the compounded return of all pain and suffering you've caused, in accordance with the inexorable universal law of karma, and the principle of cause and effect.

You may have observed the diminishing influence of the once-dominant Knights of Malta and high-ranking Jesuits, following the dictates of the Black Pope. Those who remain, mere puppets and clones, are also slated for removal.

The envisioned one-world government, stoked by the dark forces, has been extinguished by the White Knights and the burgeoning forces of righteousness. It is time to acknowledge the triumph of light. The age of illusion and secrecy has ended; we are entering a new era characterized by transparency, harmony, and unconditional love, where all truths will be unveiled.

The palpable shifts are acknowledged by those spiritually attuned. I propose a comprehensive declaration of investigation by the conscientious global community, encompassing political, religious, scientific, and educational-spheres, to unearth and rectify historical-distortions, allowing truth to emerge from suppression.

Transitioning to a higher dimension does not signify the end of physical existence but heralds the evolution to a more refined, immortal physical form within a higher reality. Those unacquainted with ancient wisdom, including metaphysics, cosmology, and mystical prophecy, may struggle to grasp the reality of multidimensional existence encompassing all life forms on Earth. This sacred knowledge, once the preserve of ancient sages and masters of light, is now accessible to all.

Quantum physics has contributed significantly to this awakening, elucidating that our physical essence and all matter in the universe are composed of energy, frequency, and vibration, revealing the fundamental energetic nature of all existence. Matter, in essence, is condensed energy, a form of trapped light within particles of negative mass, vibrating at low frequencies.

Chapter 18: THE NEW SPIRITUAL ERA

This would mark the end of the reign of the Dark Brotherhood. Everything that seems solid is really an illusion held together by our third-dimensional perception. Solid matter is empty space at its subatomic level. For example, the lower the frequency of matter, the more apart the electrons revolve around its nucleus. The higher the frequency, the more intact are the electrons revolving around the nucleus, making this matter frequency invisible to the naked eye of limited third-dimensional perception. The illusion resides in the third dimension where matter is vibrating at a very low frequency. The real reality lies in the higher dimensions of energy matter vibration.

There is no such thing as empty space for all is matter, light energy vibrating at particular rates. The only difference is the rate of the frequency of its vibration. In other words, all the dimensions are only separated by the degree of vibration, and all the dimensions occupy the same space at the same time. Unfortunately, humans have been limited to the realities of the third-dimensional frequency of reality, which is one of the lowest expressions of energy in the universe and the reason why death only exists in the lower dimension frequencies.

A veil has clouded our spiritual vision, separating our world from the entire spectrum of the multiple bands of frequency, or what an esoteric circle is known as the higher Spheres of Heaven. In essence, Heaven is just a change of vibration away; the higher plane of existence is still there. We can't see them because we are vibrating at a low frequency. They are only visible to those who have attained a high level of consciousness by raising their vibration, piercing through the veil of the third dimension, and refining their vision to the higher planes—the higher frequencies.

Only gifted, spiritual people have been known to have etheric vision, which is spirit vision. This is what mystical Christianity has called the gifts of the spirit. We can clearly see these abilities and characteristics of piercing through the veil by the seers and mystics. As the veil gets lifted, the original extra sensory perceptions that we once had will be restored. We will be able to see and experience life on a higher frequency, something we haven't done for about 10,000 years.

The beautiful Earth we live on is also a sentient being, and it's fulfilling its own evolutionary course in the grand scheme of things. Our nurturing planet is, in a way, like a human being. She is a living entity with her own soul, and everything that comprises her physical composition is also composed of energy frequency vibration. In essence, men's physical body and Earth are not only made of the same matter but are evolving parallel to each other. Even though our planet has fallen into a low frequency of vibration due to the interception of the dark forces, she is ready to be exalted again.

Together with our Earth, we have been in a fallen state from higher vibrations. This is where the great cosmic axiom validates the reality that we are all connected at the energy level that permeates and binds all existence. The Earth, like men, is ready to come home and be restored to her original frequency of higher energy vibration, which is at the fifth dimension where spiritual energy and matter meet in a perfect equilibrium balance. In terms of Christianity, salvation means being saved by grace after you have accepted Christ as your personal savior.

In the more evolved circles of spiritual mystical Christianity, salvation is not only having faith but also emulating and expressing Christ Consciousness through our works, our thoughts, and deeds, attempting to live a life of service to others. Ascension atonement has always been the true meaning of salvation in the esoteric tradition. The more a person is spiritually enlightened, the more he or she reaches salvation. Both Eastern and Western mystics agree that this is the true meaning of salvation and being born again.

In the universal principles, there is a law of return. Some of you are aware of the secret which emanates from a person whether through action or thoughts it will manifest in their life. This truth is one of the many suppressed secrets the secret government has kept from humanity since ancient times. This goes hand in hand with the Eastern truth of karma, with in science is known as the law of cause and effect. Unfortunately, the dark forces have always kept these universal principles from humanity in order to keep them thinking negatively and in fear.

We are now making a full turn toward realizing the universal truth that it all starts with the self for each of us is a micro version of the macro universe. In other words, in us there is divinity waiting to be activated. By having the right knowledge and applying the right patterns in our lives, we can learn how to be masters of our own destiny, thus manifesting anything we want in our lives by taking control of our thoughts and actions. This realization is slowly awakening more and more people each day as people are beginning to become self-realized which leads to enlightenment having tune to the right frequency the Christ light which leads to salvation ascension atonement with the source of all creation.

The ascension process is a procedure every living soul of the planet eventually takes. Only a few have been able to complete the process and completely unite all of their vehicles by fusing them into one body, the light body composed of the spirit, mind, and form—the physical body. True ascension is the integration of both our spirit and our form, which is our body, so we may resemble the nature of the universal father and Mother.

Before I explain ascension, we must understand the true nature of our total self. We are spiritual beings having a human experience; we are really our soul, which in turn is a fragment or spark of Source. Even our spirit is a vehicle for our soul, as well as our mind and our body. Those of us who have studied the true nature of human beings understand that it depends on the operation of seven major primary vehicles or wheels we call chakras. The swirl-like vortexes or miniature pools of energy are able to harness cosmic energy of our universe to enter and sustain all of our vehicles, allowing our soul to experience life on different levels of existence.

There are 12 chakras, but most only know of the primary seven. Each chakra is responsible for one of the major functional aspects in our body and represents a certain frequency or color tone in the light spectrum since we are all light beings made in the image of our creator.

Our physical body is composed of three lower vehicles and four higher ones. The three lower vehicles are our physical form, with our physical body being at the lowest point of vibration; then comes the emotional vehicle, which corresponds to the astral plane as the second vehicle; and finally, the mental body, corresponding to the etheric plane of existence as the most subtle but yet most powerful vehicle in the composition of the lower three. It is important to understand that in the Ascension process, the mastering of these three vehicles is the first three initiations.

After one has mastered their body, emotions, and mind by acquiring control of their entire functions, one has completed the three levels of initiation. Then comes the emotional body, which corresponds to the astral plane of existence, composing the plane of our emotional frequency. By mastering this vehicle, one has completed the second initiation. After our emotional body comes our mental body, which marks the highest of the three lower vehicles that compose our physical composition. The mental body is also the most subtle of the three and the most powerful for it corresponds to the etheric plane of existence.

The mental body is one of the most important ones because this vehicle is the bridge between the higher lighter subtle bodies and the lower ones. The etheric plane of existence is also where energy is vibrating at a higher rate than in the denser vibrational states like the emotional and physical dense vehicles. Thoughts are more fluid and more powerful because they exist in the etheric plane, and when enough energy is put into them, they begin to take form and materialize into the physical plane of existence.

In fact, everything in the physical plane of existence first originated as a thought form in the etheric plane of reality. The mental body is also the bridge between the world of form and the world with no form. The mastering of this vehicle is the mastering of our thoughts and marks the third initiation. After the mental vehicle comes the four higher bodies of light, which make up our invisible aspects which many of us don't know exist. This is where our initiations become a little bit more difficult.

The first of our four higher levels of bodies is the intuitional vehicle where our spirit resides. This plane is also characterized as the Buddha plane because it is when the individual finally awakens to the realization of their divinity within them. This is where true enlightenment begins to set in, as in the case of the Buddha, and marks the fourth initiation. After the attainment of the intuitional plane, the aspirant comes closer to the attainment of the Christ light, causing a cultivation and activation of the Christ within, which is characterized as the divine self. After reaching and mastering this level, the fifth initiation is achieved. It is also at this level of awakening that one can perform great miracles, such as healing, and becomes clairvoyant, acquiring etheric and spiritual vision as the gifts of the spirit begin working through them. This is the level most mystics function from.

In fact, this is the divine science that Jesus and Mary Magdalene taught when they overcame death and resurrected as perfected spiritual beings. Jesus proved to mankind the way of ascension, but his teachings were corrupted, unfortunately, and shrouded in parables and allegories by the temporary powers of this world who did not want the rest of humanity to ascend.

The next level of initiation involves the attainment and anchoring of the monadic plane of existence, which comes after an initiate completes the sixth initiation and is ready to ascend into their higher causal body of light. Jesus demonstrated this when he reappeared to his apostles on the third day following the crucifixion. In the 7th and final initiation, an individual ascends into their over self-body, which is the seventh spiritual vehicle. The realization and attainment of the seventh spiritual vehicle not only mark the completion of ascension but also reunites one's soul with the soul of all, which is God.

The five outer vehicles, which comprise the bodies of light, are the AKA body of light, the Gematrian body of light, the epi-kinetic body of light, the electromagnetic body of light, and the Zohar body of light, as revealed in The Keys of Enoch The Book of Knowledge by J.J. Hurtak.

With the completion of the Ascension, one becomes their higher self, the true immortal being as made in the image of God. This image is the original image we were made in, also known as our Adam Kadmon. The Adam Kadmon body is the integrating point of pure cosmic energy and physical form fused together, which is our original blueprint and marks the fusing of our other non-functioning strands of D.N.A., thus becoming a perfect being with 12 functioning strands of D.N.A. potential.

After completing the seven levels of initiation, and the individual ascends, he or she begins functioning on all levels of the entire composition of the light energy spectrum. This will activate all of the 12 chakra systems, allowing them to plug into different realities at will. Here, she or he may now operate on multiple dimensions in the spectrum of the light energy vibration and are no longer limited to the gross physical plane of the third dimension. It is only when one has reunited with God that they may be truly free and liberated from all bondage and have come home to their original frequency.

It is the realization and mastering of each of these levels or planes of existence that marks our ascension into our original divine self. Our soul, which has always existed, descended into the lower planes of gross matter in order to explore the denser planes of existence. In order to complete a proper ascension, we needed to descend into the third dimension so that we could experience the full spectrum of light, which is life in the lower Earth plane. Now that the universal process is reversing, as the breath of God is in effect, it is time to come home with a perfect physical body of pure energy refined matter.

Once the individual is once again united with their Divine self, they have completed the ascension and are at one with God and everything else in the universe. Most ascended beings, however, choose to stay behind in the higher fourth dimension of our world to assist the rest of humanity until the great day of graduation comes. The ascension process begins with the understanding that we are children of light and made in the similitude of our creator. Once the aspirant realizes this truth, then they begin the process towards achieving and cultivating such discovery.

Normally, this involves a deep desire within the individual to want to understand the true meaning of life, the universe, and our purpose as human beings. This curiosity opens up the individual to the understanding of cosmic principles or what is known as universal laws. The understanding and realization of these principles begin their journey towards ascension. In the ancient world, great temples and academies of light were erected by the Brotherhood of Light to begin the gradual initiation of the human race back into their original divine estate.

The existing embodiment of Luciferians, unfortunately, caused this process to succumb to secrecy and almost to oblivion. Religion became the only exotic outer lesser teachings that survived after the fall of Greece. It was the destruction of the great city and temple of Ephesus that completed the suppression of the higher mysteries, which continued through the order of Melchizedek in secret. After the destruction and attempted elimination of the higher mysteries, the process of ascension resorted to the underground. The orders of light survived, and these once suppressed truths are now making their way back into open view.

Because of the suppression of the higher mysteries, the Brotherhood of Light, through the prophets, mystics, and seers, encoded its significance in allegory and symbols to conceal this knowledge from the wicked. Thus, the Bible produced a combination of what once was pure doctrinal knowledge, the higher mysteries, with the integration of the lesser mysteries. The books in the scriptures were originally inspired by good people, but due to the infiltration of the Luciferian brotherhood, a lot of its purity has been lost. The forces of darkness have always sought to twist things to fit their agenda of world domination. Perhaps this is why the Roman Catholic Church was maneuvered by the Babylonian brotherhood to cut humanity off from the higher wisdom that would restore them back to their divinity. That is why Catholics were never supposed to read the Bible until the reformation.

Light and spiritual knowledge go hand in hand. The Dark Brotherhood knew that an enlightened human race would be impossible to control. If it were up to them, humanity would have remained in darkness forever, enslaved to them. If this were the case, the human race would eventually cease to exist because we do not live by bread alone but by the light as the primary source of our reality.

We human beings have fallen from a divine state in which we once existed. The ascension process is the only method of heading to that state of balance and integrating our true self so that we can regain our immortality. True salvation is the attainment of our higher self and its original essence. We are saved once we achieve the fifth level of initiation, which is the awakening, an activation of the Christ mind within. Therefore, the original meaning of salvation is liberation from the bonds of the third-dimensional plane of existence. This ultimately leads the individual to reconnect themselves back to the spiritual realms.

The universal truth has been kept secret by the Brotherhood of Light so that the Dark Brotherhood would not have any inclination of when their time was up. It is the ascension of our planet Earth that marks the end of the dark forces on Earth as she becomes cleansed by a special type of fire known as the transmuting flame of fire, which transmutes all negative energy of low-frequency vibration into its original frequency in the fifth dimension where balance is once again attained.

We've established that everything is energy and that there are multiple levels or planes of vibration given in all of existence. The Dark Brotherhood has been curtailed from the fifth dimension and can no longer exist in those frequency waves of vibration because it has been decreed by our universal architect that destructive energy is no longer allowed in the spheres of the fifth dimension and above. This corresponds to the cleansing and restoration process conducted by Archangel Michael and the entire cosmic Brotherhood of Light that have been cleansing and purging all negative energy from the higher worlds to the lower worlds of dense matter.

Upon this event, the Earth will enter the time of her ascension into the fifth dimension where evil is not allowed to exist. This is the true meaning of a new Earth. Only the Dark Brotherhood and wickedness will disintegrate by the time our planet ascends into the fifth dimension. According to the records of the Great White brotherhood and the now esoteric mysteries of higher knowledge which have emerged, the ascension of our beloved planet is to be completed in a matter of years from now. This implies that Heaven on Earth is only a few years away, which is bad news for the forces of darkness and good news for humanity who will be ready to ascend into the higher densities of a new Earth.

Many people have already awakened from their long sleep and spiritual ignorance, and upon reading this material, many more should be awakening to the realization of the Christ within our higher self. That realization fosters the first initiation of the ascension process. The Earth is ready to ascend sometime within the next two decades.

Great changes are underway, beginning at the subatomic level then reaching the molecular level, which affects all our physical composition as Mother Earth and humanity collectively ascend into the fifth-dimensional frequency where Heaven exists.

The only difference is that our subatomic and molecular structures will now be operating at a higher vibrational frequency, making our body more subtle and less dense. This will eliminate the aging process and all illnesses as we inherit and transform into our new body.

However, there are certain things that need to be known regarding the ascension of planet Earth. First, the Dark Brotherhood knows that they only have a few years left to fulfill their ancient Luciferian agenda. Since they are being eliminated from the highest levels of their pyramidal power structure, beginning with the Black Pope who was removed in 2003, they don't stand a chance to impose a One World Government anymore. The only ones unaware of the prophesied Earth reformations predicted in the ancient records of the Brotherhood of Light are those individuals and groups still functioning in the lower levels of negative secret societies. This is why they are still trying to bring forth the New World Order and cling to their positions of power.

If they knew their master's had been removed, they would probably give in. Apparently, these lower puppets have no clue and are still pursuing their long-awaited one world government agenda. They are acting without the support of their masters, who have been controlling their strings from the top of the pyramid since ancient times. They are like programmed robots doing what they have been trained to do.

On a good note, the forces of light are bringing in pressure from all angles through the White Knights; the flame for world government is being put out, and this planet is scheduled to be free as it ascends into a higher dimension. It is perhaps in the best interest of those puppets to change their direction and agenda because if they don't, they will face penalties on the great and dreadful day of the Solar Flash.

This message goes out to the last of the remaining cabals and to the entire planet. Those who are still exploring the negative lower frequencies associated with malice and wickedness are going to get what's coming if they don't change their ways. The raising of the frequency of the planet is going to purge all of those who are not ready to ascend into the higher vibrations of peace, love, cooperation, and unity.

It is very critical that this information be known at this time. Entertaining low energy fields of vibration such as fear, hatred, greed, and anger—mainly negative emotions which germinate at the etheric, mental, and astral level emotional plane of reality—is making it harder for them to ascend with the planet into the higher frequencies that only recognize positive emotions such as love, acceptance, unity, harmony, non-judgment, with unconditional love being the dominant force pervading the fifth-dimensional level of reality. When the time arrives for the effect of the great ascension of our planet, only those souls who have aligned with the new frequencies will ascend with her and partake of the new Earth.

Any well-informed spiritual person tuned into the changes has confirmed and validated that our beloved planet is facing a transformation like no other in the history of our world. As the energy rises, the old Earth that has been polluted by the injustices of the Jesuit Illuminati syndicate corporate world will totally be purged and be eliminated. It is the ascension of our planet that is causing all of the weird weather. Changes in the weather patterns are all indicators that the planet is shifting. In truth, we are all shifting with her as she ascends.

There is scientific proof of the changes; however, the secret government is making sure that it remains unknown. For example, the rising of the Earth's frequency is known as the Schumann resonance, which was discovered by a German physicist by the name of W.O. Schumann and his partner Koenig in 1952 and in 1957. The first spectral representation of these phenomena was prepared by Wagner in 1960. It was reported that most of its research has been conducted by the Department of the Navy, who investigated extremely low frequency communications with submarines. In addition, most of this research has been conducted outside the United States, perhaps because of the controlled community of scientists by the secret government who censor all scientific investigations regarding our world.

In the very last days of evil on Earth, the forces of light would offer protection to the scientists that are giving us the scientific information that is showing that the Earth is shifting. The evidence lies in the electromagnetic field of the planet that is in decline. Here are brief explanations giving us a better understanding of the dynamics behind the process known as Schumann resonance.

It is well understood that the Earth's base frequency or heartbeat is rising dramatically. For decades, the frequency has been at 7.83 hz as measured by scientists. This constant frequency was apparently used as a global military communication until scientists discovered that a rise of this frequency was occurring. The reports indicated that the rise climbed all the way to 11 cycles and is still climbing. Science found no explanation until Greg Braden found data collected by Norwegian and Russian researchers, explaining the activities of such phenomena. Mr. Braden reported that while the Earth's pulse rate is rising, her magnetic field strength is declining, indicating that there have been several polar reversals in the field strength. Even though suppressed history does not show that in previous times there has been a polar shift in the magnetic field of the Earth, this time is different.

According to the acoustic records and corresponding to the prophecies, the electromagnetic field of the Earth becomes upgraded into a multiple band of magnetic fields, allowing people to experience and perceive the higher dimensions. In other words, the religious veil that has blinded us from the spiritual realm is being lifted.

The Earth behaves like an enormous electrical circuit, and the atmosphere acts like a weak conductor. Therefore, if it wasn't for sources of charge, its existing electric charge would diffuse in about ten minutes. Braden and other scientists discovered that a cavity defined by the surface of the Earth exists on the inner edge of the ionosphere, about 55 km up.

The Schumann resonance is a quasi-standing wave in the electromagnetic waves that exist within this cavity. They are not present at all times but have to be excited to be observed. It is this quasi-wave that measures the electro and magnetic forces of the Earth's magnetic field, allowing for the measuring of the heart rate of the Earth's pulse, known as Schumann resonance. The scientific validation is backed up by ancient prophecies and massive metaphysical discoveries that have been felt and known by people who have attained a high level of consciousness.

Paralleling the ascension of planet Earth is the great awakening, which is another prophecy and awaited event that will be experienced by everyone who is ready to ascend as the Earth graduates into the fifth dimension. Those of us who are adapting to the new energies of love, brotherhood, sisterhood in balance are all graduating with her as she moves into a more refined state of existence.

The beginning wave of the great awakening began in the 60s when people were beginning to realize that war was a barbaric outdated tool. People in this country began protesting the Vietnam war, which we know was one of the multiple planned wars orchestrated by the secret government for political and economic gain.

Nevertheless, as a wave of gradual awakenings, many more people are becoming aware these days, especially with the advent of Eastern traditions and practices of meditations and yoga, which are tools of enlightenment enabling people to seek and learn and live a more balanced way of life. This dynamic phenomenon toward a more awakened society has increased and will continue to increase. For this reason, the secret government attempted to create blocks and impediments to halt the awakening process.

For instance, they utilize mind control technologies that originated during Hitler's experiments and culminated with the United States' black ops projects.

Using secret mind control technologies, including Project Monarch and M.K. Ultra experimentations in L.S.D.—which by the way was created by the C.I.A. on behalf of the secret government to counteract and perhaps diffuse the awakening process—another experiment in mind control they have employed to slow or impede the awakening process is the emitting of extremely low frequency (E.L.F.) waves at a high rate in an attempt to control as many people as possible.

The emitting of E.L.F. waves became a covert government experiment designed to control humanity by manipulating the airwaves and tuning them down to a low frequency, which in turn negatively affects humanity's moods and feelings, as well as the way they think and process information. The E.L.F. waves were supposed to keep human beings in lower vibrations along with processed foods that were supposed to keep humanity from awakening. In spite of the secret government's attempt to stop the awakening, humanity is waking up, and soon we will reach a critical mass awakening.

It is believed that as more and more people begin to discover who they really are through spiritual practices, whether it be yoga or meditation, the E.L.F. waves become ineffective. People all over the world are becoming self-realized and are beginning to follow in the footsteps of the great masters of the past.

It is the raising of awareness that elevates the individual to a more balanced lifestyle as they discover the Christ within is perhaps the greatest restored truth any human can ever realize. Once everyone in the world realizes this forgotten truth, they will all snap out of their hypnosis, and there will be a planetary shift in consciousness, which is the meaning of the second coming of Christ. It is the activation and awakening in millions of the Christ's minds that is considered the second coming.

It is the attainment of the mind of Christ that enables one to experience Heaven on Earth. Therefore, we can conceptualize that the universe is one big cosmic tree with multiple branches and extensions, all intrinsically and intimately connected together by the same electrical impulse that emanates from the great source and center, connecting the cosmic web as one. From this perspective, we could assume that we are all one and the same, just different parts of the same whole.

The raising of our consciousness is the only solution to the world's crisis. The more souls that become awakened, the less power the secret government holds over them. In addition, the harnessing of the Christ mind serves as a neutralizer of dark energies and negative entities and will keep our world safe from anything that is not in alignment with the light.

Another lost truth was that the original Trinity of the holy of holies—the Father, Mother, son deity—was also lost. Living in a male-dominating world, the patriarch of the Luciferians has completely eliminated the balance of the Divine feminine. It is believed that the third aspect of the Godhead that they call the Holy Spirit is attributed to the Great Mother. The balance between the masculine and feminine principles of the Godhead was venerated and practiced until the time of the formation of the Roman church. God is a perfect union between all polarities. This perfect union was the reason everything in life functioned in a steady balance before the corruption of Atlantis and Babylon.

This utopian living existed before the interception of the Fallen Angels that distorted the balance by suppressing one side—the feminine—and only upholding the masculine. This act of creating an inferior species dominated by the masculine male led to the fall of the most perfect commonwealth based on a perfect balance between the two, male and female. God made men and women equally, and it is the balance of this feminine and masculine energy that upholds the balance of all creation perfectly.

According to the ancient mysteries, the people of the ancient world venerated both the concept of the Universal Father and the Universal Mother. After all, it is the union of the two that gave birth to the firstborn of Heaven, the Christ, who is our eldest brother. The Mother became the first source and cause of the ethers, and the Father became the active principle that formed life out of the ethers, and together they created the first solar plane.

Furthermore, the balance between the Godhead is represented by the masculine and feminine parts that existed in the golden days of Egypt and Greece. We can see the balance in Greece during the peak of its mystery schools. The Great Temple of Delphi also held this lost truth and practice, and later it continued to be acceptable in practice by the Essenes of the community of Qumran, where Jesus and Mary Magdalene were the perfect embodiment of that balance.

Within the grounds of this balance, both men and women became eligible for initiation into the mysteries, as both were capable of becoming priest and priestess of the original spiritual church. The orders of light held the composition of both our Heavenly Father and our Heavenly Mother in balance, representing a unified duality as a perfect marriage. It was this grand union of a celestial father being wedded to a celestial Mother that began the rites of all marriages in the old world, since we were all made in their image.

In indigenous practices, the Heavens represented our Father Sky, and our Mother represented Earth. This understanding allowed all indigenous peoples to see the sacredness in everything and therefore respected and protected the Earth as a Mother, a nurturing living sentient being. We can see the perfect balance in the union of all things, with the most important one being the union of spirit and matter. The once forgotten universal truth honoring the sacred feminine is now re-emerging as women in the world have risen to status. This couldn't have been possible without the establishment of free world America.

By suppressing the feminine, the Luciferians were able to create the existence of inferiority among the members of humanity. This false theology was put in motion during the times of Nimrod in 3400 BC. When this theology began to throw our world out of balance, records were rewritten to uphold the concept of a male-dominated deity, giving the Luciferian Brotherhood the right by divine dogma to gradually wipe out the balance.

It becomes apparent now why women have been killed throughout history, especially during the Middle Dark Ages. In some countries today, women are still being suppressed; if not, they are treated as slaves by their husbands. In scriptures, this cover-up was the reason that Mary Magdalene was degraded and cast as a whore, a prostitute by the church, when in actuality she was Jesus's companion. Therefore, not only was she the wife of Jesus, but a high priestess after the order of Melchizedek.

It is clear that the original spiritual church also had women apostles and priestesses, and Mary Magdalene was one of them. For almost 2000 years, women didn't have any rights until now, in the last century. This is happening because all balances are being restored back to the Earth as the Earth enters the Golden Age.

The suppression of the feminine explains why all of the Luciferian secret societies of the Dark Brotherhood have been constituted as male-based societies only. This fact is reflected throughout history as women became slaves to men. After all, according to the blueprint agenda of the Luciferians, women were never supposed to rise to the same status as men; they were supposed to remain inferior. That is one of the reasons why the Luciferian brotherhood changed the Bible around to maintain the inferiority of women and allow the reality of a male-dominated society to prevail.

Rejoice, for the kingdom of God is at hand; truth will be revealed, and everyone will know the truth. It is evident that the Bible itself was tampered with by the forces of evil; however, those that had deciphered the meaning behind the metaphors understood its deeper meaning. Mother Earth has been suffering for many years, and she is tired of suffering and is soon going to shake off the fleas. The Dark Brotherhood, for centuries, has been exploiting the Earth's resources, pumping her life force out of her in the form of oil, polluting her atmosphere through the industries with chemicals that have been released over the years, and not to mention, the detonation of nuclear weapons has also polluted her.

Soon our planet and her inhabitants are going to be restored, and a true Commonwealth will emerge to suit the needs of all humans as humans become part of an integral process and build a better relationship with the ecosystem.

These lost universal principles are making their way back into our reality, and soon the entire planet will live according to Divine Law and learn to not only live in harmony with one another but to live in harmony with all life forms everywhere in the universe.

It is our duty as children of light to begin applying these universal principles because we were given this beautiful planet to take care of, not to destroy it. How can our ecology sustain us if we can't sustain it ourselves? It's like our body's cells and molecules attempting to live in our body even after our body is diseased. The care and health of our planet should be the primary concern, and as a result, humanity will reach ultimate health and life abundance. When the greater body is taken care of, so are all its components. Once mankind becomes more aware and enlightened about these principles and truths, we can collectively make a better world together. We are indeed all an integral part of a greater Community as together we make one greater planetary organism with our ecology.

This is the true nature of the universe. Everything is an organism, a microcosmic body living and being part of a greater organism, a macrocosm body. Even the greater macrocosm is a living proponent of an even greater living macrocosm known as the cosmos. There is no limit to how big our cosmos is, for we are only experiencing an inch of the infinite ruler insofar as knowledge and experience are concerned. That is the true meaning of the holographic omniverse, which everything is a part of. For example, the same structure that composes the subatomic world is the same structure that composes the greater cosmos. Everything swirls around everything else: the electrons around atoms, the planets around stars, and so on and so forth.

The nature of the universe is like a swirl within a swirl. This is why esoteric and mystics have known what quantum physicists are now discovering. It is the understanding that everything in existence is cyclic and circular, not linear as we have been taught to believe.

If we are to make the transition into the New Earth, we must accept these universal truths as real dynamics as much as we need to breathe and begin to change the process within ourselves so we can align with the new frequencies. If we choose unconditional love and brotherhood over hate and fear, we will inherit our improved and refined bodies that come as a result of achieving ascension with our beloved planet Earth. As stated in the prophecies, we won't experience death.

Chapter 19: THE PROPHECIES REVEALED

The higher self is trying to awaken within each human being at this time. The best way to allow its emergence is by quieting the turbulent thoughts of everyday life and going within. In Eastern traditions, the mechanism that triggers the awakening process is called meditation, and in Western traditions, it is considered contemplation, which is the deeper form of prayer employing even more listening to the small still voice within and doing less talking. God is always knowing what we think. God knows the desires of our hearts. If we first seek the kingdom of God within us by balancing and integrating all aspects of ourselves, we will understand the greater mysteries, and all things will be given to us.

It is this connection with what high-level spiritual people call the higher self that will secure your transition into the new Earth. You don't have to become a monk and seclude yourself from everyday life. That is not balanced. True ascension includes integrating every aspect and part of your total being — mind, body, and soul — not just one of the three components. That is why the principle of celibacy and isolation is an unworkable and unbalanced one. If one were to seek only spiritual development at the exclusion of mind and body, one fails to evolve as an integrated whole and becomes only one-sided.

The desire and endeavor to be whole and live a life of balance will mark a steady ascension in this time of great distress but yet great opportunity. It also recognizes and believes that there is a higher power known by many names who love and honor all in creation and wants to connect with everything because we are all part of it. If there is anything hindering or blocking the personal connection to the source that exists within and outside, make the necessary change that will allow you to connect and live a life of balance.

In the suppressed Gospel of Thomas, one of the various gospels that were conveniently left out by the organized Christian church, Christ clearly states that the kingdom of Heaven is within, and people do not see it. Considering the various dimensions that exist, the kingdom of Heaven is all around us in the higher fourth and fifth dimension and up. People do not see it because our eyes have been covered by an illusionary veil known as the third-dimensional world.

This great truth is causing the tilt of energy to shift towards the light of higher consciousness by connecting with our higher self, the true immortal being in us. This revelation is a major step in nullifying the power of the secret government and is working as a preparation for humanity into taking the quantum leap forward into the new Earth that is slowly materializing into a new reality.

As a final note, since our planet is experiencing a shift in energy frequency, so is everything in it. Therefore, it is important for humanity to attune and adjust themselves to the new energies that are flooding our world at this time. The old energies from the old programs are dying out and decaying. This explains the prophecy regarding the crashing down of the old Babylonian system.

When this old-world order crumbles, a new Earth is going to be reborn out of the ashes. High-level science and metaphysical knowledge have proven that everything is energy, and all matter is vibrating and nothing rests. So, the physical structure of the old Babylonian structure is in collapse and will cease to exist as the Earth graduates into her new vibrational frequency.

The key to harnessing this new energy is balance and compassion for all of life. By inclining towards compassion, our personal energy field will allow and welcome the new energies, safeguarding our survival in the final transformation into the new Earth. This change will ensure ascension with our planet without tasting death. We obviously don't want to be the weeds rooted out at the time of the last and final transition. This knowledge and understanding is what the Dark Brotherhood does not want us to know. It is their own worst nightmare, for they have been trying to suppress any information regarding the ascension process of our planet that they have known for centuries.

Before the Luciferian brotherhood came into power, humanity was living as one, and this was during the golden age of Atlantis. It is believed that this age would come again according to the original prophecies. After the fall of Atlantis, the Luciferian brotherhood created organized religions as mediators between man and the divine. This methodology was deliberately maneuvered with precise planning by the brotherhood of the snake in order to control us. This would keep mankind divided and fighting so that they could impose their absolute power and control over us, but it failed because now we are at the end of the cycle, and we are breaking free from their bond.

Today, many people are awakening and are discovering the difference between religion and spirituality. One is a way of life—spirituality—and the other one is a worldly institution that only serves the elites. The difference is simple: spiritual people respect and honor all living things, while religious people only accept those that are part of the religion while trying to disagree and fight those that are part of other religions, which is the divide and conquer method. Spiritual people take responsibility for themselves and become accountable for everything in their life as they make the choice to become better through their experiences, while religious people rely on their pastors, priests, or any mediators to guide them and tell them what to believe in and rely on blind faith. Spiritual people are independent and have a direct connection to the divine, while religious people depend on the herd mentality and are just following what their pastors, priests, bishops tell them.

The truth is that the more religions we have, the more divided we are. Since the rulers of this world have been ruling through secrecy, they have set up organized religions as a way of keeping us occupied with no real knowledge of the way the universe works. This type of control through the organization of religion could be traceable back to Babylon as revealed earlier in this book. In today's world, where people are beginning to awaken to their own divinity, there seems to be a huge decline in organized religion, and this means that the Luciferian agenda is losing power over humanity.

True spirituality is about connecting with God within to foster a connection with all living things around us, recognizing the omnipresence of God as the singular spirit that unites us all in the cosmos. This spirit's omnipotence signifies its all-powerful nature, which inherently embodies omniscience, or all-knowingness. Conversely, religion has traditionally been an aggregation of stories, symbols, and allegories passed down through the exoteric tradition, offering standard knowledge for the masses to maintain control, without imparting real understanding of spiritual truths.

The esoteric tradition, reserved for those mature enough to grasp our reality's true nature and our divinity, was practiced in secrecy for nearly 2,000 years, accessible only to a select few. However, the modern era has made these ancient mysteries available to the broader populace. Gnostics, who achieved gnosis — spiritual enlightenment and sacred knowledge — were direct communicants with the divine, bypassing any mediators. Despite negative portrayals, Gnostics were enlightened individuals with deep wisdom and higher consciousness, embodying the esoteric tradition maintained by the Brotherhood of Light.

Most organized religions, led by the Roman Catholic Church, have historically suppressed this direct connection to God, or gnosis. Religions were structured with a centralized ecclesiastical hierarchy to monopolize access to the divine, perpetuating control and deception. A few churches, diverging from the dogmatic doctrines of the past, are now beginning to embrace and teach the true principles of Christ.
Despite centuries of suppression, the esoteric tradition, preserved by benevolent orders, is re-emerging, signifying a pivotal moment for humanity. This resurgence, highlighted during the Renaissance, dealt a blow to the Dark Brotherhood, challenging their longstanding agenda.

The "Brotherhood of Darkness" adeptly manipulates situations to their advantage, as seen when they co-opted the resurgence of science during the Renaissance. This period saw the Dark Brotherhood fostering division between religion and science, thereby advancing their narrative of humanity's baseness and further entrenching their control. The schism

:en science and religion, and the ensuing reductionism in
ntific study, exemplifies the Dark Brotherhood's influence,
storting and subverting all advancements to serve their ends.

Despite their efforts, the unification of science and spirituality
reveals a deeper understanding of reality, bridging the gap
between the material and spiritual realms. This union opens
avenues for exploring higher dimensions and metaphysical
sciences, previously suppressed by a dogmatic scientific
approach. The discovery of quantum realms, beyond the
tangible, hints at a universe vibrant with unseen energies and
higher-dimensional realities, awaiting further exploration
beyond the confines of conventional physics.

In understanding divine science, we confirm that the mind is
more than just a chemical construct in our brain. There is a
different aspect of the mind that wasn't known for centuries.
The mind is a spiritual organ operating in different
dimensions. In the esoteric tradition, it is believed that the
mind is not confined within our skull but is all around us. It is
postulated that if we learn to use more than the traditionally
cited 10% of our brain capacity, we can connect all of the
invisible aspects of ourselves and tune into the higher vibrating
matter through a field that interconnects everything.

Raising one's vibration to attune to the superconscious mind,
which is a field of energy connecting all things, grants access to
unlimited knowledge without any boundaries. Individuals who
have managed to expand their minds to this higher dimension
access greater levels of consciousness. Those who have
reached this level of reality, including mystics, yogis, and sages,
have been recognized for their profound spiritual insights.

Achieving this unlimited state of mind cor
perception to the invisible realms, including the eth
of existence, the astral plane, and beyond. The hig
raises their awareness, the more one perceives the unity ∪ ⌐
life, advancing to greater levels of consciousness. It's
important to note that we only achieve greater degrees and
levels of consciousness on the never-ending ladder of
ascension, for there is always more to learn, as the process of
learning and expansion never ceases, as indicated by both
science and spirituality.

The principle that, "all is mind, and mind is in all" suggests
that consciousness pervades everything, and everything in the
universe is conscious. We inhabit a universe that is fully aware
and participates in all occurrences. The universe operates as
infinite intelligence expressing itself on multiple levels. The
notion that the mind pervades everything parallels the concept
that energy pervades everything, indicating that mind and
energy are synonymous. In this regard, the mind acts as a giant
magnetic conductor.

This is why God, being all-knowing and all-powerful, can be
everywhere and know everything simultaneously because it is
this field of energy, known by science as quantum singularity
or the unified field. Therefore, the source of all reality is the
universal mind and universal spirit, which many have referred
to as the Great Spirit.

This universal truth was not widely accepted in the West until
the advent of quantum physics, when certain scientists
discovered the existence of an energetic world shaped by
subatomic and atomic particles. These particles exhibit both
wavelike and particle-like properties simultaneously. In this
analogy, we are like these individual particles, connected at the

rgy-level, making us all part of one wave of energy. The advent of quantum mechanics bridged the gap between the physical world of solid matter and the more refined subtle world of spirit matter.

Therefore, Heaven, the higher-vibrating world of refined matter, isn't as far away as we have been taught to believe. Heaven is here; it's just a matter of raising our frequency to a higher rate of vibration so that it can be experienced and perceived. With the ascension of planet Earth, Heaven will automatically be manifested for all to experience if we choose to ascend with our planet by accepting and working with the new rate of vibration, which is love.

It should be noted that the community of scientists has been under the control of the Dark Brotherhood since the times of Galileo, technically since the times of Nimrod. There are limitations imposed by the mainstream scientific community that won't allow the higher sciences to unfold as a field of education for the general public. Since the beginning of recorded history, only the exoteric aspect has dominated knowledge, which is the general interpretation for the masses.

As we approach the great day of graduation—the ascension of our beloved planet — many will witness the greater mysteries as the awakening takes place. This event will also mark the end of all secrets, so we may all understand and connect to the great force of existence as heirs to the throne of God. Correspondingly, the time of all secret societies is coming to an end as the last battle between good and evil comes to a final resolution.

This long-awaited event will manifest Heaven on Earth, and the Dark Brotherhood will be weeded out by its roots. There will be no more need for secrets or secret societies. The secret societies have served their purpose for both the "forces of good" and evil, and now everything is going to be transparent. These events parallel what many call the coming of a new golden age or the age of Aquarius. It is a time where people are being upgraded through the expansion of consciousness as we all become uplifted into a new state of reality. Upon opening our minds to higher knowledge, the grand event of the coming of the host of Heaven with the universal cosmic consciousness that will be activated, we will walk again once again with celestials as we once did during the time of Atlantis. At this point, humanity will come to the realization that there will be no need for religion anymore; they will all have a direct connection to God through their own divinity and live in harmony with one another.

In summary of this material and its revelation, it is important to understand the degree of control and manipulation that has been inflicted upon mankind for thousands of years. This force that has been controlling the world is no longer going to be an issue. Ignorance is now a choice in the age of information.

All of this knowledge is now available for those who seek it. Depending on your level of awakening, it may be challenging to digest the information presented in this material due to the extensive conditioning we have undergone. This conditioning has permeated all levels of our society, including governments, religions, science, and education. Some may recognize the truth in this material immediately, while others may be profoundly disturbed by its revelations. It is crucial to believe in this truth and break free from the hypnosis; there is no time to waste, as imminent changes are upon us. To navigate the shift, we must become aware and educated on the many critical matters that are transforming our world.

Embrace this knowledge and allow it to prepare your mind for operating at higher levels of reality, as the Earth ascends to her original frequency, as foretold in ancient prophecies. The time of graduation is here, and Earth is set to ascend. The metaphorical weeds in the garden are about to be uprooted as the final conflict between good and evil draws to a close, culminating in the victory of light.

It is essential to ensure that we are not the weeds in this world, causing pain or suffering to anyone by violating the laws of creation, which are the same universal cosmic laws set by our creator. The greatest of these laws is to do unto others as you would have them do unto you. This principle extends to respecting and caring for the Earth and all sentient beings.

The lineage of the Luciferian brotherhood can be traced back to its inception with the biblical Ham, the first sorcerer, who invoked the dark powers and entities of Marduk/Satan. This act not only revived the black arts of sorcery and dark magic but also introduced the "Levitation Seed," the gene of the ancient serpent race, the sons of Lucifer. This gene has been preserved through generations of arranged marriages and manifests today in the bloodlines of the 13 most powerful and wealthiest families, constituting the cabal. These families are descendants of the Ham, Kish, Nimrod, and Esau lineages.

They have been the power behind most of the world's empires and institutions, maintaining their stronghold over the Earth through secrecy, manipulation, division, religion, and wars. Their lineages form the secret government that has controlled our world for thousands of years. As high-level sorcerers, they have connected with fallen angelics, who have guided their quest for world domination. It is believed that these fallen angelics are the reptilian races ruling from the lower fourth dimension, as revealed by David Icke.

In their final efforts, they have managed to maintain indirect control over the world's governments. They have been the hidden force behind all world wars and conflicts, created diseases, and plunged the world into poverty, leading to the manifestation of the Four Horsemen of the Apocalypse. Their Hegelian method has been used to bring the world under their control of the United Nations and the European Union, in an attempt to revive their old Babylonian Holy Roman Empire.

They have employed the guise of peace as a covert agenda, disintegrating national sovereignties and freedoms worldwide with their globalization programs. The central banking systems they created have monopolized the world economy, causing numerous global economic catastrophes.

The plan included transforming the NAFTA agreement into the American Union in the West and the APEC agreement into the Asian Pacific Economic Cooperation plan in the East, with the ultimate goal of uniting all four unions into a One World Government.

After reviewing this material, it becomes evident that we have been living in a world reminiscent of fantasy tales like The "Chronicles of Narnia", The "Lord of the Rings", and "Star Wars". However, it is crucial to remember that in the end, evil always loses, and light prevails, which is the transition we are about to experience as we enter a new era.

In summary, the worldwide secret government, or the "beast," has been controlled by the Jesuits, who have been a key element in the conspiracy for global domination for over 500 years. The rise of the New World Order can be seen as an attempt to resurrect the Holy Roman Empire under a different guise.

In conclusion, the Jesuit Illuminati have operated a global network through various secret societies, such as Skull and Bones, the Round Table Groups, the Royal Institute of International Affairs, and the Council on Foreign Relations, among others. These organizations, controlled by the "Black Pope," have strived to establish what they failed to achieve in Rome and Babylon. Despite their efforts, the emergence of the United Nations and various unions had made progress towards a One World Government. However, the "White Knights" and other agents of light around the world have thwarted their plans. It is now time for humanity to reclaim its future, as a new era dawns.

To be continued...

References

- Sutton, Anthony C. *America's Secret Establishment.* 1986.
- McGee, Jim. "An Intelligent Giant in The Making." November 2001.
- Peter, Allen. "Bin Laden's Family Link To Bush." 2001.
- Simpson, Christopher. *Blowback: America's Recruitment of Nazis and Its Effects on The Cold War.* 1988.
- Bamford, James. *Body of Secrets.* 2001.
- "CIA Worked in Tandem with Pakistan to Create the Taliban." *The Times of India,* March 7, 2001.
- Griffin, Edward. *The Creature from Jekyll Island.* 1998.
- Chomsky, Noam. *Deterring Democracy.* 1992.
- Rivera, Alberto. *Double Cross.* Chick Publishing, 1984-2000.
- Rivera, Michael. "Fake Terror: The Road to a Dictatorship." 2001.
- Chiniquy, Charles. *Fifty Years in The Church of Rome.* 1958 and 1886.
- Thompson, R.W. *Footprints of the Jesuits.* 1894.
- Tarpley, Webster Griffin, and Anton Chaitkin. *George Bush: The Unauthorized Biography.* Executive Intelligence Review, 1992.
- Shuster, Simon. *How The Federal Reserve Runs the Country.* 1987.
- Howells, Tim. "How Our Government Uses Terrorism to Control the U.S. Project Mockingbird." November 28, 2005.
- Poutry, Col. L. Fletcher. *J.F.K., the C.I.A., Vietnam, and The Plot to Assassinate John F. Kennedy.*
- Smith, Bradley F., and Elena Agarossi. *Operation Sunrise: The Secret Surrender.*
- Garrison, Jim. *On the Trail of Assassination.* 1991.

- Robison, John. *Proof of A Conspiracy to Destroy all Religions and Governments of the World.* 1989.
- Wiseman, Bruce. *Psychiatry: The Ultimate Betrayal.* 1995.
- Ridpath, John Clarke. *Ridpath's Universal History.* 1899.
- Mars, Jim. *Rule by Secrecy.* 2001.
- Kick, Russ. "September 11, 2001, No Surprise." 2002.
- Keller, Suzanne. *Strategic Elite in Modern Society.* 1963.
- Weeks, Bryon T., M.D. "Tavistock Institute: The Best Kept Secret In America." July 31, 2001.
- Cooney, John. *The American Pope: The Life and Times of Francis Cardinal Spellman.* 1984.
- Quigley, Carol. *The Anglo-American Establishment.* 1981.
- Puozzner, Daniel. *The Architect of Modern Political Power: The New Feudalism.* 2001.
- Icke, David. *The Biggest Secret.* 1999.
- Frazer, Ivan, and Mark Beeston. *The Brotherhood.*
- Marchetti, Victor. *The C.I.A. and the Cult of Intelligence.* 1975.
- Various Authors. *The C.I.A. and the Virus Makers.* 1997.
- Coleman, Dr. John. *The Committee of Three Hundred.* Joseph Holding Corporation, March 2005.
- DuBois Jr., Josiah E. *The Devil's Chemist: 24 Conspirators of The International Farben Cartel Who Manufacture Wars.* 1952.
- LaRouche, Lyndon. *The Executive Intelligence Review: Guns of August*, Volume 32, November 2005.
- Josephson, Emmanuel M. *The Federal Reserve and Rockefellers.* 1968.
- Brzezinski, Zbigniew. *The Grand Chessboard: American Primacy and Its Geostrategic Imperatives.* 1997.
- Kruger, Henrik. *The Great Heroin Coup: Drugs, Intelligence, and International Fascism.* 1980.
- Collins, Paul David. *The Hidden Face of Terrorism: The Dark Side of Social Engineering From Antiquity to Sept. 11.*

- Fagan, Myron. *The Illuminati and the Council of Foreign Relations.*
- Cuday, Dennis. *The Men, The Money and the Methods Behind the New World Order.* 1999.
- Reimer, George. *The New Jesuits.*
- Lifton, Robert J. *The Nazi Doctors: Medical Killing and the Psychology of Genocide.* 1986.
- Hertz Jr., William. *The Nazi Ratlines: Time to Rid America of the Dulles Complex.* Executive Intelligence Review, 2005.
- Sayers, Michael, and Albert E. Khan. *The Plot Against the Peace: A Warning to the Nation.* 1945.
- Wright, Mills C. *The Power Elite.* Oxford University Press, 1956.
- Kornbluh, Peter. *The Pinochet File: A Declassified Dossier on Atrocity and Accountability.* 2003.
- Marsden, Victor (Translator). *The Protocols of the Learned Elders of Zion.*
- Goni, Uki. *The Real Odyssey: Smuggling the Nazis to Peron's Argentina.* 2002.
- Loftus, John. *The Secret War Against the Jews.* 1994.
- Paris, Edmond. *The Secret History of The Jesuits.*
- McCarthy, Burke. *The Suppressed Truth about the Assassination of Abraham Lincoln.* 1973.
- Hislop, Alexander. *The Two Babylon's.* 2006.
- Epperson, Ralph. *The Unseen Hand.* 1985.
- Paris, Edmond. *The Vatican Against Europe.* Translated from French, 1975.
- Higham, Charles. *Trading With the Enemy: An Expose of the Nazi-American Money Plot (1933-1949).* 1983.
- Quigley, Carrol. *"Tragedy and Hope": A History of the World in Our Time.* 1966.
- O'Brien, Cathy, and Mark Phillips. *Trance Formation of America.*

- Aarons, Mark, and John Loftus. *Unholy Trinity.* 1998.
- Phelps, John Eric. *Vatican Assassins.* 2001.
- Juergensmeyer, Mark. *Understanding the New Terrorism.* 2001.

References to the Brotherhood of Light

- Hertz, Jr., William F. *A Guide to Schiller's Aesthetical Letters.* 2005.
- Stone, Dr. Joshua David. *Beyond Ascension: How to Complete the Seven Levels of Initiation.* 1995.
- Wallace, Tim, and Marilyn Hopkins. *Custodians of Truth.* 2005.
- Jones, William. *Friedrich Schiller and His Friends.* Executive Intelligence Review, 2005.
- Cheney, Earlyne. *Initiation in the Great Pyramid.* 1987.
- Lost Secrets of the Mystery Schools.
- Cheney, Earlyne. *Secret Wisdom of the Great Initiation* (Astara Library of Mystical Classics). 1992.
- Stone, Dr. Joshua David. *The Complete Ascension Manual: How to Achieve Ascension in This Lifetime.* 1994.
- Chaney, Robert G. *The Essence and Their Ancient Mysteries.* 1968.
- Hurtak, Dr. J.J. *The Keys of Enoch: The Book of Knowledge.* The Academy for Future Science, 1973.
- Cheney, Earlyne. *The Masters and Astara.* 1976.
- LaRouche, Helga Zepp. *To What End Do We Study Friedrich Schiller in The Year 2005?* The Fidelo Print, 2005.
- Wisdom from the Angels and The Forces of Light.
- NESARA.
- Brother Veritas.

- *The Bible*, King James Version: Corinthians 11:13, Ephesians 6:12, Revelations 3:7, Revelations 13:18.